TAINTED GODDESSES
Female Film Stars
of the
Third Reich

TAINTED GODDESSES

Female Film Stars of the Third Reich

CINZIA ROMANI

Translated from the Italian by
ROBERT CONNOLLY

Foreword by
RICHARD C. HOTTELET

GREMESE

TRANSLATOR'S ACKNOWLEDGMENTS

I would particularly like to thank Joseph Radon and Erich Hissel for their assistance in the Filmography section of this book. Extensive thanks are also due Nancy Davis, Laura Eppy, Vittorio Ansuini, Elise Sachs, Ingeborg Godenschweger, and Richard Plant, as well as the librarians at the Goethe House, New York, and the staff of the Celeste Bartos International Film Study Center of the Museum of Modern Art, New York, for a variety of information about the German film world, 1933–1945. Without the help of all of the above, my translation would have been less accurate. Last, I am indebted to Donn Teal for his expert editing and suggestions.

Robert Connolly
New York
1991

First publication in the United States (1992) by
SARPEDON

Originally published in Italy as
Le Dive del Terzo Reich
by Gremese Editore, Rome

Cover:
Apostoli & Maggi

Photocomposition by
Graphic Art 6 s.r.l. – Rome

Printed and bound by
La Moderna – Rome

Copyright GREMESE
2001 © E.G.E. s.r.l. – Rome

ISBN 88-7301-463-1

CONTENTS

FOREWORD

by Richard C. Hottelet

Why should Americans be interested today in a group of movie stars and their directors who readily accepted the rewards of going along with the Nazis? Many of the names are hardly known in the United States. Most of their films have not been seen here. There is no pull of nostalgia; but then, this book is not a fan magazine. The dramatis personae—all attractive women—flesh out the thesis presented in the perceptive Introduction: the German film industry, like the whole of German culture, was manipulated to serve the goals of National Socialism.

Adolf Hitler, the party's first propaganda chief, did not need an evil genius. But he had one in Joseph Paul Goebbels, who employed every nuance of corruption and cooptation. He fashioned the national mood so as to consolidate Nazi power, prepare for war and then fight beyond all reason. Some films he oversaw were pure propaganda; however, carefully calibrated escapism was always part of the mix. Goebbels' star system provided the needed actors and actresses. This gaunt, dark little man with a clubfoot—the antithesis of the Aryan hero—had a reputation as a womanizer. He could assign roles and pay well.

It is absurd to think that the people Goebbels engaged were all Nazis. Many or most were simple careerists with the normal quantum of cowardice. One must have lived and worked in Germany, as I did from 1937 to 1941 and in the Soviet Union of the 1946 Zhdanovchina (Stalin's purge of all wartime liberalism in art and literature) to appreciate the pressure to conform. The civic courage of a Pastor Martin Niemoeller (or of an Andrei Sakharov) in standing up to an omnipotent, murderous state is a rare and remarkable heroism. Those who had their own compelling standards of taste and decency fled Germany if they could, or withdrew from serving the Nazi state. The rest went along. Even here there were special cases. The great Henny Porten remained in Berlin to the bitter end, faithful to her Jewish husband. One is reminded of Kirsten Flagstad, reviled for returning to occupied Norway to rejoin her spouse.

Self-righteousness and hindsight are poor guides for judgment. Goebbels' stars were indeed drawn by the lure of fame and money. They were also pushed along by the public stage management that conditioned them, and everyone else, to feel part of a great patriotic movement. The stars were utilized in many ways, such as standing on prominent street corners rattling little cans, collecting coins from their adoring fans for the Nazi Winter Relief. Political intelligence is not characteristic of the average movie queen, matinee idol or even serious actor.

The book focuses on women for a reason which it elaborates well. Including such fine actors as Emil Jannings, Mathias Wieman and Heinrich George might have made it even more instructive. As it is, some talented people made some good motion pictures. The information assembled here fills what has been a big gap for those interested in 20th-century film.

Wilton, Connecticut
1991

RICHARD C. HOTTELET, a student at Berlin University 1937–38, was resident in Germany until 1941 (when he spent time in solitary confinement by the Gestapo on suspicion of espionage). A foreign correspondent for United Press and stationed with the U.S. Office of War Information in London, 1942–43, he became a journalist with CBS News from 1944 to 1985.

Wolfgang Liebeneiner and Sybille Schmitz in "Abschiedswalzer" (Farewell Waltz), 1934.

INTRODUCTION

Nosferatu and *Faust*...*Der Golem*...*Metropolis* and *Das Testament des Dr. Mabuse*... *Der blaue Engel*...*Das Kabinett des Dr. Caligari*...classic German films of the Twenties and early Thirties, all of them. Many Americans living today recall with delight their appearance on this country's silver screen. All of them preceded the coming of the Nazis.

Adolf Hitler came to power in January 1933. For the German film industry this meant operating in a political climate the whims of which they would have to accustom themselves to in a hurry. This, even though the majority of the nation's directors and actors had never even read the *Völkischer Beobachter* (The People's Observer) or *Mein Kampf,* the bible of the Nazi movement. The films produced by the German motion picture industry under Hitler's tumultuous reign have, for the most part, never had a large audience in the United States, except in a few "art theaters" in major American cities. Even their stars are, for most of us, unknown quantities. This book will help us become acquainted with them and learn about the restrictive world in which they worked.

A few weeks after the Führer's installation in the Chancellory of the Reich, activity ceased at the film studios at Babelsberg, just west of Berlin, and actors put off examining new scripts until more was known about the position of the new regime. Almost immediately the *Gleichschaltung*—the absolute control of federal, state, provincial and municipal activities by the state—became an irreversible phenomenon, the inherent brutality of which had been sensed by those Germans who as early as 1932 had sought refuge abroad. Directors Fritz Lang, Hans Schwarz, Wilhelm Thiele and Erik Charell had left Germany; actresses Marlene Dietrich and Elisabeth Bergner had gone to London and elsewhere, actors Fritz Kortner to Vienna and Peter Lorre to Paris, along with the brilliant screenwriter Billy Wilder and the prominent composer Werner Richard Heymann.

It could be said that the best artists of the German film industry of the 1930s quickly discerned the obsessive distortions of the soon-to-be-seen anti-Semitic films and the heavy-handedness of those of propaganda. Statements issued after the war by the many members of the film industry who remained were pathetic attempts to justify their behavior; it is not easy to believe the recantations and protestations of ignorance of directors Veit Harlan or Leni Riefenstahl. Nothing was more convincing than the flight from Germany of the artists who foresaw the disaster.

Moreover, Joseph Goebbels, appointed Minister of Culture and Propaganda on March 28, 1933, two weeks after his appointment and during an informal meeting at the Kaiserhof Hotel in Berlin, described clearly the mandate that was to be handed to the film industry:

> We must free ourselves of the opinion that the present crisis is a material one; the crisis of the cinema is rather of a spiritual nature, and will continue to exist unless we have the courage to reform the German cinema from its roots...There can be no doubt that the National Socialist movement will intervene in the economy and in all cultural matters, and thus also in the sector of film. I would like to cite a few examples in order to indicate what is artistic and what is dangerous to film. Certain films have produced an indelible impression on me.[1]

And here Goebbels named the four "models" that "die Herren vom Film"—directors and producers— should seek to emulate: the Soviet Union's *The Battleship Potemkin,* the United States' filming of *Anna Karenina* as *Love* (1927), and the German world's own *Die Nibelungen* and *Der Rebell.* It is interesting to note that, aside from the last film—whose director, Luis Trenker, was always well received in the highest Nazi circles—the others represented, in order, products of the abhorred Bolshevism, of the American cinema (defined as "degenerate" by the Nazi press) and finally the school of Fritz Lang. (Nonetheless, only two days after Goebbels' discourse, Lang would see his film *Das Testament des Dr. Mabuse* [The Testament of Dr. Mabuse, 1932] banned, "for the legitimate motives of disturbing the peace and public safety."[2]

Actor Willy Fritsch at the peak of his fame.

Goebbels' plan of action is already highly revealing in these apparent contradictions, which seem to confirm the schizophrenic character of the film industry of the Third Reich and at the same time to manifest its aspects of modernity and meticulous planning. Obviously, in observance of the new Nuremberg Laws, Jews were to be eliminated from the film world. Nevertheless, it was the gifted screen-writer Erich Kästner (a victim of the *Schreibverbot,* or ban on writing, in 1942), of Hebrew origin, who conceived the screenplay of the enormously successful *Münchhausen* (The Adventures of Baron Münchhausen, 1943), although he was obliged to appear in the credits under the pseudonym of Berthold Bürger. "Let us free the cinema from the hands of the Jews" was a widespread slogan in 1933, but such reservations would be set aside when composers such as Paul Abraham or Friedrich Hollaender were needed to write the songs for the film operettas and musical revues that were turned out in large numbers during the wartime period.

In Germany, unlike the United States, filmmaking had from its beginnings been considered a serious art form, rather than merely a business. German anti-Semites noted that Jews had gained what they deemed was undue influence in the world of film, and were responsible for the steadily increasing number of theaters throughout the nation as well as for the inflated salaries being paid to stars and directors; and that all of this pointed to the "Hebrewization of the film industry." Screenwriter Hans Zöberlin summed up this latent anticapitalism and anti-Semitism as early as 1931: "The Jews have turned the art of film into a business."[3]

"The star must die, if the cinema is to live," declared E. Krünes in an article in *Die Filmwoche* (Film Week),[4] the star, after all, being the invention—so said the Nazi leaders—of philistine Jewish capitalists in Hollywood, and having little to do with film "art." And yet we know that Goebbels, during the years of his ministry, sought to build up a stable of stars as similar as possible to Hollywood's.

.After 1933, it becomes evident how the controversy over the star system was used to reveal the "degenerate" character of the Weimar *Systemzeit,** when Margo Lion and Marlene Dietrich performed their licentious routines in disreputable cabarets, and a dancer (Henriette Hiebel) who called herself La Jana, the embodiment of carnality and dissoluteness, was seen in the theaters of Berlin's West End, under the gaze of "parlor Communists," each with his intellectual girl friend.

During the Weimar period, the phenomenon of the "liberated woman" had developed at the same time as the growth of the parties of the Left. The Twenties witnessed the emergence of such figures as acclaimed poet and playwright/novelist Else Lasker-Schüler, who worked in cafés, slept under the stars and gave birth to a child without benefit of matrimony, and the novelist/poet Claire Goll, another symbol of unconventional womanhood. The Nazi Party set out to make a clean sweep of these scandalous examples of perverted women.

Untiring in his elimination of everything that did not reflect "the German spirit and the German mentality," Goebbels dismissed the actress Elisabeth Bergner as a "tubercular Jew." Healthy Aryan women had ample hips, muscular thighs, well-rounded arms and blond hair—like Kristina Söderbaum. On the other hand, Goebbels was not unmindful of the danger of a "revolution" in the German film industry if the images dear to the public were wiped out overnight. His attempt to woo back Marlene Dietrich in 1936 was not successful. He sent the actress Mady Soyka to London to bring the "Blue Angel" back to Berlin with an offer of forty thousand pounds in cash and a contract giving her anything she desired; her response was a brusque refusal.

Goebbels was profoundly aware of the *practical* importance of star personalities, especially female ones. Lilian Harvey, who earned 58,000 marks a film (plus another 250,000 in foreign currency) drove through the streets of Berlin in a dazzling white cabriolet with the license plate IA-1111; her partner, Willy Fritsch, at the peak of his career earned 20,000 marks a month. The pages of *Film-Kurier* (Film Courier) or *Licht-Bild-Bühne* (Light-Image-Scene) of those years of the regime are filled with accounts of the public's storming the UFA-Palast or the Capital am Zoo, where the latest film of Zarah Leander was being presented; of autograph hunters; of the sales of sentimental postcards of Hans Albers and Käthe von Nagy on the Kurfürstendamm; and of the grateful thanks of movie actors from the stage after premières. Even the policeman at the corner of the Potsdamer Platz cherished the dream of one day seeing Willy Fritsch and Lilian Harvey get married, just the way they did on screen. It didn't seem strange to anyone that the studios spoiled their stars.

Paradoxically, while the press of the early Thirties severely criticized American permissiveness, the Berlin Wintergarten created a troupe of dancers whose very name, Hiller Girls, was suspiciously similar to the more famous British precision-dancing Tiller Girls.† Except, however, that the Hiller Girls, as Maria Milde,⁵ who was one of Frau Hiller's girls in 1938, wrote in her 1978 memoirs, aspired to be "more disciplined, more graceful and more sincere."

This concept of the greater discipline of the Teutonic dancing girls brings up a theme of primary importance to Goebbels in his dealing with the "film problem": the relationship between the American models and their Germanic copies. In fact, up until 1939, the year in which the Ministry of Propaganda banned the importation of films from the United States—following the release of Anatol Litvak's *Confessions of a Nazi Spy,* one of the first anti-Nazi American films—U.S. films brought, at least into the theaters of the larger cities, the American Way of Life. The musicals of Fred Astaire and Ginger Rogers were especially popular (although *Top Hat*, 1935, was banned by the German censors, as well as *Gold Diggers of 1937*), as were *Broadway Melody of 1938,* which was shown for more than two weeks at the Marmorhaus cinema in Berlin, and *Born to Dance* (1936), distributed in Germany as *Zum Tanzen geboren.*

---

*Germany's attempt at democratic government was, after the civil November Revolution of late 1918, called the Weimar Republic, named after the city of Goethe and Schiller. There the first session of the National Assembly took place on February 6, 1919. (Berlin remained as capital.) "Weimar *Systemzeit*" refers to the Weimar period's many ill-fated changes of government and ideas about government—a period of many "systems," and none of them good.

†The Tiller Girls were created in England in the late nineteenth century by former ballet dancer John Tiller. They were seen in New York first in 1899 and were still a group as late as the 1960s.

Urging producers to at least take note of the most interesting examples from America, Hans Hinkel, State Commissioner of the Ministry of Propaganda, wrote to Goebbels on December 12, 1944: "Producers must keep abreast of the current American production in order to study the artistic and technical progress of our enemies."[6] Not only were American working methods not condemned; the importance of learning from Hollywood, given the success of its films, was confirmed by the screenings organized every fourteen days by the Ministry of Propaganda to draw from American musicals ideas that could be applied to German *Revue-Filme* (films that might be either "revues" or musicals). It was precisely this policy of comparison with the "American Dream" that would be the guiding principle of the Reichsfilmkammer (Reich Chamber of Film) created by Goebbels.

I. *The Structure and Background of the German Film Industry Before the Third Reich*

The socio-economic conditions of the German film industry before the advent of the Nazi era laid the groundwork for a governmental control of the industry. Following capitalistic guidelines of production, however, the fledgling film industry also tended toward maximum industrial backing. Lavish investments in the "Dream Factory" had aroused, as far back as the first decade of the century, the interest of the ruling class in the new medium, but during World War I the times were not ripe for a film industry centralized and guided by the state.

The earliest bases of German film development had been the Deutsche Lichtbild Gesellschaft and Universum Film Aktien Gesellschaft. The latter in particular (better known as UFA) had been created to perform a double function: to serve important capital interests and, at the same time, promote conservative ideology.

The story of the German film industry coincides in many ways with the history of UFA, which was created on December 18, 1917. Conceived as a *national* society for film production, UFA always had, from the beginning, the requisite elements for becoming a dangerous propaganda instrument, especially in the hands of energetic speculators such as newspaper magnate and entrepreneur Alfred Hugenberg. In 1927 this powerful businessman allegedly "saved" UFA from the hands of the Americans with an act greeted by the press as an "event of national importance." It was during these years that UFA production was becoming more and more closely linked to the power groups of German heavy industry.

If on one hand the films produced by UFA were sometimes clearly intended as propaganda, on an artistic level they were often *Kolossals,* often intimate social comedies. The great merit of the organization was that of always securing the services of the outstanding talents of the classic German cinema, especially after 1921, when the producer Erich Pommer assumed control of the organization. Despite competition, UFA became one of Europe's leading production houses.

At the end of World War I, an alliance between capital, the political body and the film industry was achieved. Germany's great banks, soon to be linked, would protect the nation's motion picture companies. Meanwhile, however, in the 1920s increased production costs and galloping inflation hounded the industry. During the Weimar Republic, the state assured the private economic base, but did not take decisive steps to lighten citizens' fiscal burden. The economic collapse of 1929 dealt a severe blow to the industrial organization of the still-young German film companies, which had indeed been in a permanent state of crisis since the end of the war.

Defeated, and with loss of much of its territory, Germany suffered, too, from the Allies' (Great Britain, France, and the United States) demand for war reparations. "Even under the Dawes Plan (signed in August 1924), which was designed to reform the reparations payments situation, they were to amount to one billion gold marks in 1925, rising to 2.5 billion in 1928 and with no total amount due stipulated."[7] Disastrous inflation followed.

Even though the introduction in 1924 of the so-called *Rentenmark* to stabilize currency seemed to help the film industry, and even though foreign loans helped to lessen unemployment, the industry lost money between 1924 and 1928, in this period the ten leading studios registering a deficit of 122.5 million marks. Although a reorganization of the industry had been set in motion, the internal market barely covered 10 percent of production costs, without taking into consideration that Germany was literally inundated by a flood of American films at the same moment as a ban came, on the export of

4

most German products. Only with the decree on *Kontingentfilme,* "quota films," was it possible to curb the invasion of American movies. This was an agreement made by the government with the film studios, stipulating that for every foreign film distributed, one German film would have to be produced. Thanks to this decree on quotas, the film industry was able to survive in the years of economic slump, 1924–25 to 1929.

To cope with the lack of capital, UFA signed a contract, called "Parufamet," on February 6, 1926, with the American company Famous Players Lasky (Paramount) and Metro-Goldwyn-Mayer. The contract stipulated that UFA, in exchange for a loan of 17 million marks and the distribution of ten German films in the United States, agreed to play 20 films of the two American companies—which came to 50 percent of the playing time—in its theaters.

With the collapse of "bull" speculation on the New York Stock Exchange in October 1929, loans to Germany were suspended, and consequently the film industry felt the effects of what soon became a grave economic crisis. The fear of failure paralyzed producers, while many theaters were forced to close their doors. Thus, by the end of the Twenties, UFA was, along with Tobis and Terra, one of the three studios to survive a general economic collapse that came at a time when many technological changes were necessary for the conversion from silent to sound films. By the summer of 1930, in fact, a quarter of all German theaters were already equipped for sound, and a "patent war" raged between America's Western Electric and Germany's Klangfilm Tobis, unleashed by the sensational discovery of sound. In the early Thirties, with the dispute by now favoring Tobis, the German film industry became an oligopoly of a small number of studios, solid and enterprising according to the basic dictates of free competition; and it was at this point that the new regime intervened directly to set up the state-directed "Dream Factory."

II. *The Organization of the Reichsfilmkammer*

The basic institution from which the Nazi regime set out to coordinate cultural activities was the Ministry of Culture and Propaganda (Promi, or Propagandaministerium), created by decree on March 11, 1933. The thirty-five-year-old Joseph Goebbels was appointed its director. Chief of the Central Office of Propaganda of the party since 1932, Goebbels continued to supervise all propaganda activities of

Lilian Harvey kicks up her heels in "Capriccio," 1938.

the Nazi Party,* while participating in the public sector as minister and as president of the Third Reich's Chamber of Culture (Reichskulturkammer). On March 25, 1933, Goebbels was installed in his office in the Wilhelmplatz, situated in front of the Führer's Chancellory. From this imposing building of the Promi, entirely renovated by Albert Speer, Hitler's favorite architect, Goebbels would control for over a decade all cultural activities of the nation.

An efficient staff of old Party members and of many young officials under forty guaranteed the success of the operations of control and manipulation. The Reichskulturkammer comprised seven sections: radio broadcasts, press, literature, fine arts, theater, music and film. Paragraph 4 of a Promi decree published on November 1, 1933, stated: "Whoever contributes to the preparation, reproduction, revision of a spiritual or technical nature, to the diffusion, to the maintenance, to the publishing, or to duties relating to the publishing, of the cultural patrimony must be a member of the branch of the Chamber in charge of his activity."

In order to clearly define Promi's area of influence on the film industry, on July 14, 1933, the "Law on the Establishment of a Temporary Chamber of the Cinema" was published. This temporary Filmkammer, born as a public corporation, had the "duty of promoting the German film industry in the overall economic picture, of representing the interests of individual film groups in the Reich, in the various regions...and of balancing the activities of those who exercise their profession in the film industry."

Paragraph 3 of the law stipulated that membership in the Filmkammer was mandatory for "anyone who produces, prepares and projects films or who contributes to their creation," with the provision that "membership in the Filmkammer may be refused or a member dismissed when facts exist which demonstrate that he does not possess the reliability necessary to carry out filmmaking activity." By a law issued on September 22, the provisional Filmkammer acquired an official character and was incorporated into the Reichskulturkammer. Goebbels then undertook a total restructuring of the Filmkammer, getting rid of the old corporate council and reserving for himself, as sole president, control of all the organization's internal activities. The renewal of Germany's film industry achieved by the creation of the Filmkammer was aided, on one hand, by the capillary nature of its regional organization (every German region had its *Gaufilmstelle,* or regional film center); on the other, by the close relationship existing between the Filmkammer and the Bank of Film Credit (Filmkreditbank), founded on June 1, 1933, to "furnish partially, also to independent production houses, necessary financial assistance."[8]

The establishment of the Filmkreditbank (FKB) was an important means of government control over film activity. Into its administrative bodies were inserted reliable Party men such as Walther Funk—responsible for the financing that had led to the FKB's foundation. Funk, a department leader at Promi and a key figure in the negotiations between the Nazi Party and German industry, in 1939 would become president of the powerful Reichsbank.

To get an idea of the ties existing between financial capital and the economy of the film industry one need only consider that the representatives of Germany's most powerful banks were members of the boards of directors of the film studios, and decided on the granting of, and the extent of, credit. Consequently, the activity of the FKB was concerned not so much with the actual financing of the film companies as with mediation between film producers and the suppliers of credit. In its administrative function as well, the FKB was different from "normal" banks; apart from a Bureau of Dramaturgy (Dramaturgisches Büro), which examined the plots of films in order to estimate their commercial value, there was also an Office for the Control of Production (Produktionskontrollbüro), to calculate costs from the first to the last day of shooting.

Another element of the Nazi regime's economic-ideological control over film production was the *Prädikatsystem.* The use of "awards," or critical evaluations of a film: predicates—issued by a censorship committee—had already been adopted during the Weimar Republic, for films of cultural importance. As early as 1918, the Ministry of Prussian Culture had established in Berlin an institute to judge so-called *Lehrfilme* (educational films), to which could be given certificates of tax reduction. From 1924

*National-sozialistische Deutsche Arbeiterpartei, or German National Socialist Worker's Party—full name of the Nazi Party.

Kristina Söderbaum aims right at the heart in "Opfergang"
(Sacrifice), 1943.

Joseph Goebbels, patron of the film industry of the Third Reich.

Bavarian children visiting the
Führer and Dr. Goebbels on
the Obersalzberg, below
Hitler's Berchtesgaden retreat.

on, this institute began examining full-length features as well, and in 1926 the "grading" of films for *künsterlich Wertvoll* (artistic value) was introduced. In the same period, a censorship bureau was created in Bavaria, similar in structure and function to the one in Berlin. These film institutes worked independently of the government's organs of censorship, since their object was primarily to increase the number of films of cultural value.

The new regime took advantage of the opportunity to intervene directly in production by means of the *Prädikatsystem* awards given out by the Reichsfilmkammer. On June 10, 1933, a decree was issued reducing taxes on "awarded" films—from 10.5 percent to 8 percent. Then Goebbels, to induce producers to maintain even greater allegiance, took steps to widen the range of film awards. Of the more than 1,300 German films made in the twelve years of the Third Reich, many of them received multiple awards—an indication that their producers and directors were generally conformant to the tastes and dictates of Hitler and Goebbels.

The quantity of awards distributed in the Third Reich—equal to roughly one-third of all the full-length films produced—shows that the instituting of the system was enthusiastically received by producers. From an organizational point of view, Goebbels contributed to tightening the bonds between the censorship process and the evaluation of films (during the Weimar period the official censoring and the giving of awards were two separate steps). The awards also represented a notable source of savings for the state as well. According to the calculations of the chief of the Reichszensurbehörde (Reich's Censorship Bureau) in 1937, a film that cost 500,000 RM had to earn 750,000 marks for the distributor and 2.5 million for the theater managers in order to amortize its cost. With the assignment of an award—even one—the film obtained a tax reduction of 4 percent, or 90,000 RM. On the basis of this estimate, with 40 full-length films awarded, the film industry saved around 7.2 million marks in taxes every year; the industry therefore looked extremely favorably upon the *Prädikatsystem* and, thanks to it, a kind of self-censorship evolved.

As for the Reichsfilmkammer, its internal structure was subdivided into various sections, each provided with consultative bodies and subcommittees, divided into: general administration, politics and culture, artistic supervision, economics, personnel, production, circuits of distribution, theaters, filming and projection techniques, cultural films, advertising films and legitimate theaters.

Amazingly, by the end of 1933 the framework of the film complex projected by Goebbels rested on solid legal and economic foundations. As Goebbels himself would say later, the German film was "ready to go throughout the world as a messenger of German culture and of German creative ability."[9]

III. *Joseph Goebbels, Patron of the German Cinema*

With Joseph Goebbels there began a new phase in the use of the film medium for political purposes. Neither Hermann Esser nor Gregor Strasser, both responsible for propaganda prior to the coming to power of Hitler as Führer, had thought of the use of film beyond that of visual support in electoral campaigns or for the diffusion of party information in circles already permeated by the Nazi ideology. According to "star" Nazi cultural philosopher Alfred Rosenberg, as well, the film activity of the Nazi Party should have remained on the level of "simple newsreel reports of National Socialist manifestations, to be utilized as propaganda by the NSDAP."[10] Goebbels, however, thanks to his pragmatic view of the "film question," and by virtue of the bond soon built up between the private film companies and the Filmabteilung (Film Department) of the Party, went far beyond Rosenberg's limited horizons, projecting a truly modern use of the so-called *Traumfabrik*, or "Dream Factory." What's more, to help insure the success of that factory, Goebbels did not hesitate to issue an edict that all film criticism must be positive. No negative reviews were to be printed in the media.

Goebbels' diaries,[11] which have perhaps contributed most to creating the image of the minister as a film lover—almost maniacal in his eagerness to fix in his mind certain images of "American films, good and bad, very good, but also very bad"—are a confirmation of his dedication to film. From a thematic point of view, the diaries contain many of the projects that Goebbels would later try to put into practice. In them, behind an acute perception of diverse aspects of film life of the day—the arguments with director Veit Harlan, the severe control of newsreels, the encouraging of light

9

entertainment films ("strategically important"), the private screenings for Hitler and Rommel—we find not only the daily routine of a minister who personally goes over scripts and films looking for possible themes "in contrast with the spirit of the times," but also the ideology of the strategy of propaganda.

Some pages of Goebbels' diaries have the evocative power of certain old photographs in which the viewer clearly perceives the passage from reality to its reflected image. "In the evening," noted the minister on September 30, 1942, "we had a screening for Rommel of the new color film *Die goldene Stadt* [The City of Gold, 1941]. He had never seen a color film before, and hadn't gone to the movies at all for several months. He was extremely impressed by the film"; and on February 14 of the following year, about the film *Das Bad auf der Tenne* (The Bath in the Barn), he wrote: "Unfortunately the direction was poor, and instead of an amusing film the result was a second-rate tale of rural life."

During the war years Goebbels, while he could not dedicate as much time to the viewing of films as previously, nevertheless continued to suggest cuts and changes in those that he deemed required reworking. Director Veit Harlan attributes entirely to the minister the responsibility for conceiving the anti-Semitic *Jud Süss** (Jew Süss, 1940), even down to minute details: "He [Goebbels] had commissioned an added scene from the Ministry of Propaganda. I am firmly convinced that it was Goebbels himself who wrote the scene. I had to film it and insert it."[12] From the filming of *Kolberg* (1945), an epic picture in which Germans native to the town of the same name try to hold out against Napoleon's forces, the director, asserting his own position of protest in the face of orders from the minister, would recall: "Goebbels ordered me, without batting an eyelash, to substitute for *'Ein feste Burg ist unser Gott'* the *'Niederländisches Dankgebet.'* I reminded him that the Dutch prayer of thanks had been written 50 or 60 years after the Battle of Kolberg and was therefore an anachronism. 'Nonsense!' Goebbels answered. 'Who's ever going to know that?' And so at the end of the film they sang the Dutch prayer."[13] It is certainly undeniable that the minister often stepped in to make changes in cases of what he perceived as deviation from totalitarian ideology—Luther's melody, *Ein feste Burg*, was well known, very popular and too religious for the basically anti-religious Nazis, and might have turned many Germans' thoughts to the "good old days" before Hitler—but it is also true that the memoirs of many of his colleagues, like Harlan, who, at World War II's end, have sought to distance themselves from their wartime past, often appear tendentious and unfair.

The recollections of another filmmaker, Arthur Maria Rabenalt, also reveal more the desire to shake off responsibility than to contribute to the reconstruction of actual facts. About the banning of his film *Ein Kind, ein Hund, ein Vagabund* (A Boy, a Dog, a Vagabond, 1934), Rabenalt wrote: "A simple musical comedy. . . banned for its romantic elements of humor, satire, irony. . . because Hitler hated its lighthearted surrealism."[14] Goebbels, on the other hand, who always seemed to take pains to distinguish between the artistic use of film and its political possibilities, voiced *his* opinion on the Rabenalt film and on one of Georg Zoch, *Die Liebe siegt* (Love Wins Out, 1934) this way: "The films were not banned because they go against the political interests of the state, or because they contrast with the fundamental ideas of the Nazi *Weltanschauung* [world view], but rather because they are weak and lacking in taste and style. . . . Both films are banned to show producers that the regime will not allow film producers who have no artistic conscience to lower the level of taste of the German people."[15]

As the war progressed, Goebbels' criteria for the selection of proper film material became increasingly rigorous. As he noted in his diary on May 23, 1943: ". . .very little is happening at the front, and what is happening is certainly not suited to the mass public." It is this tone that, while it reflects the grave condition of Germany, expresses the type of film communication—indeed, the very genre of film—chosen by Goebbels for speaking to the masses: the manipulation, by sophisticated formulas and techniques, of any unfortunate military event and the increasing filming of escapist fare.

Nevertheless, it should be remembered that, according to the testimony of one director of the period, Wolfgang Liebeneiner, a Silesian German, it was possible to elude even the implacable

---

*One of the most famous historical novels by German Jewish author Lion Feuchtwanger (1884–1958)—and certainly *not* anti-Semitic as written. Among Feuchtwanger's other works were *Josephus* (1932) and *The Oppermanns* (1933). *Jew Süss* was written in 1925.

surveillance of Goebbels. Every director, in preparing the so-called "ministerial copy," which was to be personally viewed by the minister, could edit that copy in such a way that it would be judged to be in keeping with the dictates of the Hitler regime.

The image of a Goebbels interested solely in propaganda films has been fostered, to a large degree, by contemporary scholars of the cinema of the Third Reich, who have created it by a kind of biased inductive reasoning. Both the French writers Francis Courtade and Pierre Cadars, and the American author David Stewart Hull,[16] give more emphasis to the German production of films of a nationalistic nature—for example, the *Blut und Boden** (Blood and Soil) films and those exalting the glory of the German Air Force, as well as films of the German mountains and films exalting the Fatherland—than to the production of films intended as simple entertainment. Not that the gap between escapism and propaganda is always a wide one, or that the elements of entertainment and the regimentation of the masses are so rigidly separated; *Triumph des Willens* (Triumph of the Will, 1935), one of the most celebrated examples of the propaganda film—which celebrates, with imaginative film techniques, the 1934 National Socialist Congress in Nuremberg—is in structure more like a film musical than a documentary. Various stylistic elements transform this celebratory festival into a musical revue-type film: the bodies moving to the rhythm of the military bands, the S.S. (Schutzstaffel, or "protection echelon") filing by in perfect geometric order, the torchlight processions creating spectacular patterns of light. "The Nazi mass assemblies, as we see them today in films or in photographs, have lost their original power: the flames burning at the sides of the stadium of Nuremberg, the endless expanse of banners, the marches and the choruses offer to the modern audience a spectacle not unlike those American musicals of the Twenties and Thirties that Hitler loved to watch every evening,"[17] writes George L. Mosse, a propos of the "new esthetic of politics" to which the Nazi leaders seemed, even early on, to be particularly attracted.

* *"Blut und Boden"* films celebrated the commonality of Germanness and stressed the land and farmers in contrast to urban areas—as part of the commonality.

Zarah Leander confides in Paul Hörbiger in "Die grosse Liebe," 1942.

Glancing through the pages of Goebbels' diaries of the period 1942–43, one notes that out of seven premieres of propaganda films, the minister attended only that of *Der grosse König* (The Great King, 1942). Goebbels examined the new films in private screenings, usually a month before their public presentation; his presence at premieres would have emphasized the importance attributed by the Ministry of Propaganda to specific films.

An interesting particular: of the 288 notes contained in Goebbels' diaries, only 16 (5.6 percent) have detailed comments on newsreels and propaganda films, whereas 79 (27.4 percent) deal with films having a hidden political message. This is a logical proportion, actually, since of a total of over 1,300 films made during the Third Reich, 47.8 percent were comedies; 27 percent *Problemfilme* (films about serious social or ethical issues); 11.2 percent *Abenteurfilme* (adventure films); and only 14 percent can be considered, strictly speaking, propaganda films. The production of light entertainment films *(Unterhaltungsfilme)* remained relatively constant, even when we might have expected a different orientation of the industry: in 1939 they reached their highest level, with 36 percent of the total production; and in 1942, the year of the Germans' greatest military expansion, they came to 34.6 percent, against 25 percent for *Propagandafilme*. Goebbels, obviously fully cognizant of the potentiality of ideological manipulation through "entertainment," did not fail to set forth his theories on the subject during his public appearances: "Entertainment is not a marginal aspect of public events, nor can its importance be ignored by the political command," he pronounced at a cinematic congress in Berlin for Hitler Youth, on October 12, 1941. Film, he believed, was "an educational means of the first class for the nation, comparable, given the extent of its influence, to elementary school."

Among Goebbels' notes that concern the problems of influencing public opinion through entertainment, the shrewdest and most interesting are those that reveal his conceiving of propaganda as part of a much vaster network linking it to other film genres: *Zirkusfilme* and *Kriminalfilme*, *Gangsterfilme* and films of fantasy—which is surprisingly modern. "In this time of great hardship," he wrote on March 3, 1942, "the film and the radio must bring entertainment to the people. Good spirits must be maintained, because a war of this dimension can be won only through optimism." Between the controlled and the permitted, between the bloodless lobotomization of the masses and their carefully guided recreation, lies Goebbels' propaganda technique.

IV. *The Musical Film and the Propaganda Film: Two Faces, One Head*

The lack of a real separation between films of propaganda and those without immediate political messages has been noted by Gerd Albrecht in a highly perceptive volume, *Nationalsozialistische Filmpolitik* (Stuttgart, 1969). His observations upset the traditional relationship between the lighthearted moment and the ideological moment (accepted by other German critics, such as Ulrich Gregor and Enno Patalas, who find a clear division between propaganda and mere light entertainment), and establish a parallel function between the light comedy and the work with a political message. Both genres use a clear and direct tone, comforting the spectator, who is encouraged not to reflect and not to exercise his critical faculties. The world that they portray removes all doubts (the good guys must be Nazis, sincere, blond and healthy; the bad, Communists, Jews, blacks and sometimes carriers of disease), eliminates social problems and elevates the deserving to the realm of happiness. An advertisement in a 1935 issue of *Filmwelt* (Film World) for the Austrian musical film *Der Himmel auf Erden* (Heaven on Earth), directed by E. W. Emo, promises: "Heinz Ruhmann und Hans Moser bringen Ihnen Himmel auf Erden" (Heinz Ruhmann and Hans Moser will bring you Heaven on earth).

In *Die grosse Liebe* (The Great Love, 1942), a typical *Liebesfilm*, the actors live out the vicissitudes of World War II between Berlin, Paris and Rome. On one side, we see wartime events; on the other, the anguished expression of Zarah Leander waiting for her Luftwaffe pilot, and the Hitler Youth going off to die. Over all: the leveling atmosphere of the world of uniforms and, in the clouds, the aerial squadrons toward whom the star, at the end, lifts her grateful gaze.

The *Liebesfilm* is the genre in which it is easiest to banalize the ideological message; since 1939, when the basic theme of almost all German films became the war, it came to represent the ultimate test of love for both the men who depart and the women who remain behind. In 1940, over 23 million

Fritz Camper (seated, with mustache), Carola Höhn and Johannes Heesters, standing, in "Der Bettelstudent" (The Beggar Student), 1936.

spectators were moved by the musical *Wunschkonzert* (Request Concert), in which the wartime conflict was served up in a mixture of songs and items from newsreels (by now the daily diet for spectators, who, once inside the theater, couldn't escape). Even here the war penetrated deeply into the basic structure of the film: now the departure for the front, now the U-boats, now the infantry, now the crowd cheering the departing soldiers. The songs, sung by Marika Rökk and the trio Heinz Ruhmann–Hans Brausewetter–Josef Sieber, served to allow the audience to catch its breath between the attacks on and the counterattacks of the Luftwaffe. Once again we see the linking together of the homeland and the front, of the amorous skirmishes in one and the real battles in the other.

Karl Anton's *Wir tanzen um die Welt* (We Dance Around the World, 1939) remains the most remarkable example of how it is possible to throw together the most disparate musical ingredients—uniformed chorus girls performing military marches, gigantic metronomes beating time as their lacquered boots advance, the Jenny Hill Girls goosestepping down the stairs—and come up with a patriotic film. Obliged to dance from Copenhagen to Lisbon, from Genoa to London, wherever they go the girls sing the *Leitmotiv:* "Tanzen und jung sein / Siegen und jung sein / Lachen und jung sein / Das sind wir, das steht auf unserem Panier!" (Dance and be young / Win and be young / Laugh and be young / This is what we are, this is what we carry in our baskets!). The film was distributed in Germany during the Christmas following the Polish campaign.

An attentive observer of the moods of the masses, Goebbels noted in his diary the link between the production of light entertainment and the favorable progress of the war: "The spiritual and cultural guidance of the people will become increasingly important during the war...It is strategically important to keep up the morale of our people. We forgot to do it during the First World War, and we paid for it with a tremendous catastrophe. In no way must this be allowed to happen again."

V. *The Nazi Cinema and "Classic" German Cinema*

It would seem natural to suppose that, with the exception of wartime patriotic and propaganda films, the filmmakers of the Third Reich would draw upon the notable artistic patrimony of the pre-Hitler German cinema. It is, however, a widespread opinion, found in both German and non-German criticism, that when the Nazis came to power they made *tabula rasa* of the school of director Max Reinhardt and the lessons of Ernst Lubitsch, of the intimate, small-cast *Kammerspielfilm* and costume films, of the Weimar tradition of the "social" film and the *Wiener-Komödie,* or Viennese comedy. But by this line of reasoning one ends up by losing sight of the historical / dialectical bond that links the "Viennese" operettas of Willi Forst to the *Kostümfilme* of Lubitsch, the flood of films on the lives of famous composers that enjoyed great popularity just after the advent of sound and the spectacular revues of Paul Martin and Reinhold Schünzel to the film musicals of Erik Charell (*Der Kongress tanzt*; Congress Dances, 1931) and Wilhelm Thiele (*Die drei von der Tankstelle*; The Three from the Filling Station, 1930), and that links, as well, H. Steinhof's *Hitlerjunge Quex* (Hitler Youth Quex, 1933) to P. Jutzi's Marxist film *Berlin-Alexanderplatz* (1931). In the early sound films immediately preceding the Nazi period we find, in fact, the stylistic and thematic models that the film directors of the Third Reich will appropriate, soft-pedaling (or eliminating) certain types of comedy or satire typical of the pre-Hitler product. Certainly the works preceding the *Gleichschaltung* are to be preferred from a stylistic point of view to those that followed, constantly intent as they were upon trying to put across an ideological message.

The well-crafted comedies of Georg Jacoby, which rank among the best of the "light" films of the Hitler period, do not stand up to comparison with the sparkling and inventive works of Erik Charell. Even if the lesson of the Weimar movies leaves evident traces in the films of Goebbels' "Dream Factory," and even if certain pupils and colleagues of Ludwig Berger and Reinhardt were still working in the industry—visibly carrying on the teachings of their masters—there was a notable decline in quality. And the more Nazism advanced, the more all talents dwindled. One simply cannot listen to the over-sweet songs of Franz Grothe with the same pleasure that one has in the inimitable works of Werner Richard Heymann. It was doubtful that the baroque, full-bodied Zarah Leander could compete with the rarefied glamour of Marlene Dietrich, or that it was possible to "invent" a second Erich Pommer, the producer of infallible taste, responsible for the enormous success of the first *Tonfilmoperetten* (having foreseen the danger, in 1933 Pommer returned to Hollywood to work for M-G-M, where he had originally acquired his vast experience).

Once the domination of the swastika was established, with the resulting flight of the elite of the film industry, as well as in other fields, everything suddenly seemed ersatz. The use of substitute, lesser talent would be upheld as warranted ideologically. Jazz, as a product of *Niggerei,* was banned from musical films, its place taken by Strauss waltzes and Bavarian folk music. German composers of popular music—Theo Mackeben, Franz Doelle, Leo Leux, Peter Kreuder, Michael Jary, Georg Haentzschel—did their best to transform the officially approved but outmoded version of the fox trot into something more acceptable by dressing it up with more modern arrangements and instruments. Nonetheless, given the ever-present danger of "musical bolshevism," the result was usually the inevitable mixture of fox trots, tangos and polkas. It is no accident that in Ucicky's *Die Postmeister* (The Postmaster, 1940) it is a Russian dancer who abandons herself to the frenzied rhythms of a wild folk dance, moreover with bare breasts, or that in Max Kimmich's *Germanin* (Sleeping Sickness Medicine, 1943) it is the members of an African tribe, also bare-breasted, who perform a native dance. Nazi *Prüderie,* detecting the presence of evil in the uninhibited body movements and in the rhythmical undulations to the sounds of "degenerate" music, identified the enemies of morality with those of Nazi ideology.

The unnatural attitude of the regime regarding sex is well illustrated in the *au naturel* appearances of Kristina Söderbaum. When the actress is seen nude, as, for example, in *Immensee* (1943)* and in *Das unsterbliche Herz* (The Immortal Heart, 1939), not only is she seen for a mere few seconds and from a distance, but her nudity is a "bath of fresh air and sunlight," carefully distanced from any

---

*An 1849 novel by Theodor Storm; the name is of a fictitious lake.

Marika Rökk wants to see things clearly in "Es war eine rauschende Ballnacht," 1939.

eroticism. Instead it brings to mind the athletic exhibitions of the nude female gymnasts of the ground-breaking film *Olympia* (released 1938) of the 1936 Berlin Olympic Games or the sporting activities of the members of Kraft durch Freude (Strength Through Joy), a government-sponsored social program of low-cost travel abroad.

A dispute that broke out between two organs of the Nazi press in 1935 illustrates the extent of the prudishness of those years. The object of the scandal was an innocent calendar for farmers, with each month displaying a healthy German maiden in the altogether. The *Deutsches Volkstum* (German Folk Heritage), normally an ardent supporter of eugenics theories, objected to the lack of sense of decency of those photographs, but the *Schwarzes Korps,* an official organ of the S.S., replied harshly that this criticism was a symptom of the "degradation of the German race" [18] and of the "systematic destruction of all that is beautiful and noble." Only a "depraved sensualist" could find anything unhealthy in the representation of Germanic beauty; to find indecency in the wholesome pinups of the farmers' calendar was to be lacking in respect for German womanhood.

Peculiar as it may seem, it was one of the minister's "lieutenants," when not Goebbels himself, who chose the chorus girls one by one, on every occasion that a film called for them, because there was in Nazi Germany no permanent company of dancers. This lack of professional organization, due in part to low pay and the only sporadic need for dancers, is confirmed by Arthur Maria Rabenalt, a specialist in musical and circus films of the period, who points out that Germany was confronted by "the economic impossibility of creating a company of dancers for an individual film, training it and rehearsing it for [merely] this particular assignment."[19] In any case, the impression of amateurishness resulted not only from the lack of money (although the constant attempt to equal the American models required investments of enormous sums), but also from the scarcity of qualified talent — to which was added the artists' constant fear of making a wrong move.

Aware of its limitations, the film industry of the Third Reich hid its ineptness under the veil of puritanism: Marika Rökk was unable to dance as well as her American model, Eleanor Powell, and so in her films she rides horseback, does gymnastics, sings, shoots rifles and disguises herself — anything to avoid having to appear as soloist in a dance number. In *Leichte Kavallerie* (Light Cavalry, 1935), when she applies for a job with a circus, the director looks her over from head to toe and then feels her biceps, exclaiming, "You have real talent!" Later, the actress, transformed into an equestrienne, leads a troop of horsewomen, and as she rides by, the public whispers, "Isn't she fantastic — what talent!" We are told flat out that she is fantastic, but during the course of the film we do not witness a single example of real virtuosity. In all fairness, in her biography Marika Rökk herself admits being "a singer who had the nerve to dance."[20] But more than dance, Marika *tänzelt* (hops around), to use the expression of the critic of the Berlin *Filmwelt:* "To see Marika Rökk hop around, swing on the trapeze, tap-dance and fly across the screen . . . is to be irresistibly swept into the exhilarating vortex of the joy of living."[21] In Georg Jacoby's *Kora Terry* (1940), for example, the only scene calling for any kind of bravura display turns out to be a few moments of a tap dance, ventured by Rökk while balancing her sister Mara (also Marika Rökk) on her head. Despite the dual role and the combination of dancing and acrobatics, one is still left with the impression of a stunt that didn't quite come off. But not even in the films featuring spectacular production numbers, such as *Es leuchten die Sterne* (The Stars Shine, 1938), do we see a solo dancer or a tracking shot of the entire group of dancers. With an effect that calls to mind anatomical precision, the moving dancers are shot vertically (neck–waist, hip–knee, etc.) because the Nazi cinema is still thinking in terms of the legitimate theater and a strict rhythm.

Zarah Leander's first scene in *Die grosse Liebe,* in which she is accompanied by an elaborate ballet, is a long shot, much as we would see it in the theater. While in the American musicals chosen as models there is almost an excess of tracking shots and movement in general, here there is a tendency to conceive of the shot as the petrified, unyielding piece of a monumental mosaic that cannot be taken apart. This technique of editing — in which the dynamic element is rejected and the figures are dismantled in an orderly fashion — is suited to the Nazi sexual phobia: the barely suggested movement annuls the body's signals. Henriette Hiebel (alias La Jana), for example, wears a bikini in *Es leuchten die Sterne,* but quickly minimizes its erotic effect by barely moving. In *Stern von Rio* (The Star of Rio, 1940), the musical film with which she won the heart of the German public, there is another aborted attempt at seduction: as Concha, a Brazilian dancer, her magnificent hips and thighs go for naught as she is allowed to consume her sensual ardor by performing a pair of swift high kicks. It is the death of sensuality in favor of the healthy wartime substitute.

The purifying of erotic stimuli, however, does not hold only for the women: none of the male heartthrobs of the Nazi cinema, have, to our eyes, much to offer. Johannes Heesters, Hans Söhnker, Willy Birgel, Hans Albers, Willy Fritsch—to name only the most famous—seem modeled after the archetype of the man who is sports-loving, open, tirelessly loyal, and whose appeal is strictly that of the good husband and father. His "exploits" take place in the forests and in the mountains, under the banner of the clean-living German *Bund,* or "brotherhood." At best, he may proffer a bit of tenderness, as when Heesters in *Gasparone* (1937), based on Carl Millöcker's operetta, breaks into song (since he can't dance), asking in a timid voice: "Kann ich ein Liedchen singen?" (May I sing a little song?).

Only toward the end of the war did the industry loosen up somewhat, in *Die Frau meiner Träume* (The Woman of My Dreams, 1944), and allow a glimpse of the midriff of Marika Rökk, who tears her skirt falling from a motorcycle. The changing climate of war was bringing about uncertainties even in the rigorous policies of Nazi censorship, in which escape from the routine was permitted after the German setback at Stalingrad.

Even by the mid-Thirties, the sterilizing of film's erotic elements, drained of all meaning by the national-patriotic ideology, had led to a loss of vitality. In *Glückskinder* (Fortune's Children, 1936), director Paul Martin, one of the few German specialists in sophisticated comedy, attempted to duplicate the American *It Happened One Night* (Frank Capra, 1934) in plot and style. The story devices of both films were similar: Willy Fritsch (read: Clark Gable) finds himself in New York, with no job; Lilian

An actress portrays the Myth of the Hero's Death in "Sieg im Westen" (Victory in the West), 1940.

Harvey (read: Claudette Colbert) is drifting through the city, even though she is the niece of a millionaire. Thrown together by adversity, they end up sharing a bedroom. Decorum must be maintained, however. In the American film the solution is a blanket (the "wall of Jericho"); in the German film it is a shelf bristling with cactus plants. The similarity of ideas is no more than mechanical, however, and the German film is sadly lacking in the verve and good humor of the American original. Then, to bolster the perfectly *conventional* structure of his film, Martin has the snobbish young lady marry the penniless reporter after it turns out that in reality she is not the niece of an oil baron, but just an ordinary girl. Capra, too, has the journalist marry the young heiress, paying his tribute to the classic "happy ending," but in the fights between the two he recognizes the problem of class differences and satirizes social injustices. The wit, the zest and the vitality of the American original become flat and colorless in the hands of the German director.

The excision of anything that might be considered suggestive is particularly evident in the satirical *Amphitryon* (Reinhold Schünzel, 1935), where Jupiter (Willy Fritsch) descends from Mt. Olympus to pass a night with Alkmene (Käthe Gold), but falls into a drunken sleep just when the passionate creature is about to yield to him. In this case, as in many others, it was decided not to remain faithful to Heinrich von Kleist's early-nineteenth-century comedy, upon which the film is based, in order not to stir up illicit passions. And what about the rewriting of Gottfried Keller's 1881 story *Regine?** In Erich Waschneck's film version, the three salon intellectuals of the tale lose their homosexual identity, to become merely three meddling gossips. In *Es war eine rauschende Ballnacht* (It Was a Wild Night at the Ball, 1939), even Tchaikovsky, who was known for having no particular interest in women, is presented to us as a manly and impenitent heartbreaker. Also highly distorted by the fear of nonconformity, the propagandistic *Hans Westmar* (Franz Wenzler, 1933), taken from the 1932 novel *Horst Wessel*, by Heinz Ewers, eliminates the scene in the club for transvestites, which is graphically described in the book.

VI. *Women's Roles in the Nazi Cinema*

What are women for the Nazis? Essentially: wives ("German women want above all to be brides. . .they don't want to be comrades, as the Red windbags tried to convince them"[22]) and mothers ("The education of young women is based on the duty of bringing children into the world"[23]). Since Hitler's regime sought immediately to construct its own stereotypes, sweeping away the gains of the Weimar era, women passed quickly from the human category to that of symbolic reference. The suffragette and the intellectualized woman were symbols of the hated *Systemzeit*. During the 1920s, in fact, more than 11 million women worked in offices and factories. The influence of the unions had increased, as had that of women's organizations, most of which dissolved spontaneously at the coming of Nazism — so as not to become branches of the various Nazi women's leagues.

"German women have no nostalgia for the factory, the office and not even for Parliament. The warmth of a home, a loving husband and a host of happy children are what matters most to them," a theoretician of the "volkisch" ideology declared with confidence. With equal presumption, the ideologist Alfred Rosenberg emphasized that the role of the woman consisted of "keeping the race pure."[24] The function that women, as a social unit, needed to fulfill within the sphere of the totalitarian system was thus linked above all to reproduction; in 1934, Hitler had said to the members of the NS-Frauenschaft (National Socialist Organization of Women): "Every baby that a woman brings into the world is a battle waged by her for the existence or non-existence of her people."

The link between the concepts of female-maternal and of the supremacy of the race was strengthened by institutions such as Muttertag (Mother's Day) and a Mutterkreuz (Mother's Cross) of iron for the mothers of four children, of silver for mothers of six and of gold for mothers of eight. The natural calling of the German woman was therefore further reinforced as being: maternity. It is sufficient to reread the words with which Hitler illustrated the program of his party in 1932: "The party of our National Socialist women's movement contains one point alone, and that point is called: the baby."[25] Despite the prudishness of the National Socialists, they pardoned unmarried young ladies

---

*Actually, an episode in the Swiss writer's long *Singedicht* (Poem of Reason).

who had illegitimate children—in the name of the supreme female function of furnishing manpower to the Fatherland.

In the same manner as Italian fascism, Nazism banished women from public life with a series of laws aimed at sending them back into the home. With an ordinance of June 30, 1933, the state fired, on the spot, all married women, who took jobs away from their husbands; banned women teachers from giving private lessons; regulated by means of a quota the influx of women students to the universities; and eliminated courses for women in hospital training. In 1934 the Ministry of Public Instruction took measures against mixed schools, stipulating that the percentage of female students in the secondary schools could not exceed 10 percent. In the same year, only 1,500 female candidates for the exam of matriculation were promoted. Furthermore, out of 39 schools existing in Germany in 1939 for the ideological training of Hitler Youth, only two were allotted for young women. Even education constituted a sphere from which women were to be banished. The Bund Deutscher Mädel (Association of German Girls), composed of young women fourteen to eighteen years old, from the organizational point of view, depended in fact, upon the Hitler Youth, and its activities were limited to prepatory courses for childbirth, even if, bizarrely, together with lessons in home economics, *erotische Bastelstunden,* "courses in erotic training," were organized.

The rapid growth of these courses of home economics for the young women of the Hitler Youth also served to further define the position of women in the regime. Sewing and cutting lessons, gymnastics, fresh-air baths and instruction in household tasks all contributed to using up the time and energy necessary that would have otherwise been channeled into pursuing truly creative goals. Adolescents from ten to fourteen were required to enroll in the Jungmädel (League of Young Girls), and at the age of eighteen women served a year in mandatory work communities: NS-Frauenschaft, Deutsche Frauenwerk (German Women's Work), and Mutter und Kind (Mother and Child). These were organizations aimed at carrying out the national-patriotic programs for restructuring German society.

Setting forth a precise hierarchy of values, regional Party leader Gregor Strasser, writing in the pages of the *Völkischer Beobachter,* as far back as November 17, 1931, sustained that women's work was above all "work of the party." There were three types of work that seemed to him most suited to women: "1. auxiliary activities of an economic nature (cooking for the S.A., sewing, looking after wardrobes, etc.) and hygienic activities; 2. educational, pedagogical and cultural duties; 3. economic-national training of German housewives."

The limiting of women's activity to "work of the party," interpreted as exclusion from the actual life of the party and instead preparing cool drinks for the soldiers, did not meet with unanimous approval. In 1933 the National Socialist Sophie Rogge-Börner led a women's protest movement, with the manifesto "The German women entreat Adolph Hitler," which asked the Führer to admit them, as well, into the effective life of the party. Not surprisingly, the request went unheeded. Hitler had stated in 1931: "Women, if they become involved in the parliamentary system, and see its inner workings, will be sullied by the experience—and less feminine." As if this were not enough, in 1934 the "domestic year" was established. It was yet another way to keep girls who had just finished their studies busy—this time by sending them to work as domestics for families in exchange for only room and board. The idea was not well received, however, by many upper-class families, who often refused to send their daughters off to work for nothing. The result was that, in 1938, the "domestic year" was declared mandatory.

The regime looked with pride on its policy of demographic expansion, and to further its goals of the creation of a pure race had no qualms about establishing the organization of the Lebensborn in December 1935. This program introduced reproduction centers (literally, "founts of life"), where unmarried mothers "valid from the racial point of view" could give birth to their babies in secret and then leave them to the S.S. The clinic of each center was staffed with a doctor, a nurse and an administrative secretary, all duly enrolled in the NSDAP. If a mother wished to rid herself of her child, it automatically became an *S.S.-Kind.* Babies born deformed or retarded were eliminated.

A matrimonial advertisement appearing in the *Münchener Neuste Nachrichten* (Munich Latest News) in February 1935 sheds light upon the myth of the woman at the service of the *Volk.* It is a *doctor* who is seeking a wife: "52-year-old physician, pure Aryan race, veteran of Tannberg desires male offspring through civil marriage with healthy woman, of long-established Aryan descent, virgin, young, without pretensions, capable of heavy work, thrifty, low heels, no earrings. Discretion assured. Write to: AEH 151 0944 M. Neuste N." There emerges from this insertion the image of a woman divested of any individuality, neutralized by the disappearance of traditional sexual symbols (no high heels, no jewelry), ready for the great task that the man reserves for her, the reproduction of male children. The technique of subordination is clear: reducing the woman to her alleged primary biological function is one way to deny her her emotional and sexual impulses.

Even on screen the woman had but two choices, both crippling; either she created a family or, in the case of "irregular" behavior, she disappeared before the end of the film. It is obvious, for example, that Kristina Söderbaum's suicide in *Die goldene Stadt* was not accidental; an admonitory function was served by showing the death of the girl who let herself be seduced by her cousin and by big-city life. Also emblematic was the character of Aels, played by Söderbaum in Veit Harlan's *Opfergang* (Sacrifice, 1944), a film taken from a novel by R. G. Binding. In the original, it is the protagonist, Albrecht (played by Carl Raddatz in the film), who dies, and not Aels; but this finale was not pleasing to Goebbels. In 1940 a report submitted by the Sicherheitsdienst, the security service, among whose duties was the writing of detailed accounts of the public's reaction to films, pointed out: "It is inopportune to encourage a propensity toward adultery at a time in which many families are separated because of the call to arms of their men."[26] Hitler himself mentioned that Goebbels insisted that it must be the *woman* who pays: "The woman guilty of having caused the breakup of the couple must die, and not the man. Matrimony must remain sacred above all else, not only in consideration of those who are at the front, but of the homeland itself, in the minds of the people."[27] *Opfergang*, in fact, sets one woman, Aels the Adulteress, against another, Oktavia the Wife (Irene von Meyendorff). Just as one is bound to things of the earth (she loves nature, and therefore also "free love"), the other is of a more spiritual character (Oktavia is quick to forgive, unconcerned with worldly values, does not bathe in the nude like her rival, etc.). In Aels, a passionate attachment to life is counterbalanced by an obsession with death. This aspect of her character is apparent when she tells Albrecht that she has had her favorite dog put to sleep because it was incurably ill. Here, in a certain sense, Aels is sanctioning euthanasia, in the same manner as the heroine of Wolfgang Liebeneiner's *Ich klage an!* (I Accuse!, 1941), Heidemarie Hatheyer.

Continuing with the "guilty" woman . . . in *Kora Terry* we see the death of Kora, who, as Berlin's *Illustrierter Film-Kurier* explained, "seems identical to her sister Mara, but in reality has a totally different character: her restless nature, her thirst for fame and riches bring about her downfall." The joys of true love are achieved only by the devoutly longed-for solution: marriage (which must also be elaborate, since this is such a deep-rooted convention in the culture of the German *petite bourgeoisie*). The romantic dreams of young women naturally revolve around the storybook figure of Prince Charming. In one of her films (*Karussell*, 1937, dir. Alwin Elling) Marika Rökk works in a gas station. Thanks to her resourcefulness, she marries the wealthy nephew of an antiquarian, giving a totally new direction to her life, which otherwise would have been spent filling up customers' tanks. In the operetta *Gasparone*, Nasoni (Leo Slezak), governor of the imaginary country of Olivia, sings a paean to marriage: "Glück kann es nur im Joch des Ehestandes geben!" (There can be true happiness only on the marriage day!). During the finale, the three couples who are about to marry sing in unison, "Heiraten, heiraten, das ist schön!" (Marriage, Marriage, It's Wonderful!"), inviting the spectator to save himself from the dangers of unbridled sensuality through the safety of matrimony. If marriage is wonderful, to give up a job, no matter how pleasant it may be, for home and hearth, is even more wonderful. Marika Rökk, the star of a Franz Doelle musical, *Und Du, mein Schatz, fährst mit* (And You, My Darling, Come Along with Me, 1937), makes this clear when she says No to a glittering career in the theater in favor of conjugal tranquility.

Which is precisely what Eleanor Powell does *not* do in *Broadway Melody of 1936* (Roy Del Ruth, 1936), bursting onto the screen with a virtuoso tap dance on the roof of a Manhattan apartment building, and then, backed by a bevy of M-G-M chorus girls in sequins, dazzling a Broadway theater audience in a breathtaking production number. No one can deny that a star has been born, one who wouldn't dream of going back to her sleepy home town. The endings of the two films are poles apart, for while Powell becomes a Broadway star, Rökk rejects the frenetic world of show business. The refusal not only serves to avoid possibly embarrassing demonstrations of talent, but also to manifest the anticapitalist spirit implicit in the Nazi ideology. "I'm not a commodity that can be bought by a bank account," says Marika to the film's shady Gloria Liners, a deceitful "friend"; as for the director of the revue, he is portrayed as the embodiment of the theatrical figure rendered totally neurotic by a "world of lunatics."

The forsaking of a career to return to the home is a recurring theme in Nazi light entertainment films, especially those aimed at the women's market. In *Die grosse Liebe,* for example, Zarah Leander is transformed from a celebrated music-hall star to a nurse at the front. The fact that Marianne Hoppe, in Helmut Käutner's *Auf Wiedersehen, Franziska!* (1941), gives up her career in handicrafts to go back home and wait for her constantly traveling journalist husband signifies the reestablishment of order: God, the Fatherland and Family. The film dwells at length on the details of Franziska's business of making and selling toys, and points out that it is this small commercial activity that has relegated her to the margins of the truly productive society. It is suggested that her pseudo-independence is actually a burden; what she really needs is not so much escape from solitude as the affectionate presence of the globe-trotting reporter. The first time he enters Franziska's house, Michael exclaims, "And you live here all *alone*?"; then, when she has finished singing the praises of autonomy, speaking contemptuously of a sentimental girl "possibly with a broken heart," he explodes: "Franziska, how can you lie so terribly?" At this, she admits that she has been thinking of nothing but his return, and embraces him. What is condemned is the desire for emancipation; what is advocated is the simplicity and sincerity of the young women who patiently wait.

For the same reason, Marika Rökk, in Harald Braun's *Hab' mich lieb* (Take My Love, 1942), just after having drunk the first glass of *Sekt* (champagne) of her life, offered to her by the Egyptologist (Hans Brausewetter) who has invited her to his house, sings: "Ich möchte so gerne/ich weiss nur noch nicht was?! / Mein Herz möchte dieses, mein Verstand möchte das!" (I'd like to so much/but I only know that/my heart would like this/my mind would like that). The conflict between the heart and the mind, pleasure and morality, surrender and control is quite simply the conflict between "throwing oneself away" and "marrying respectably."

Marianne Hoppe (left) in "Auf Wiedersehen, Franziska," 1941.

Lilian Harvey and Thomas Cziruchin in "Glückskinder," 1936.

Behind the myth of marriage one perceives the morality of the status quo in the female condition: it is unwise to live without a husband, it is prudent to cut oneself off from a vaster social responsibility. In the already narrow female world there are few allusions to women friends, who generally cause problems and sometimes serious personal crises. In Carl Boese's *Hallo, Janine!* (1939), Yvette (Else Elster), colleague of Marika Rökk in the part of a dancer, typifies the jealous friend. For the star of *Und Du, mein Schatz, fährst mit,* there is no worse friend than Gloria, an acquaintance who doesn't hesitate to have Marika accused of theft in order to ruin her career. In Erich Waschnek's *Regine* (1935), the result of the heroine's friendship with three women is the destruction of her marital happiness. Solidarity between sisters doesn't exist; in *Kora Terry* the good sister shoots (by mistake, admittedly) the bad one. One might almost say that the German film industry had accepted as truth the theories of the converted Jew Otto Weininger, who in his *Geschlecht und Charakter* (Sex and Character, 1904) affirmed that woman was the principal enemy of the emancipation of women.

Consequently, happiness for women lies in confinement at home and in the reduction to the minimum of outside relationships; and this is achieved through the absence of a job, with its resultant stress and complications. And so even though virtually all the stories of light entertainment films of a romantic nature take place in big-city settings (Berlin, Vienna, Hamburg, Paris, New York), and where there is an urban concentration there exists work, almost never do we see heroines who are salesgirls, factory workers, hairdressers, fruit-sellers or pharmacists. It is not by coincidence that the two "ladies" of the Nazi screen, Olga Tschechowa and Lil Dagover, always play actresses, journalists, sculptresses, writers, fashion designers and pianists. Here we are laboring under the great bourgeois myth of "refined" professions, totally purged of all unpleasantnesses. Or there are the films of Zarah Leander, Marika Rökk and Ilse Werner, where singing and dancing represent the esthetic equivalent of work; the numbers done by these German stars are also presented as the result of hours of exhausting rehearsals; but most of all they are pure spectacle. When Lilian Harvey glides in and out of the arms of Willy Fritsch, or Marika Rökk pirouettes on a glittering trampoline, the actual physical effort involved is minimized by the cameraman's artistry.

22

Unpleasant reality explains the fact that during the war years the regime called upon women to take jobs in defense industries, and the Kindergärten, closed during the Depression, were reopened. Nevertheless, in the immense film output of the period (except for the UFA newsreels) there does not seem to be even one image that would give us a glimpse of daily life as women actually lived it. Zarah Leander normally wears "simple" movie-queen dresses; Marika Rökk cannot resist sipping *Sekt* at the tables of a casino between one musical number and another; Willy Fritsch accompanies Lilian Harvey from the dressmaker to antique shows; Henny Porten gives tea parties for her friends—all of this while outside the theater the crackling of machine-gun fire can already be heard.

Despite what we see in the films, after the dismissals of the early years of the regime, the percentage of females working in Germany was steadily increasing. In 1933, 29.3 percent of the women had been working in industry; in 1936 the percentage went down to 24.7 percent, then was stabilized at 25 percent in 1938. At the same time, however, whereas in 1933 4.2 million women were employed in industry, handicrafts and commerce, by 1938 their number had increased to 5.2 million. Another schizophrenic aspect of Nazi policy, then: while on one hand there was a massive drive encouraging women to go back to their homes, on the other they were steadily being thrust into the work force—and were paid one-third less than men.

Besides the "good" marriage and the rejection of outside work, another hallmark of the female universe was that of sexual disguise. Not only were actresses obliged to follow the dictates of misogynist fashion designers, who distorted their figures with man-tailored suits and bulky furs, but in certain films they had to disguise themselves in order to succeed in their career. Actually, the device of transvestite dressing was often found in German films, even before 1933. Liesl Karlstadt often appeared in men's clothing in the films of Karl Valentin, as did Marlene Dietrich in the works of Josef von Sternberg. Distressingly, the Nazi cinema makes use of the expedient not only because of its inherent theatricality, but to show that the woman is really a man *manqué*.

To judge from *Viktor und Viktoria* (Victor and Victoria, 1933), directed by Reinhold Schünzel, a woman has more of a chance in life, more possibilities, when she assumes the mannerisms and the appearance of a man—although in this delightful film the light touch and the permissiveness of the Weimar comedies is still evident. With an intent considerably different from Schünzel's, director (as well as Reichsfilmintendant) Fritz Hippler presented the actor Curt Bois dressed as a woman in the anti-Semitic *Der ewige Jude* (The Eternal Jew, 1940), as a sign of perversion. (The film also pictured Jews as living in filth, their houses rat-infested.)

The theme of transvestism as a key to social success is found again in Hermann Kosterlitz's *Peter* (1935), in which Franziska Gaal plays the role of an itinerant singer who disguises herself as a man in order to get a job on a newspaper. A young doctor (Hans Jaray) takes an interest in her future, and their friendship is transformed into love when he discovers the true sex of the "youth." In Geza von Bolvary's musical *Abschiedswalzer* (Farewell Waltz, 1934), the ambiguous Sybille Schmitz, as the poetess George Sand, wears the elegant morning coats and trousers of the period ("in order to gain access to the literary circles," explains the illustrated brochure of the *Illustrierter Film-Kurier*); she goes back to women's clothes, however, as soon as Chopin appears on her amorous horizon.

But the utmost in transvestite virtuosity is achieved in Karl Ritter's *Capriccio* (1938), a romantic *Lustspiel* (comedy) in which Lilian Harvey plays the part of Madelone, the niece of a general who has raised her as a boy. When told she is to be married, she escapes from home disguised as Don Juan de Casanova. She manages to keep her identity hidden, aided by her name, which is more suited to a man, and by the loose jackets and riding breeches that conceal her figure. In *Seine Tochter ist der Peter* (His Daughter Is Peter, 1936), director Heinz Heilbig states that to be born a man is almost a gift from God. In the film, a man (Carl Ludwig Diehl) treats his daughter, Elisabeth (Traudl Stark), like a boy, even calling her Peter. His wife, however (Olga Tschechowa), wants her to be feminine and so takes her to the city to introduce her to the world of women. But after the mother has bought her silks and laces, toy stoves and dolls, she discovers that the little girl prefers the tomboy life she has been taught, and throwing stones with the boys to little girls' pastimes. The *Leitmotiv* of the film introduces the theme of the identity crisis of women: "Heute bin ich so, morgen so/Manchmal weiss ich selbst nicht wieso/Scheinbar will die Welt, dass man sich verstellt/Komisch ist die Welt" (Today I'm this

Zarah Leander

A pensive Zarah Leander in "Es war eine rauschende Ballnacht," 1939.

way/tomorrow that way/Sometimes I don't know why/the world wants us to put on a facade/The world is bizarre).

Woman thus finds herself obliged to imitate "superior" models. Nazi films of the epic-military genre also propagated the ideal of Aryan virility, as opposed to female passivity. The dominating factor in these films is *Kameradschaft* (comradeship) among soldiers and the utmost disdain for danger, values summed up in the ideal of the *Bund,* the masculine elite founded upon ideological affinities (the *Volk,* the Fatherland, the Führer). As far back as 1932, in Rudolf Meinert's film *Die elf Schill'schen Offiziere* (The Eleven Officers of Schill), the fundamental misogyny implicit in the concept of the *Bund* takes the form of exhorting women to renunciation. The words to the little march sung by the Prussian soldiers are significant: "Liebes Mädchen, lass' die Traurigkeit/Heut' ist zum Küssen keine Zeit? Wir bleiben Kameraden!/Kameraden und wenn die Welt voll Teufel wär!" (Dear girl, away with sadness/Today there's no time for kisses/We'll be comrades/ comrades, even if the world be full of devils!). Even though war hardly seemed imminent in 1932, the men are already "comrades," using lack of time as an excuse to avoid the entanglements of love.

The contrast between masculine idealism (soul and *Volk*) and coarse female materialism (marriage and reproduction) forms the plot of *Blutsbrüderschaft* (Brotherhood of Blood, 1940), in which two aviators (Hans Söhnker and Eduard von Klipstein) are in love with the same girl (Anneliese Uhlig). At the outbreak of World War II the two forget rivalries and jealousies in the name of the Third Reich, and, leaving for the front, also forget the one who was the cause of all their misunderstandings. Hans Bertram, a German aviation ace between the two world wars who later became a director, scored a success with a similar theme in the adventurous *Kampfgeschwader Lützow** (Combat Squadron Lützow, 1941). The story is told in three chapters: two Luftwaffe pilots (Heinz Welzel and Hermann Braun) become friends during an air raid against "perfidious Albion"; they discover that they have the same girlfriend (Marietherese Angerpointner); while she remains in Germany, seeking comfort with her mother, the two men, closer friends than ever, resume the forays against England. Another film with the same narrative line (two aviators in love with the same girl triumph over jealousy, thanks to the war) is Karl Ritter's *Besatzung Dora* (The Crew of the *Dora,* 1943).

But while the hero of the military films directs all his energies—which would otherwise be squandered in amorous activities—toward serving his country, what constitutes proper behavior for woman? The answer is clear: she is to emulate the comportment of the female stars of the film world, which, like all other industries, has its myths. A statement by Fritz Hippler, Reich Film Artistic Director (Reichsfilmdramaturg), confirms the importance of these myths, which the public must consume:

> The film, beyond the personal bond between the spectator and the actor, elicits also the desire to be like him. The way he clears his throat and how he spits, how he dresses, how he moves, if and what he drinks, what and how he smokes. If he is a prude or a man of the world—all this has its effects, not only in the theater but in the private life of the spectator as well. After seeing a film of Albers, the boy who lathers you up in the barber shop *is* Albers. . . In the same manner, it is undeniable that the woman shown in the film influences the ideal of beauty of the mass public. For this reason it is impossible to overestimate the importance of the casting of film roles. Not only because they have to like this woman or that one in this or that film. No, the woman carefully chosen for her physical appearance as well as for her ability and her inner attributes can influence, unconsciously yet in a decisive manner, the general level of taste and the ideal of beauty of a great number of men.[28]

The leaders of the industry were thus well aware of the fact that women were not to be flesh-and-blood creatures, but idealized symbols, the embodiment of Nazi virtues.

---

*German military units were frequently named after national heroes. Adolf von Lützow (1782–1834) was a leader in the wars of liberation from Napoleonic occupation.

If the myth of Hitler's divine ladies has been defined so far in its general characteristics, now let us examine the differences *within* the system, as handed down to us in films, photo collections, clippings, autographs and archives in which some of the most curious mementos have been found. The appearance in 1956 of a group of the most famous stars of the Third Reich in a gala evening at the Titania-Palast in West Berlin proved enormously successful with the public. To the joy of the lovers of "legends," the most glamorous men and women of Goebbels' film world paraded across the stage, having arrived punctually in the German metropolis to keep their rendezvous with the past. The first to appear was the queen of the silents, Henny Porten, who in 1910 was already starring in films for Oskar Messter, father of the German film industry; then Lil Dagover, the grande dame of the drawing room, and Dorothea Wieck, the latter remembered for the severity with which she played the headmistress in *Mädchen in Uniform*; then the little blond Karin Hardt, the charming Gretl Theimer, who made the public's heart beat in three-quarter time, the elegant Fern Andra, the stately *Salondame* Gerda Maurus, the sparkling Lilian Harvey. The first of the men to appear was Hans Albers, still as blond and energetic as he was in his adventure films; behind him came the well-groomed Ludwig Trautmann, Johannes Riemann, Carl Ludwig Diehl. Then it was the turn of an actor who had begun his career in Berlin, trying to steal parts away from Albers, just as Albers did with him: Harry Piel. Both specialized in playing the tough guy with the heart of gold, Albers in a blond version, Piel dark-haired, but with a slight difference: the former took women in his arms, while Piel preferred to tame lions, parrots, dogs and chimpanzees. That evening, years after the war, thousands of formally dressed people paid homage to the legends of the Nazi era, showing, incidentally, that during that regime the stars of escapist films had been far more popular with the public than those of propaganda films.

It can hardly be said, therefore, that Hitler's Germany imposed on an unwilling public actors with an outdoorsy, Aryan bearing such as Luis Trenker or actresses bursting with good health such as Kristina Söderbaum. This is borne out by the many nostalgic old-timers whom one finds today in the antique shops of Berlin and Hamburg looking for photographs of Harvey in her cream-colored sportscar, or the many young film fans—children of the nostalgia boom—seeking old issues of *Film-Kurier* or *Licht-Bild-Bühne*. (Nonetheless, despite the fact that the phenomenon of the star system in the Third Reich achieved almost Hollywoodian proportions, an entire sector of contemporary research concentrates continually and exclusively on the films of propaganda.)

And now, since the existence of a Nazi star system has been established, it is fitting to furnish specific examples and ascertain which stars personified the various forms of ideal womanhood of the era.

1. THE LADIES "Werdet nie Damen, bleibt deutsche Mädchen und Frauen!" (Never become ladies, remain German girls and women!) exhorted regional Party governor Julius Streicher in November 1937, speaking to a gathering of young Hitler Youth women in Berlin. And yet the Nazi cinema is filled with "ladies." Acting the "lady" was evident in certain ways of pouring tea, giving receptions, exchanging gossip, exclaiming, "Oh, mein Gott!" in difficult situations—as seen in the films starring Olga Tschechowa, Lil Dagover and Henny Porten. The three actresses are the personification of fashionable life, but one based on the ideal of a tranquil maturity lived out in economic security. In their homes, a subtle mood of bourgeois solidity pervades the tastefully decorated rooms, where one feels instantly that their mistresses are skilled in the art of receiving guests graciously. The "science of femininity" was embodied by Olga Tschechowa, who, at the end of her screen career, acquired an esthetician's diploma and founded a "beauty empire" with branches throughout the world. Perhaps because she represented bourgeois decorum par excellence, the Führer proclaimed her Staatschauspielerin (Actress of the State) on January 30, 1938.

A character of respectability and dignity is also the hallmark of the performances of Lil Dagover, a "splendid and sumptuous figure, truly regal, a regality perfectly suited to the needs of the screen," as the critic Gianni Puccini defined her.[29] The figure of Henny Porten also personified the Teutonic ideals of wisdom and sentimentality, particulary in her portrayal of Frau Wilhelmine in the Carl Froelich

Marthe Eggerth and Jan Kiepura, a Viennese husband-and-wife singing team — both of them half Jewish — left the Third Reich in 1938 for film careers in America and elsewhere.

Familie Buchholz series; but here the tone is one of healthy good sense. Porten glorifies the maternal nature more than the *Salondame,* with the placid expression of an artist who has chosen "the technique of naturalism — a naturalism softened by a vein of spontaneous tenderness that is an inherent trait of this actress."[30]

A world that is stable and secure, in an atmosphere of unrelieved philistinism, is portrayed in the films of these three actresses. Their films may be stodgy, but they give a picture of elegant German life of the period, closed off and with a relative sense of security. While average people on the street greeted each other with the mandatory "Heil Hitler," and women wore their uniforms even off-duty, the characters played by these maternal and fashionable stars continued to call out their mellifluous "Auf Wiedersehen," in these *Gesellschaftsfilme* that serve up a fictitious, make-believe world.

2.   THE FEMMES FATALES   Although the Lulus and the Blue Angels had been banned from Nazi screens, certain national-popular actresses carried on the genre of the *femme fatale* — although in a considerably altered fashion, less exotic and less dangerous. Zarah Leander symbolized the flight from reality, the escape into dreams. The haunting quality of her deep contralto voice mesmerized the German public, who filled the theaters whenever her films were shown. The most authentic star of the period, whose success was perhaps in part due precisely to the fact that she was *not* German, she cultivated the myth of the perverse woman in her off-screen life as well. Only men were invited to her parties, which featured the finest caviar, champagne, aquavit and cognac. In those festive circumstances it was possible "to know the amazing Leander in a completely new light. She is not only an exceptional hostess, but her own best guest. She eats enough for three. She drinks . . . as only the Swedish can

drink."[31] Despite these gossipy reminiscences of Curt Reiss, Leander must have really led a life of excess, since she was obliged to embark on rigorous reducing cures before beginning each new film. Italy's Gianni Puccini, sent by *Cinema* magazine in January 1941 to inform Italians about working conditions in Germany, had this to say about the actress, whom he met in the studios of Carl Froelich during the filming of *Der Weg ins Freie* (The Way to Freedom): "Dressed like Seramis in a sumptuous, low-cut gown of saffron yellow, the mouth sensual and regal at the same time, the body massive, from a distance of three feet she somehow seemed like a figure out of *Gulliver's Travels,* appearing suddenly among the Europeans, a fascinating but certainly not human souvenir from some strange world." The foregoing is scarcely the description of a seductress capable of replacing Marlene Dietrich.

Nevertheless, the lack of a more competitive vamp, the ominous awareness of living in a confined world that was destined to disappear with the war, contributed to the veneration of Zarah Leander, whose roles embody the figure of the eternal *femme fatale.* She is the star of a timeless Reich, the voice of a possible oblivion, an oblivion that, since it serves as a safety valve, had a precise political function in Hitler's Germany. The sensual appeal of Brigitte Horney also helped relieve the general melancholy, as she celebrated the passing of time with a song aimed at helping the spectator to accept the present: "So wie das Meer ist das Leben / Ewige Ebbe und Flut" (Life Is Like the Sea/A Sea That Ebbs and Flows). And her Ruby, the waterfront girl who squanders her youth on sailors, is the finest performance of her career. Sybille Schmitz, her ambiguous face framed by a mass of mahogany-colored hair, also belongs to this group, as does Brigitte Helm, a silent- and sound-movie actress who retired from the screen in 1935. Lida Baarova carried her screen persona into real life; it was because of her that Magda Quant Goebbels assigned confidential agent Karl Henke to investigate the minister's private life. Goebbels had decided to abandon his wife and six children for the beautiful Czech actress. But Hitler issued an order that could not be disobeyed, and Count Wolf von Helldorf, chief of the Berlin police, ordered Baarova to return to her country. The affair almost cost Goebbels his position at Hitler's right hand. Even the Minister of Propaganda himself had fallen prey to the myth of the star, which he had helped to create; not even he could resist the spell of the *femme fatale.*

3. THE DEFEATED   The antithesis of the sinful woman is the sentimental one, who falls in love in order to suffer, idealizing her slavery in adoration of the loved one. This type is exemplified by Kristina Söderbaum; in Veit Harlan's *Jugend* (Youth, 1938), she plays Annchen, a girl who speaks and acts like a victim in a society constructed to render women incapable of self-preservation. When Annchen, who has never known her father, allows the student Hans to court her, the following dialogue takes place:

> Annchen: "It's just that my uncle, my poor uncle. . . !"
> Hans: "Annchen, try to control yourself a little!"
> Annchen: "He was so good to me and I'm so bad, I'm so bad inside!"
> Hans: "Annchen, you aren't bad, really you aren't. There now, don't cry!"
> Annchen (in tears): "I don't deserve someone who is good to me!"
> Hans: "Annchen, you're so dear and sweet. I could forget everything for you — kiss me, kiss me!"
> Annchen: "I have to think about my mother, whether she loved my father as much as I love you."
> Hans: "Oh, Annchen! Those are things that happened long ago! Don't think about it now — this time it's completely different!"
> Annchen: "I can imagine just how it must have been. This is the way we women are. If we trust a man, then he deceives us."

Submission to the man, a feeling of self-guilt, and sacrifice define the behavior of the defeated woman. "You have to put up with everything in this life; it isn't easy, but with time you learn." This line, spoken by Luise Ullrich in Josef von Baky's *Annelie* (1941), typifies the attitude of the woman who has learned to endure every kind of unhappiness. In Harald Braun's *Nora* (1944), Ullrich plays a woman who believes that being a respectable wife is more important than one's own happiness. Unlike Ibsen's *A Doll's House,* upon which the film is based and where the woman tries to escape from the bonds of conjugal life, this *Nora* presents a woman who feels and acts according to the rules laid down by men. Ullrich, however, made a specialty of the woman defeated by love, and in *Regine* she dies a "beautiful" death, one that is esthetically beyond criticism, naturally wearing the dress she wore on the day of her engagement. In *Ich klage an!* (1941), on the other hand, the heroine dies at the will of her husband. Justified or not, euthanasia appears to be the only possible solution for the actress (Heidemarie Hatheyer).

Bewitching laces for French actress Lili Damita in "Die Berühmte Frau" (The Famous Woman), 1930.

4. THE GIRLS NEXT DOOR   The largest and safest category in the world of women of the Nazi screen was that of "the girl next door." Its representatives offer protection against the assaults and the betrayals of the vamps. Offering no cause for worry, they are frank and open, like Lilian Harvey or Renate Müller; they need only to be guided back to stability by the tutorial element (the husband). Theirs is a homespun sensuality; there is no erotic danger in Grethe Weiser's laughing eyes, nothing suggestive in the straightforward behavior of Paula Wessely, the latter Viennese but light-years away from the trollops of the Jewish playwright Arthur Schnitzler's *Reigen*.* In their films, Ilse Werner and Marianne Hoppe spend most of their time at home, waiting for the men who, after having grown up with them, have married them. Even if she works, the star of *Auf Wiedersehen, Franziska!*, who invites her friend Michael to her home, where she lives alone, shows that the only thing on her mind is marriage. The dialogue cited below merits reading in its entirety:

> Michael: "And you live here all *alone?*"
> Franziska (laughing): "Alone? No. You could hardly expect *that*. No, the independence and the fact that one can quite well . . . After all, this makes one freer. And that surprises you, doesn't it? But you are not disappointed, are you? Oh, it would be just awful if you found here a sentimental girl—possibly with a broken heart, only because once, at the railroad station, you said quite sweetly, and also quite brusquely, 'Goodbye, Franziska.' I knew, anyway, that all we had couldn't last. . . . Come, I'll show you my apartment. . . . Hey there, can't you talk? Your face has become thinner. Have the women you've met brought you such heartache—the many women, all over the world?"
> Michael: "Franziska, how can you lie so terribly?"
> Franziska: "Well . . . I . . . what else could I do? I had no idea that you still cared for me. All this time I've done nothing but wait for this, for you to come back." (They embrace.)

The social and economic movitations for her waiting are clear. In *Glückskinder,* when Lilian Harvey, wearing a cook's apron, sings: "Ich wollt' ich wär ein Mann" (I wish I'd been a man), her three male friends—Fritsch, Sima and Kemp—echo her sentiments: "Denn nur der Mann kann *Herr* der Schöpfung sein" (Because only man can be master of the universe). Even this popular song in a few words reminds us of the virtues of the socio-moral status of the *Hausfrau,* once the cute little girl next door or the brightest schoolmate.

If, of course, a girl is as quick-witted and attractive as Renate Müller, she will have no trouble finding a good position, as she demonstrates in *Die Privatsekretärin* (The Private Secretary, 1930). This pretty and well-dressed office colleague bears a remarkable resemblance to the models who advertise Junker gas heaters. The body that is well proportioned but does not awaken forbidden desires, the glowing skin and clear-eyed gaze of one who has nothing to hide, not even in the shower—these constitute the ideal of the average German girl of the period: the good companion, and future model wife.

5. THE HIGH-SPIRITED GIRLS   A virtual textbook of the kind of self-assurance that is a guarantee of marriage can be found in the person of Käthe von Nagy—voluptuous mouth, inclined to pout; an air of confidence in the most dangerous situations; restless gestures that disappear at one glance from her man. When her *Prinzessin Turandot* (Princess Turandot, 1934) offers charades and riddles to bring a touch of merriment to the court, her aplomb makes it clear that within the walls of a living room she would be equally capable.

Marika Rökk's exploits on the trapeze constitute the maximum of efficiency combined with a certain amount of self-possession. Whereas Rökk in *Hab' mich lieb* resorts to hitchhiking in order to arrive at the theater in time for her rehearsal, with the excuse that her grandmother is dying, this doesn't prevent her from slapping the driver of the car (Hans Brausewetter), who, as soon as she is aboard, makes a pass at her. This slap is highly significant: it says, "I may seem free and easy (I am a dancer, I will hitchhike if necessary), but I am not an easy mark." The slap blocks the advance, but in such a good-natured manner that the spectator thinks: this is what self-confidence is for our girls. When

---

*Or *Round Dance* (1900), signifying the dance of love—or exchange of love partners. Filmed in France as *La Ronde* (1950).

Monika (Marika) is kicked out of her house for not paying the rent, who is it who takes her in but the slapee, who, as it turns out, is a renowned Egyptologist. He offers her a drink because "Wer Sorgen hat, hat auch Likör" (whoever sorrows needs liquor). The fact that our girl drinks too much and falls asleep on the sofa of a man she doesn't know is not a reflection on her morality. The Egyptologist, in fact, behaves, as might have been expected, as a perfect gentleman, setting her down gently on his own bed, where she will sleep undisturbed. The meaning intended in this case is: the girl is uninhibited and easy-going, but not to the point of failing to demand respect. The myth of the virtuous little devil once again reflects the ideology of the regime regarding morality: the Nazi woman is upright in character, will not let her honor be compromised even in the most dire predicament and, above all, will never give up her own healthy high spirits.

VIII. *Fascinating Fascism?*

If in this brief discussion of German film the star system and totalitarianism often seem intermingled, it may be useful, in concluding, to touch on the dangers of "fascinating Fascism" — a topic to which the American writer Susan Sontag devoted a long article in *The New York Review of Books* on February 6, 1975, and which was reprinted by West Germany's *Die Zeit* on May 2 and 9 the same year. Miss Sontag begins her article by calling our attention to two books, the American edition of Leni Reifenstahl's album of photographs, *Nuba,* and Jack Pias' *SS Regalia,* in her analysis of the rekindled interest among the young and not-so-young in the world of the Nazi dictatorship.

In recent years, Germany itself has witnessed a notable revival of interest in Nazism, accompanied by numerous films and plays dealing with the period. In the summer of 1977, the long lines at the box offices of West Berlin's Karlstor and Filmkasino, which were showing Joachim C. Fest's *Hitler, eine Karriere* (Hitler, a Career, 1977), showed that the image of the Führer, assimilated with all the other symbols of the reactionary myth, had by no means faded from the minds of the German people. The film, compiled from newsreels, was a valid contribution to the new wave of reevaluation of Nazism. Even if Hans Jürgen Syberberg's *Hitler, ein Film aus Deutschland* (Hitler, a Film from Germany, 1978) was intended by its author to be an anti-Nazi film, its length (seven hours) had the effect of mythicizing the Nazi horror through the sheer piling up of images. It is all well and good for Syberberg to repeat that Nazism lurks in each one of us; the manner in which he has represented it has elevated it to mythical status.

It is more comforting to observe that the film of Daniel Schmid, *Schatten der Engel* (Shadow of the Angel, 1976), taken from a play by Rainer Werner Fassbinder entitled *Der Müll, die Stadt und der Tod* (Garbage, the City and Death), which shows a constant interchangeability of roles — even a Jew can become a Nazi, and that Nazism is returning, because it is in our heads — was poorly received. Nevertheless, one can say that Nazism "sells," that it exerts its fascination even today, on the nostalgic, as on those who claim that it is necessary to document oneself and, proceeding to a confrontation with the past, let oneself be "dispassionately" influenced by it. And what about those people who go through the flea markets in search of records of the martial music of the Third Reich, the choruses of the Hitler Youth, or the speeches of Goebbels? At least it means that the product is doing well on the market.

Susan Sontag has shown that the films of Syberberg are distorted sources of information, since too often what the spectator carries away are the perfect synchronism of the mass movements, the careful composition of many scenes and the choreographic nature of others. It is of little importance that, in Syberberg's film, Hitler is impersonated by a marionette; it is sufficient to consider that *Hitler, ein Film aus Deutschland* constitutes the "ideal" continuation of the trilogy of the German director on Ludwig II of Bavaria. Even critical positions are engulfed by the mass media.

After seeing Leni Reifenstahl's *Der Triumph des Willens,* David Bowie, a star created by the rock music industry, exclaimed: "Hitler wasn't a politician — he was a mass media genius! The way he could manipulate the public! The girls got carried away, they were sweating. . .We won't see anything like that again."[32] Apparently Bowie saw the film several times in order to learn from Hitler how to subjugate his own young fans. This "operation nostalgia" must be handled with care. Particularly when the past can seem more appealing than the present.

Marlene Dietrich in "Die Frau nach der man sich sehnt" (Eng. title, "Three Loves"), 1929 — but this "Engel" would leave for America before the coming of the Third Reich.

HENNY PORTEN

THE BEGINNINGS AND THE DEVELOPMENT OF THE German film industry were paralleled by the artistic evolution of Henny Porten, not only a talented artist but the German actress par excellence. "Sturdy and blond, she reminded you of the Walkyries and the bronze statues of Germany in German town squares," Georges Sadoul, a French journalist/author of the time, said of her, referring to those physical characteristics of abundance and womanliness that made her the "all-German star." In her behavior, on and off the screen, Henny Porten was never a "diva," never posed as a sophisticated woman of the world or as a vamp. Her image was rather that of the respectable middle-class woman, the loyal woman who will accept defeat if she cannot prevail by means of her virtue alone.

The actress, who was born in Magdeburg in north-central Germany on January 7, 1891, and died in Berlin on October 15, 1960, came from a theatrical family. Her father, Franz Porten, sang as a baritone and was for a time an actor with the Stadtheater of Magdeburg. The biographies of the actres relate an incident of her early childhood of a somewhat prophetic nature. One evening, Franz Porten invited home an Italian dancing master, a certain Buccilesi. When he saw little Henny dance a few steps he was so impressed that he asked permission to take her to the ballet school of La Scala in Milan. Porten, certain that his daughter's talent would blossom even without ballet lessons, refused. And he did not have long to wait. Henny Porten was in fact one of the few German actresses to enter films without having any prior theatrical experience. Her entry into the world of film took place in 1906 — still the era of pioneers — through the efforts of her sister, Rosa Porten, who already worked for Oskar Messter (1886–1973), founder of the first German production company. Henny appeared in short film dramas, barely 300 feet in length, to the accompaniment of a gramophone (even then there existed crude attempts at synchronizing sound to film), in which she would mime duets from *Lohengrin* and other operas with her father.

During a walk in the outskirts of Berlin, the two Porten sisters happened to see a group of little blind girls, in twos, each holding the other's hand as they crossed the street. Henny was so deeply touched by what she had seen that when she got home she tried to reenact the scene. Rosa, who also wrote screenplays for Messter, immediately dashed off a story, *Das Liebesglück der Blinden* (The Happy Love of a Blind Girl), written to order for Henny. The idea appealed to Messter, the film was made in 1910 and the company was flooded with letters asking the name of the "pretty blond blind girl" (in those days, many actors remained anonymous).

By the spring of 1912, Porten was the leading actress in all the films of the Messter company, motion pictures that for the most part were lachrymose and cloying and that today might seem " kitsch" and tedious, but at the time they found enormous favor with the public. These films, known as "Henny-Porten-Filme," quickly became a national institution, as popular as the spy stories of Harry Piel (the "Harry-Piel-Filme") or the comedies of the droll Ossi Oswalda. For the remainder of the decade, Porten worked uninterruptedly, playing comic and tragic parts, simple country girls and elegant society women. During this period she benefited from the support and advice of her colleague Robert Wiene, writer and theatrical director, whose films were frequently written exclusively for her. He would become famous for his *Das Kabinett des Dr. Caligari* (The Cabinet of Dr. Caligari) in 1919.

Particularly successful among Porten's films were *Feenhände* (Fairy Hands, 1916), based on a tale by French dramatist/librettist Eugène Scribe, and *Die Ehe der Luise Rohrbach* (The Marriage of Luise Rohrbach, 1917), in which Porten was teamed with Emil Jannings, who first attracted the attention of the public in this film. Both films were directed by Rudolf Biebrach.

Until well into the decade many of Porten's films had been directed by her husband, Kurt Stark. Stark died at the front in 1916; this painful experience served to make an artist of greater depth and humanity of the actress, who moved gradually toward more dramatic roles. She played an abandoned woman in *Die Faust des Riesen* (The Giant's Fist, 1917); a mother who saves *in extremis* her child stricken with diphtheria in *Das Maskenfest des Lebens* (Life's Masquerade Party, 1918); and in 1919 she had the title role in *Rose Bernd,* the film adaptation of the drama by Gerhart Hauptmann,* who went to congratulate her personally on her moving performance. Her co-star was Jannings.

---

*One of Germany's greatest nineteenth- and twentieth-century writers (1862–1946). A poet and novelist as well, his first play was the realistic *Vor Sonnenaufgang* (Before Sunrise, 1889). He received the Nobel Prize in literature in 1912.

The true flowering of German film came about after World War I. It was in this period that Ernst Lubitsch, a master of sophisticated storytelling, directed *Madame Dubarry* (U.S. title, *Passion*, 1919), with Pola Negri, and *Anna Boleyn* (Eng. title, *Deception*, 1920), with Henny Porten. A new era was beginning for German film, and for the actress as well. The latter film was a great success, and everyone agreed that Emil Jannings was perfectly cast as the tyrannical Henry VIII. Also in 1920, and again directed by Lubitsch, with Jannings, in *Kohlhiesels Töchter* (Kohlhiesel's Daughters), a rustic comedy, Porten played a dual role, that of Liesel, a titled lady, and Gretl, a Bavarian servant-girl. The comic high point of the film was the scene in which Liesel and Gretl—that is, Porten with herself—sang a duet. In both of these Lubitsch works, Porten revealed her natural talent in portrayals totally different from the naive young girls of her earlier films.

On July 24, 1921, Porten married Wilhelm von Kaufmann, a physician, who would later give up his profession to become the producer of his wife's films. (This was a marriage that would prove to be the source of grave problems in years to come.) Two years later she showed new artistic maturity in *Der Kaufmann von Venedig* (The Merchant of Venice), appearing opposite the celebrated star of the German stage Werner Krauss, and in Robert Wiene's *I.N.R.I.* (Jesus of Nazareth, King of the Jews), in which she played the Virgin Mary. Also in 1923, in *Das alte Gesetz* (The Ancient Law), directed by E. A. Dupont, she was the anxious fiancée of a Jewish actor torn between his love of the theater and his ancestral traditions. *Mutterliebe* (Mother Love, 1929), in which she played a housemaid so attached to the small son of her employers that after being fired, she ran off with him, was her last silent film.

Her first sound film was *Skandal um Eva* (Scandal for Eve) in 1930, directed by the celebrated G. W. Pabst, then at his creative peak. And although he had just finished directing the classic *Tagebuch einer Verlorenen* (Diary of a Lost Girl, 1929), with Louise Brooks, and in 1931 would make *Die Dreigroschenoper* (The Threepenny Opera), with Lotte Lenya, he could also turn out uninspired, forgettable films; and *Mutterliebe* was one of them. In 1924 Pabst had directed Porten in another inconsequential film, *Gräfin Donelli* (Countess Donelli), which was similar in theme and style to the hastily done, facile films of Carl Froelich—one of the most commercial and petit-bourgeois of all German film directors, whom Pabst was then working for as an assistant director.

Henny Porten in "Apachentanz" (Apache Dance), 1906.

Porten had founded a production company with Froelich, the Porten-Froelich-Produktion, shortly after the release of their *Mutter und Kind* (Mother and Child, 1924), one of her most successful films. Another important film made by the company was *Zuflucht* (Refuge, 1928), in which Froelich directed her in a fine performance with Czech-born actor Franz, later Francis, Lederer. Her collaboration with Froelich began promisingly and lasted for almost twenty years, but produced only a series of mediocre moralistic melodramas.

Froelich, the most "protected" and "approved" director of the Third Reich era, was of great help to Porten during the period of her estrangement from the film world. When Goebbels advised producers and directors not to employ the actress — guilty of refusing to divorce her husband, who according to the racial laws, was a *Volljude,* a "complete Jew" — Porten, who during the first years of her career made twelve films a year, and by agreeing to make one film automatically had to turn down four others, found herself, halfway through the 1930s, living on memories, shut up in her home in the Dahlem area of Berlin. Just when she was considering seeking shelter in America, where Lubitsch would surely offer her work, the Minister of Propaganda denied her an exit visa, on the grounds that her leaving Germany would produce a negative impression abroad.

In 1938, in order to make her feel that she was still needed, the Emo-Film Company in Vienna offered her a small part as a middle-aged mother in *Der Optimist,* a sentimental comedy that was a star vehicle for actor Viktor de Kowa. The same year she was given a part by the Fanal-Film Company in a mystery entitled *War es der im dritten Stock?* (Was It the Stranger on the Third Floor?).

In August 1939 the Tobis Company assigned her the role of the Duchess von Weissenfels, a patron of the arts, in Pabst's *Komödianten* (The Players). These roles were in effect given to her as favors (at some risk) by personal friends who felt sorry for her. The ultimate indignity was that whenever Goebbels visited the set of *Komödianten* to check on the film's progress, she would have to disappear. It was a virtual excommunication for the actress who more than any other had brought fame to the German film industry.

In the midst of the isolation to which she had been relegated, in 1944 there came an offer from Carl Froelich of a role in a story set in the Berlin of 1875, *Familie Buchholz.* Hers would be the leading role, that of a shrewd and down-to-earth mother whose major problem was to find the ideal husband for each of her daughters. Finally she had a part that was eminently suited to

her. But why had it taken the Allied aerial bombardments to get Porten back on the screen? For a heartwarming story of the good old days, when a daughter's broken engagement was considered an earthshaking family crisis, aimed at demonstrating that, in a country ravaged by war, on the brink of total disaster, "everything would be all right," there could be only one choice — the placid, reassuring, motherly Henny, whose very appearance on the screen was sufficient to evoke the aura of happy times gone by.

Porten made several films after that, but it was too late for her to make a real comeback. On the night of February 14, 1944, an aerial mine destroyed the house in which she and her husband lived. The two found themselves literally out in the snow-covered streets, shunned by their former friends, since the regime forbade Aryans to give shelter to Jews, and Dr. Kaufmann was a *Volljude.* How long ago it must have seemed to Henny Porten when the German newspapers proposed electing her President of the Reich, because with her "blond loveliness" and "noble brow," there was no problem that she could not resolve!

Porten in a signed postcard, c. 1925.

Komödianten   *(1941)*

(The Players)

Director: G. W. Pabst

At the International Film Festival in Venice in 1941 this film won the Gold Medal for best direction. Its director, G.W. Pabst (1885–1967), having emigrated to France with the advent of Nazism, was one of the leading figures of the German film industry between the two wars. In 1933 he went to Hollywood, where he directed *A Modern Hero,* starring Richard Barthelmess— his only American film, and a good one. He was unable to get other assignments, however, and resumed his career in France. In 1939 he announced his intention to return to the United States and become an American citizen. Instead, he inexplicably returned to Germany, where he spent the war years. Under the Nazi regime, he directed, in addition to *Komödianten, Paracelcus* (1943), filmed in Prague and starring Werner Krauss, and *Der Fall Molander* (The Molander Case, 1944), which he never completed. Although not without interest, none of these works attained the level of his *Westfront 1918* (Eng. title, *Comrades of 1918,* 1930), *Kameradschaft* (Comradeship, 1931), *Die Büchse der Pandora* (Pandora's Box, 1928) or *Das Tagebuch einer Verlorenen* (Diary of a Lost Girl, 1929), the last two with American actress Louise Brooks. After the war, his anti-racist contribution, *Der Prozess* (The Trial, 1948), smacked more of a belated attempt at rehabilitation for himself than a true indictment.

Story: from the novel *Philine* by Olly Boeheim. Script: A. Eggebrecht, V. von Colande and G. W. Pabst
Photography: Bruno Stephan
Set Design: Julius von Borsody and Hans Hochheiter
Music: Lothar Brühne
Production: Bavaria-Film
Length: 113 minutes
Country of origin: Germany, 1941
Censor's approval: August 13, 1941
Premiere: September 5, 1941, Munich
Awards: Particular Political and Artistic Value; Cultural Value; Formative for the People

CAST _____

Käthe Dorsch (Karoline Neuber*), Henny Porten (Amalia, Duchess of Weissenfels), Hilde Krahl (Philine Schröder), Gustav Diessl (Ernst Biron, Duke of Kurland), Richard Häussler (Armin von Perckhamer), Friedrich Domin (Johann Neuber), Ludwig Schmitz (Müller), Sonja-Gerda Scholz, Lucie Millowitsch, Bettina Hambach, Walter Janssen, Alexander Ponto.

SYNOPSIS _____

It is the middle of the eighteenth century, and the actress Karoline Neuber is trying to improve the lot of actors. It is not an easy task, and she is often misunderstood by the public. But she finds a benefactor sympathetic to the problems of theater people in the Duchess Amalia von Weissenfels. Actors at that

A poster of the film.

*Karoline Neuber (1697–1760) founded the first German National Theater in the 1750s.

Rehearsals at the castle of the Duchess von Weissenfels: Friedrich Domin (center) and Lucie Millowitsch (right).

time were looked down upon as ne'er-do-wells and vagabonds. Even the duchess refuses to let her nephew marry Philine, a pretty young ingenue in the Neuber troupe, believing that an actress is meant for pleasure but not for marriage. Karoline responds violently to the attacks made upon her and the company, defending her colleagues with such vehemence that she is driven out of the country. A performance given at the court of St. Petersburg ends in disaster. Abandoned by everyone and unable to find success even back in Germany, Karoline dies in solitude.

CRITICS' COMMENTS ─────

A real revelation for us was the performance of Henny Porten. For how many years have we followed on our screens this unaffected, lovable, wise and warm lady? Given a part that fits her perfectly, in this film she has reached a new level in her artistic evolution, and we hope to see her more often on our screens. . . .The film, whose importance has been shown by the number of awards it has received . . . provided the Munich audience with numerous topics for discussion.
T. W. MARTINI, *Deutsche Filmzeitung,* Munich, September 21, 1941

It is a monument to the act of creation. In relating the story of Karoline Neuber the film leads us to the eternal wellsprings from which art is drawn. . . . The only real stars are ideas. Henny Porten gives a forceful and honest performance. With exemplary assurance she succeeds in unraveling the tangled threads of the plot. She sustains with grace and dignity the emotional outbursts of the company of players in the castle.*
F. HENSELEIT, *Film-Kurier,* Berlin, September 1941

It is a poor film, in part because it tries to reflect the main theme in several parallel sub-themes. . . . Observing Karoline's noble intentions, [someone] warns her: "The theater is not the mirror of life! Life is squalid, only art is pure!". . .The film often strays far from reality. Furthermore, Käthe Dorsch is not equal to the leading role, lacking the authority displayed by Henny Porten in the part of the authoritarian duchess who sniffs snuff.
F. COURTADE and P. CADARS, *Histoire du cinéma nazi* (Paris, 1973)

Familie Buchholz   *(1944)*

(The Buchholz Family)

Director: Carl Froelich

Henny Porten offers a glass of "Sekt" to Gustav Fröhlich (left) and Jakob Tiedtke.

Carl Froelich had already directed Porten in various "Henny-Porten-Filme," and he particularly wanted her for this film, which enjoyed a great success, not only out of loyalty, but because it portrayed a world of wholesome and unchanging values at a moment in which the German people were living in constant insecurity. Beginning as a cameraman at the Messter-Film studios in the second decade of the century, then as director and producer, Froelich played a major role in the film industry of the Third Reich, and was one of the few filmmakers on whom Goebbels conferred the title of Film-professor.

Story: from the novel of the same name by Julius Stinde
Screenplay: Jochen Kuhlmey
Photography: Robert Baberske
Music: Hans-Otto Borgmann
Production: UFA
Length: 96 minutes

Country of origin: Germany, 1944
Censor's approval: January 21, 1944
Premiere: March 3, 1944
Awards: Artistic Worth; Formative for the People

CAST

Henny Porten (Wilhelmine Buchholz), Grethe Weiser (Frau Bergfeldt), Gustav Fröhlich (Holle, the painter), Elisabeth Flickenschildt (Emmi), Jakob Tiedtke (Wilhelmine's husband), Hans S. Schaufuss, Sigrid Becker, Oscar Sabo, Fritz Kampers, Irmingard Schreiter, Carl H. Worth, Günther Lüders, Margarete Schön.

SYNOPSIS

In order to find a proper husband for each of her daughters, Wilhelmine Buchholz even sets aside the novel she is writing. She decides that Dr. Franz Wrenschen, a fine-looking physician, is the right man for her daughter Emmi.

But Franz prefers Betti, who is more mature, and in any case he isn't ready to give up his freedom. Frau Bergfeldt is more fortunate than Wilhelmine; her daughter, Auguste, has her eye on the student Weigelt, while her son, Emil, is in love with Betti. Wilhelmine has her doubts about this profusion of romantic entanglements—especially after surprising young Emil Bergfeldt at the zoo with another girl, Cilly. In the end, Wrenschen will marry Emmi; Fritz, Wilhelmine's brother, will marry Erika, and Betti will break her engagement to remain faithful to the painter Holle, who has to spend three years in Rome studying. And Wilhelmine's novel is a success.

CRITICS' COMMENTS

Froelich's task, and not an easy one, was to re-create on the screen the Berlin of a bygone era, when friends would meet to take long walks together along the Spree, when families breathed an

With Elisabeth Flickenschildt.

Familie Buchholz

atmosphere of virtue, solidarity and middle-class common sense. He shows us a world that is past but not dead. Henny Porten, as we have said so often, possesses the art of knowing what to say and what to leave unsaid, as in the scene where, firm yet understanding, she tells her Emmi that she has to learn to control her own heart. The director effectively contrasts the Buchholz family and its down-to-earth matriarch with the snobbish world of the Bergfeldts. The film has the great virtue of being truly entertaining, at a time in which life for Berliners is considerably more grim than in the past.

G. IPSEN, *Film-Kurier*, Berlin, March 4, 1944

For a moment at least we are back in the Berlin of another day. Porten gives

With Emil Jannings in "Kohlhiesels Töchter" 1920.

a superb performance, with the aura of warmth and humanity that the character requires. . . .The era of 1875 has been re-created by those who love what is beautiful and enduring, with commendable taste and accuracy, particularly in the ball scenes.

E. KETTLER, *Licht-Bild-Bühne*, Berlin, March 6, 1944

A delightful comedy, which is also the symphony of a city. Wilhelmine Buchholz embodies the true nature of the Berliner—spontaneous and cordial, droll and direct. The scene between Betti and Wilhelmine, for example, is a gem of dialect humor. In a finely controlled performance, Henny Porten expresses the myriad emotions of a mother.

W. MELZER, *Der Film*, Berlin, March 18, 1944

This is the way to speak to wives! – a scene from "Die Ehe der Luise Rohrbach," 1917.

OLGA TSCHECHOWA

A scene from "Regine," 1934.

S HE WAS CALLED "THE GRANDE DAME OF GERMAN film," and in effect there were not many like her in the industry. For three decades, in almost two hundred films, she portrayed the woman of elegance, who moved with grace, self-assurance and vitality.

Olga Tschechowa was born in Leninakan (formerly Aleksandropol), in the Caucasus, on April 26, 1897. Her father, however, an engineer and Minister of Railways in Czarist Russia, came from Westphalia, in northwestern Germany. The rest of the family were mostly artists: her mother was a painter, her grandmother had been a celebrated singer and her uncle was the celebrated Russian author and playwright Anton Chekhov. Olga spent her youth between Moscow and St. Petersburg, studying sculpture and engraving, until she decided to enroll in Konstantin Stanislavski's Moskow Art Theater school. At sixteen she married her cousin Michael

Chekhov, who was already a well-known actor. The marriage lasted three years, ending shortly after the birth of their firstborn, Ada. The First World War and the Bolshevik Revolution induced her to go to Berlin at the beginning of the 1920s, where she worked designing posters until she was discovered by Erich Pommer, founder of UFA, and by F. W. Murnau, the most important German director of the period. In 1921 Murnau gave her a leading role in *Schloss Vogelöd* (Eng. title, *Haunted Castle*). From that moment on, the image of "La Tschechowa" became a fixture in the German film world.

In 1930 she appeared opposite Max Schmeling, world boxing champion and husband of the actress Anny Ondra, in *Liebe im Ring* (Love in the Ring). In Max Ophüls' masterpiece *Liebelei* (Flirtation, 1933), she found herself appearing with Magda Schneider (mother of the late actress Romy Schneider), Luise Ullrich, Paul

Hörbiger and Gustav Gründgens. In Willi Forst's classic *Maskerade* (Eng. title, *Masquerade in Vienna,* 1934), he contrasted her worldly sophistication with the innocent freshness of Paula Wessely, who was making her film debut. In *Burgtheater* (Town Theater, 1936), Tschechowa played opposite Werner Krauss.

The beautiful emigrée, by now a woman of the world whose regal bearing kept both admirers and supplicants at a respectful distance, worked in Paris, Prague, Rome and Vienna. In 1931 she had gone to Hollywood to do *Love on Command,* the German adaptation of Mal St. Clair's *The Boudoir Diplomat.* Her slight

Russian accent, far from being a handicap, only seemed to add to her cosmopolitan charm. When a part called for an aristocratic woman—beautiful, elegant and ever so slightly maternal—directors instantly thought of Tschechowa. In effect, she portrayed better than anyone else the behavioral codes of the Austro-Hungarian aristocracy. Countess Edith von Tauroff of the musical *Die drei von der Tankstelle* (The Three from the Filling Station, 1930), of Wilhelm Thiele, and Baroness Eggersdorf of Ophüls' *Liebelei* are intriguing examples of that spirit which interposes between itself and others a reassuring veil of discretion.

At the time in which she played in *Der Choral von Leuthen* (The Hymn of Leuthen, 1933), the Hitler regime was beginning to demand propaganda films from the industry, especially stories glorifying German history, such as the "Fridericus-Filme." These were movies based on the exploits of Frederick the Great (usually played by Otto Gebühr), depicting him as a popular hero, devoted to tradition and to his own subjects. They were for the most part paternalistic transpositions of the figure of the "great leader," behind which it was not difficult to discern a reference to the Führer. In *Der Choral von Leuthen,* presented at the UFA-Palast in Berlin four days after Hitler's appointment as Chancellor, Tschechowa played the part of a noblewoman who provided shelter in her castle to a Prussian platoon under Frederick's command. Also appearing briefly in the film were future directors Wolfgang Staudte (who went on, after World War II, to become a major filmmaker in East Germany) and Veit Harlan.

Tschechowa much preferred making American-style comedies, however, such as *Die gelbe Flagge* (The Yellow Flag, 1937) and *Verliebtes Abenteuer* (Amorous Adventure, 1938), as well as musicals and films of fantasy. Prominent among the latter were *Die Welt ohne Maske* (The World Unmasked, 1934), a typical Harry Piel film, and *Die unheimlichen Wünsche* (Sinister Desires, 1939), based on the romantic idea of all one's wishes being granted by means of a magic object—in this case a fur coat. In this film Tschechowa was a glamorous actress who brought about the ruin of a nobleman who spurned her for a simple cutter of silhouettes.

Tschechowa, with her air of the slightly dangerous woman of the world, often found herself in situations that put her in competition with much younger and less experienced women, as in *Zwei Frauen* (Two Women, 1938), wherein she competed with her own eighteen-year-old daughter for a young pilot; *Befreite Hände* (Unfettered Hands, 1939), in which a mature woman's passion is transformed into an unseemly display of female fury; and in *Gefährlicher Frühling* (Dangerous Spring, 1943), where she succeeds in snatching away an older professor from the arms of her plump young niece.

Her private life was as varied as her screen roles. Shortly after the war's end, she founded a film production company, which turned out to be an ill-advised venture. She had better luck with a cosmetics firm, founded in Munich in the early 1950s, and which today has branches in Milan, Vienna, Helsinki and the United States. She has been the author of several books on beauty care, which met with considerable success, as well as an autobiography entitled *Meine Uhren gehen anders* (My Clocks Tell Different Times), which did *not,* although it contained her prized formulas for certain beauty preparations, as well as the personal "philosophy of beauty" of the actress to whom the famous surgeon Ernst Ferdinand Sauerbruch said, "How I would love to dissect that wonderful body!"

Active and energetic until the end, able to accept the reversals of fortune with grace, Tschechowa knew when it was time to stop. "I retired," she said to the *Süddeutsche Zeitung* (South German News) for November 4, 1967, "because I didn't want to spoil the illusions of all those people who admired me." However, in 1971 Tschechowa interrupted her career as a business executive to appear with her niece Vera in the TV series "Duell zu dritt" (Duel for Three). Those who knew her fanatical belief in hard work knew, above all, how proud she was of never having set foot in a hospital. Even when she became gravely ill, her family respected her wish to remain in her home in Munich, where she died on March 9, 1980, at the age of 82. She lives on through her films.

With Eckhard Harendt (seated).

With Adolf Wohlbrück (later Anton Walbrook).

Gewitterflug zu Claudia *(1937)*

(Stormy Flight to Claudia)

Director: Erich Waschneck

This film, which tells the story of the comradeship between a German pilot and a British one, was made when the regime had not yet begun its campaign against "perfidious Albion," which led the industry to produce pro-Irish films such as *Der Wolf von Glenarvon* (The Wolf of Glenarvon, 1940), in which Tschechowa played the part of the Irish patriot Gloria Grandison, and *Mein Leben für Irland* (My Life for Ireland, 1941), the tale of an Irish boy who sides with the Nationalists — both directed by Max Kimmich.

Story: from the novel of the same name by Karl Unselt
Screenplay: Karl Unselt and Christian Hallig
Photography: Robert Baberske and Heinz von Jaworsky
Set design: C. L. Kirmse
Editing: C. Stapenhorst
Technical consultants for flying sequences: Joachim Matthias, Dr. Ernst Dierbach and Ranz Schlenstedt of Lufthansa

Music: Werner Eisbrenner
Production: UFA
Length: 74 minutes
Country of origin: Germany, 1937
Censor's approval: November 22, 1937
Premiere: November 25, 1937, Berlin
Award: Artistically Commendable

CAST

Willy Fritsch (Droste, Lufthansa pilot), Olga Tschechowa (Frau Mainburg), Jutta Freybe (her daughter Claudia), Gerhard Bienert (flight mechanic Hübner), Rudolf Schündler (flight radio operator Klömkes), Maria Koppenhöfer (Frau Imhoff), Karl Schönböck (William Crossley, flight captain, Imperial Airways), Heinrich Marlow (Sir Reginald Crossley), Edwin Jürgensen (Quist, the secretary), Walter Werner (James, the butler), Paul Mederow (Maxwell, the notary), Hans Leibelt (Inspector Bäuerle).

SYNOPSIS

The crew of the *Wilhelm Cuno*, the most modern Lufthansa aircraft, is made up of true friends, rather than mere co-workers. Claudia, the pretty young Lufthansa secretary, anxiously awaits the return of Captain Droste. One day he receives a telegram from his British friend Crossley, engaged on a mission in Africa, asking him to go to London to look after his old Uncle Reginald. Frau Imhoff, whom Claudia believes to be her mother, tries to thwart the romance between Droste and the girl for reasons of her own. In 1914, in London she had had Claudia's real mother, Frau Mainburg, arrested as a spy, and had taken Claudia away with her. Frau Mainburg meanwhile has become a celebrated singer, and has fought to regain her good name.

Quist, who was the accomplice of Frau Imhoff, is now the secretary of Sir Reginald, and tries to prevent Droste from coming to London and discovering the truth. Droste receives a false

Not even Olga Tschechowa can resist a man in uniform (Karl Schönböck).

order to land in Hanover, where he is arrested. Meanwhile, Frau Imhoff has been killed by Quist, and the police arrest Claudia, believing her guilty of the crime. Droste, freed, flies with Claudia's real mother to London, where the real murderer is brought to justice. Sir Reginald, dying, leaves Claudia universal heir to his estate, having discovered that she is the daughter of his son Percy. Mother and daughter are reunited, as are old friends Droste and Crossley after their tempestuous flight.

CRITICS' COMMENTS ─────

A complicated story, which doesn't let up for a moment. It has elements of a mystery—murder, money that disappears, a criminal unmasked by the police. . . . It also has fascinating technical particulars, such as air–land radio linkups, emergency landings, etc. . . . Olga Tschechowa is given every opportunity to display her singular brand of warmth and femininity. She is particularly memorable in the scene where she is reunited, after so many years, with her daughter, now an adult. . . . She has never been better.
  G. SCHWARK, *Film-Kurier*,
  Berlin, November 26, 1937

A screenplay that is a hymn to the dedication of pilots, who guide their aircraft through the worst of storms, still managing to be so punctual that one could set his watch by their time of arrival. . . . We must thank Olga Tschechowa if
the film nonetheless has the aura of a love story. As endearing as ever, she gives an extraordinary performance in what is actually a most difficult part, inasmuch as she is under suspicion until the very end. . . .The entire cast, in fact, is excellent, with a special pat on the back to the wonderful young actor who plays the milkman's helper. Our congratulations to all concerned.*
  A. SCHNEIDER, *Licht-Bild-Bühne*,
  Berlin, December 1, 1937

Erich Washneck has directed his cast with an able hand. Playing opposite the vigorous and virile Willy Fritsch. . . Olga Tschechowa gives a performance notable for its strength and sensitivity.
  M. RAAB, *Völkischer Beobachter*,
  Berlin, December 3, 1937

Bel Ami, der Liebling schöner Frauen   (1939)
(Bel Ami, the Idol of Beautiful Women)

Director: Willi Forst

Willi Forst (born Wilhelm Frohs in Vienna in 1903), star and director of this film, can be considered the most frivolous and least committed among the creators of Austro-German screen operettas. An actor and producer as well as director, Forst had learned from Geza von Bolvary the formula for putting together lightweight films with a Viennese setting, featuring a great deal of music and enjoying enormous popularity between 1930 and 1937. After acting in several films with the same team—the Hungarian soubrette Marthe Eggerth, the character actor Paul Hörbiger and the comedians Hans Moser and Theo Lingen, fellow Austrians—he turned to directing in 1933 with *Leise flehen meine Lieder* (Eng. title, *Schubert's Unfinished Symphony*), one of his most melodic films.

Forst attempted to emulate the sophisticated, scintillating works of Max Ophüls, particularly in *Mazurka* (1935)

and *Burgtheater* (Eng. title, *Vienna Burgtheater*, 1936), but the results were merely hollow and unconvincing films, set in a synthetic Old Vienna, in which Hapsburg high society carried on short-lived flirtations against a background of Strauss waltzes. Perhaps his best work is *Bel Ami,* an elegant satire of the Parisian *haut monde.*

Certain critics have attempted to analyze Forst's works in the light of an alleged anti-Prussianism (and thus of a hidden anti-militarism and anti-Nazism), based on his glorification of the Hapsburg myth, which could be interpreted as a manifest expression of hostility toward the Hitler regime. More objectively, however, Günther Peter Straschek observes: "The sentimentality and artificiality of *Maskerade* and of *Mazurka* have been palmed off as "Viennese charm," given their traditional operetta trimmings, when they might more realistically be viewed

as examples of fascistizing introspection."[1] After the war, Forst, unable to repeat the great successes of earlier times, retired to private life in Switzerland, after presenting to the city of Vienna a villa with 100,000 square meters of land around it. He died in August 1980.

Story: from the novel of the same
  name by Guy de Maupassant
Screenplay: Willi Forst and Axel
  Eggebrecht
Photography: Ted Pahle
Set design: Schlichting and Herlth
Music: Theo Mackeben
Editing: Georg Wolff
Production: Wien-Film and
  Forst-Film
Length: 101 minutes
Country of origin: Austria, 1939
Censor's approval: February 7, 1939
  (banned to minors under 18)
Premiere: February 21, 1939

Tschechowa and the irresistible Bel Ami (Willi Forst).

CAST

Willi Forst (Georges Duroy), Olga Tschechowa (Madeleine), Ilse Werner (Suzanne), Hilde Hildebrand (Madame de Marelle) Lizzi Waldmüller (Rachel, the dancer), Johannes Riemann (Minister Laroche), Aribert Wäscher (the editor), Will Dohm (the editor-in-chief), Hubert von Meyerinck (a journalist), Hadrian M. Netto (another journalist), Hans Stiebner, Werner Scharf, Egon Brosig, Tatjana Sais, Ilse Petri, Erich Dunskus, Walter Gross, Richard Ludwig.

SYNOPSIS

Paris, at the turn of the century. The gigolo Georges Duroy returns to the capital after a long sojourn in Morocco. With the aid of the well-connected Madeleine, Georges manages to make some headway in the newspaper world, but in reality his only talent is his ability to court beautiful and celebrated women. Madeleine, for a number of years mistress of the Minister of Foreign Affairs, succeeds in having him appointed Minister to the Colonies. After scandals and intrigues of every kind, Bel Ami marries Suzanne, the daughter of the minister who was his predecessor.

CRITICS' COMMENTS

Let us be honest and say it openly: Bel Ami represents an age-old aspect of the French national character. . . . The most delicate situations are handled here with such refinement that the spectator can only laugh and applaud. One recalls the first scene between Madeleine and Laroche, and the scene of farewell in the four waiting rooms, but most of all the exhilarating opera ball and the scenes. . .with the cancan and the song "Bel Ami." . . . Special praise must go to the alluring, wise and witty Olga Tschechowa, who adds another memorable portrait to the vast gallery that she has created in films and in the theater. . . . The director and his stars were greeted by thunderous applause and called back to the stage repeatedly.
A. SCHNEIDER, *Licht-Bild-Bühne*, Berlin, February 22, 1939

If Maupassant had been able to see the film adaptation of his novel, he would have been delighted. The film is light-hearted from beginning to end, without ever descending to the tasteless or the obvious. What a charming and debonair fellow this Duroy is! And clustered around him are women of every conceivable type, and all with but one obsession: Bel Ami. In the first row we see Olga Tschechowa, wise and cool-headed, the mistress of every situation. Our heart is hers for the taking. Then Hilde Hildebrand, the glittering drawing room butterfly. . . . A bit further back, Lizzi Waldmüller of the charming braids. . . . The music is intoxicating, and the audience leaves the theater humming "Bel Ami."
W. LÜTHE, *Die Filmwoche*, Berlin, March 1, 1939

"You have luck with the ladies, Bel Ami/ So much luck with the ladies, Bel Ami!/ You're not handsome, but you're charming./ You're not intelligent, but so gallant./ You aren't a hero, but just a man that they all adore." This refrain aptly sums up the figure of the debonair young man played by Willi Forst. . . . From a musical standpoint, it could serve as a model for others to emulate, with the songs introduced at just the right moment to enhance a particular mood or situation . . . with a charming score in the background throughout virtually the entire film. Willi Forst performs with uncommon taste and discretion, particularly in the final scene in the enormous banquet hall, where he opens the many doors, behind each of which one of his ex-lovers is waiting. . . . It is impossible here to single out each actor for praise, and thus we shall merely state that the most outstanding is Olga Tschechowa . . . who is not only beautiful and elegant, but an actress of extraordinary intelligence and intensity. . . . There was enormous applause when Willi Forst and the other leading players came out on stage for a bow.
A. SCHMIDT, *Deutsche Filmzeitung*, Munich, March 5, 1939

With Karl Raddatz.

LIL DAGOVER

L IL DAGOVER WAS ONE OF THE FEW STARS OF THE silent era whose career continued to flourish even after the coming of sound. Like Zarah Leander and Olga Tschechowa, she was an actress of exceptional "presence." With her smooth, even features, dark eyes with lids half lowered, and long arms of incredible whiteness, she seemed created for the joy of the photographers who competed for her services for fashion layouts. If one leafs through the annals of the silent era, and then of the films made between 1929 and 1944 in Germany, he will be amazed at the frequency with which the actress's name recurs in the cast lists.

She was born Marta Maria Lillits (or Marie Antonia Sieglinde Martha Seubert) on September 30, 1897, in Madiven, Java, where her father, a forest ranger, worked for the Dutch government. At the age of six she went to Germany, the country of origin of her parents. They died soon afterward, leaving Lil an orphan at thirteen, who would spend her adolescent years as a guest of friends and relatives in Baden-Baden, Karlsruhe, Geneva and Weimar. It was in this Thuringian city that Lil, aged seventeen, met and married the veteran actor Fritz Daghofer, thirty-five years her senior. Her biographies relate that one day in 1919, while the young matron was walking through the streets of Weimar, an unknown man approached her, struck by the extraordinarily photogenic quality that he sensed in her. Confused, Dagover returned home, just in time to find herself in the midst of a gathering of actors where the man she had seen on the street earlier took her husband by the arm to tell him of his having run across the ideal interpreter for the role of a beautiful, petulant woman in his next film. The man was none other than the director Robert Wiene, who at that moment was in the midst of preparations for the filming of *Das Kabinett des Dr. Caligari,* the most celebrated work of the period of German expressionism.

After being properly introduced to the gentleman, Lil went to Berlin to sign a contract with Decla, the production company headed by Erich Pommer, who took charge of getting her career started. Her screen debut, however, was not in *Caligari* but in Fritz Lang's *Harakiri* (Eng. title, *Butterfly,* 1919). She and her husband were divorced this same year. Dagover's part in *Caligari* (1919) was a smallish one, even considering that all the protagonists of the film were men. That brief appearance, however—with her milk-white skin and black-rimmed eyes—in the role of Jane, the girl abducted by Cesare, was sufficient to make an indelible impression upon the public. Her ascent had begun under the sign of Decla, and proceeded as swift and sure as that of the eagle in the trademark of the company.

The disparate nature of the roles given her in her first years in the industry can be seen by a rapid glance at a few of her films. In 1921 she made *Der müde Tod* (Eng. title, *Destiny*), directed by Fritz Lang; in 1922 *Phantom,* by F. W. Murnau; and in 1925 *Chronik von Grieshuus* (Eng. title, *At the Grey House*), a dramatic film based on a novella by Theodor Storm, in which she played a young woman who dies in childbirth. Also in 1925, again under Murnau's direction, she appeared as Madame Elmire in *Tartüff* (Tartuffe), with Emil Jannings, and later that year in *Die Brüder Schallenberg* (Eng. title, *The Two Brothers*), by Karl Grüne, an actor-director who had a profound influence on German films in the 1920s. The use of Dagover by important directors and the constant regularity with which she appeared on the screen, as well as her glowing good looks, which reflected the criterion of female beauty of the period, all served to advance her career. In 1925, Max Reinhardt invited her to represent "Beauty" at his new festival in Salzburg, Austria. He had evidently chosen well, inasmuch as for the next six years Dagover appeared as the personification of Beauty at the Salzburg Festival.

Lil Dagover in a fainting scene from "Schlussakkord," 1936.

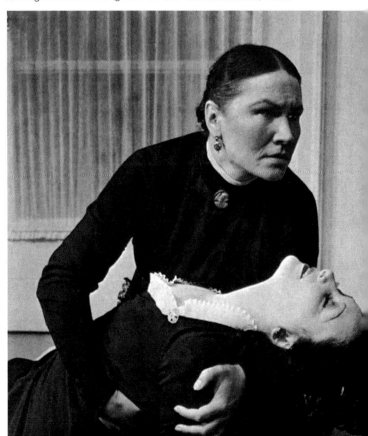

Her career especially flourished between 1924 and 1929, when she also made films in France for the Vandal & Delac Company: *Le Tourbillon de Paris* (The Whirlwind of Paris, 1928), *La Grande Passion* (1929) and the unusually long *Monte Cristo* (1929), which was shown in Germany in two parts. By now she had passed from ingenue roles to those of a mature and sophisticated woman, experienced and self-assured. Her career had reached its zenith during the final years of the silent period; the coming of sound had no adverse effect upon it. In 1929 she made *Ungarische Rhapsodie* (Hungarian Rhapsody), an ersatz Magyar extravaganza, seasoned with gypsy violins, with poor Willy Fritsch unable to decide between the mature fascination of Dagover and the youthful freshness of Dita Parlo. In Erik Charell's classic *Der Kongress tanzt* (The Congress Dances, 1931), she was a countess whose patrician profile was enhanced by a pair of sparkling paste earrings. Despite her brief appearance (for this *Monumentalwerk* of German film artistry, the most prestigious actors had been mobilized, even for the minor parts), the international audience was struck by her beauty and charm; the film, an enormous success, was made in three versions: German, English and French.

It was only a matter of time before America beckoned. In 1931 Warner Brothers brought her to Hollywood to film *The Woman from Monte Carlo,* which was premiered in Indianapolis, and enjoyed an unexpected success. The American cameramen seem to have discovered a new Dagover, livelier, less reserved, with a more mobile, expressive face, returning her "transformed" to their German colleagues, who were delighted to show off these newly discovered facets of her artistry.

Like her celebrated colleagues Hans Albers and Lilian Harvey, Dagover often made foreign-language versions of her films, dubbing herself with a well-modulated and caressing voice that not even the primitive early sound systems could spoil. In *Die Tänzerin von Sanssouci* (The Dancer of Sanssouci, 1932), a tale set in the reign of Frederick the Great, and directed by Friedrich Zelnik, she sang, displaying a highly agreeable voice.

By the beginning of the 1930s, Dagover's screen image had been clearly defined: the beautiful woman no longer in the bloom of youth but still lovely, and able to resign herself to the inevitable competition of younger women. In *Die letzte Illusion* (The Last Illusion, 1932), she gave a memorable performance as a woman of forty who loved a younger man (Willi Forst). At first he seems fascinated by her mature beauty. Their love is destroyed, however, when the woman's daughter seduces the young man. Crushed and yet dry-eyed, she accepts defeat, giving up forever her last illusion. The psychological evolution of this character is similar to that found in Hermann Kosterlitz's *Das Abenteuer der Thea Roland* (The Adventures of Thea Roland, 1932), the story of a woman who has always been alluring and sought-after, at the moment in which she realizes that her beauty is fading. Dagover gives an affecting portrayal of a woman confronting her own physical decay—the dark circles under her eyes, the lines that makeup will no longer hide.

After numerous serious roles, she finally got a change of pace in the sparkling comedy *Ich heirate meine Frau* (I'm Marrying My Wife, 1934), where, as a reporter who will do anything for a scoop, she disguises

herself as a Japanese. After appearing as Mrs. Erlynne in *Lady Windermeres Fächer* (Lady Windermere's Fan, 1935), a film made before Oscar Wilde was banned in Germany, she played a *cocotte* in the propaganda film *Der höhere Befehl* (The Higher Command, 1935). The story, laid in Prussia in 1806, concerned two officers, one British and one Prussian, both intent on thwarting the Napoleonic armies. For the role of the French actress (and spy) Madame Martin, Dagover assumed an amusing French-German accent, which, however, according to the critics, was not sufficient to make her character believable.

Her stock rose again, however, with Detlef Sierck's *Schlussakkord* (Closing Chord, 1936), the drama of a woman seeking her lost son. Dagover, who was always careful to avoid histrionics, even in her most dramatic roles, gave a moving, measured portrayal as the desperate mother. The film, which was awarded the prize for best musical film at the Venice Film Festival in 1936, can be counted among Dagover's most successful efforts of the Hitler period. In *Die Kreutzersonate* (The Kreutzer Sonata, 1937, adapted from Tolstoy's short story), a work that can be classified with the great mass of Nazi-period films that were workmanlike if undistinguished, the actress played a jealous woman. In the role of Yelaina, a woman swept into the vortex of adultery in a moment of bewilderment, she sought to express the joylessness of a love that was condemned by the prevailing morality. The adulteress, incapable of throwing off her immoral shackles, dies—upholding the Nazi ideology. For this performance, which was highly praised by Goebbels, Dagover was awarded the title of Staatsschauspielerin (State Actress). Soon after, she would begin to slip into character parts. Two decades as a reigning beauty is not at all a bad record, but her spectacular triumphs were now a thing of the past.

During the war years she did supporting roles, primarily in the lamentable *Kostümfilme* based on heroic episodes in German history. After a career of more than sixty films, of which thirty were silent, Dagover preferred to step aside, appearing occasionally in theater, returning, as it were, to an earlier stage in her career. Because of the aristocratic grace of her presence, the hint of melancholy in a smile half amiable, half mocking, Dagover had portrayed a vast gallery of women, but always with a degree of detachment. From the young girls of *Caligari* or *Der müde Tod* to the noblewoman of *Der Kongress tanzt,* from the lonely, aging woman of *Die lezte Illusion* to the grieving mother of *Schlussakkord,* her characters seldom laughed; they only smiled.

Lil Dagover died in Munich on January 30, 1980, at age eighty-two.

Opposite: Publicity pose for "Eine Frau, die weiss was sie will" (A Woman Who Knows What She Wants), 1934.

Schlussakkord   (1936)

(Closing Chord)

Director: Detlef Sierck (Douglas Sirk)

At the International Film Festival in Venice in 1936 this work was awarded the cup for best musical film.

Screenplay: Kurt Heuser and Detlef Sierck
Photography: Robert Baberske
Set design: Carl Dohnberg
Music: Kurt Schröder, and excerpts of classical music
Production: UFA
Length: 102 minutes
Country of origin: Germany, 1936
Censor's approval: June 10, 1936
Premiere: June 27, 1936, Dresden; July 24, 1936, Berlin
Award: Artistic Value

CAST

Lil Dagover (Hanna), Willy Birgel (Maestro Gravenberg), Maria von Tasnady (Charlotte Gravenberg), Maria Koppenhöfer (the maid in the Gravenberg house), Peter Bosse (Hanna's son), Theodor Loos (the pediatrician), Albert Lippert, Kurt Meisel, Erich Ponto, Hella Graf, Paul Otto, Alexander Engel, Eva Tinschmann, Walter Werner, Carl Auen, Erich Bartels, Johannes Bergfeld, Ursula Deinert.

SYNOPSIS

After the suicide of her husband in America, Hanna returns to Europe seeking her son, Peter. He has been adopted by the famous conductor Gravenberg, who hoped in that way to be able to save his marriage. With the aid of an influential friend, Hanna is engaged as a nurse by the Gravenberg family, who have no idea of her real identity. But her excessive affection for the boy betrays her; a police inquiry delves into Hanna's past, and she is suspected of murder just as she is preparing to leave with the boy. Charlotte Gravenberg, the conductor's wife, has died of an overdose of morphine, and it was Hanna who had administered the fatal dose. All evidence seems to point to her guilt, when a family maid reveals that Charlotte herself, before dying, admitted that she was committing suicide. Hanna is exonerated of all charges; together with her son and Grevenberg, whom she has loved for some time, she can look forward to a new life.

With the suave and romantic Willy Birgel.

CRITICS' COMMENTS

Rarely does a film achieve such great success. Sierck, who seems to possess an innate theatrical gift, shows with this film that he ranks with the most important contemporary filmmakers. One thing in particular distinguishes him and his mode of directing: with

Sierck there are no stars, in the conventional sense; all his actors are stars from the moment they appear on the screen. Lil Dagover is, as ever, the consummate professional. . . . Willy Birgel gives a particularly fine performance. His restrained yet intense portrayal was repeatedly applauded in mid-scene. . . . Congratulations also to charming little Peter Bosse, who can stand comparison to the most famous international child actors. At the end the players were warmly greeted by the audience.

A. LIPPERT, *Das 12 Uhr-Blatte,* Berlin, date uncertain

There is an actress in Berlin of such talent that she dominates an entire film, even in a secondary role: Maria Koppenhöfer. She is the faithful maid and confidante of the lovely Frau Charlotte, wife of the conductor Gravenberg. . . . Willy Birgel is excellent, in a relatively passive role. He portrays to perfection the artistic passion and the need for love of the mature man. At the beginning Lil Dagover seems badly utilized by the director, and moves like a kind of flighty socialite. But in the scene of Charlotte's death she is truly moving. We tip our hat as well to little Peter Bosse, who captured the audience in the scene with his marionette theater. . . . The most honest and affecting product to come from the German film industry in recent years.

SCHNEIDER, *Licht-Bild-Bühne,* Berlin, July 25, 1936

A hat of egret feathers for a timeless beauty.

With little Peter Bosse.

Lady Windermeres Fächer

Das Mädchen Irene   (1936)

(The Maiden Irene)

Director: Reinhold Schünzel

Story: from the play of the same name by Reinhold Schünzel
Adaptation and screenplay: Eva Leidmann and Reinhold Schünzel
Photography: Robert Baberske
Set design: Ludwig Reiber
Costumes: Ilse Fehling
Music: Alois Melichar
Editing: Arnfried Heyne
Production: UFA
Length: 100 minutes
Country of origin: Germany, 1936
Censor's approval: October 8, 1936 (banned to minors under 18)
Premiere: October 9, 1936

CAST

Lil Dagover (Jennifer Lawrence), Sabine Peters (Irene Lawrence), Geraldine Katt (Baba Lawrence), Hedwig Bleibtreu (the grandmother), Karl Schönböck (Sir John Corbett), Hans Richter (Philip), Elsa Wagner (Frau König), Roma Bahn (the baroness), Alice Treff (Lady Taylor), Erich Fiedler (Bobby), Olga Limburg (the duchess), Gertrud Wolle (the teacher), Georges Boulanger (a violinst), Hilde Scheppan (a singer).

SYNOPSIS

Jennifer Lawrence, the queen of London's fashion world, and the explorer John Corbett want to get married. Jennifer, however, doesn't want to take this step without discussing it first with Irene and Baba, her daughters from a previous marriage. While Baba accepts the idea of having a new father, Irene, who lives only for the memory of her dead father, creates a situation of tension within the family. After much hesitation, Jennifer decides to marry anyway, and Irene, desperate, runs away from home. The girl tries to drown herself in a river, but is saved by her sister Baba and her childhood friend

A cooly sensual profile shot from "Lady Windermeres Fächer," 1935.

Bobby, who bring her back to her mother. Jennifer reveals to Irene certain unpleasant facts about her father, which lead her to see him in a different light. The girl realizes that she has been wrong, and Jennifer marries John, free of any sense of guilt.

CRITICS' COMMENTS

There are two types of public taste: there is one that will accept anything as long as it comes from a movie screen, and there is another that can distinguish the good from the bad. It is possible to pander to its worst sentimental instincts, but there also exists the possibility of offering honest works that reflect the world of genuine sentiments. . . . The virtue of this film lies in the fact that it shows adults the right way to arrive at the hearts of young people. . . . Lil Dagover is the refined woman of the world who can make a place in her life for parties and important friendships, and for her duties as a mother as well. Certainly, sixteen-year-old Irene doesn't exactly make things easy for her; but, after all, isn't Karl Schönböck the kind of father whom every girl dreams about having?
    I. WEHNER, *Der deutsche Film,*
        Berlin, October 9, 1936

It must be admitted that the role of Jennifer, gracious, mature and wise, ready to sacrifice her own desires for family harmony, could only be played by Lil Dagover, who has been the grande dame of the German screen for so many years. . . . Her many years of artistic activity and the great satisfaction that she derives from her profession have formed and defined this singular performer. . . . There are doubtless many other actresses in Germany who, like her, have been before the public for years and who have remained remarkably youthful. But there is no other actress who embodies so completely the character of the mature and refined woman.
    A. SCHMIDT, *Deutsche Filmzeitung,*
        Munich, October 10, 1936

With Sabine Peters (left) and Geraldine Katt.

Streit um den Knaben Jo (1937)

(Clash Over the Boy Jo)

Director: Erich Waschneck

Erich Johannes Waschneck (1887–1970), this film's director, entered the film industry in 1926, and became a producer in 1932; he was the head of the Fanal-Film Company, among others. In 1935 Waschneck published a short novel entitled *Christina.* Among his most successful films were *Acht Mädels im Boot* (Eight Girls in a Boat) and *Abel mit der Mundarmonika* (Abel with the Harmonica), both in 1932.

Story: from the novel of the same name by Hedda Westenberger
Screenplay: Wolf Neumeister and Ilse M. Spath
Photography: Robert Baberske
Music: Georg Haentzschel
Production: Fanal-Film
Length: uncertain
Country of origin: Germany, 1937
Censor's approval: September 14, 1937 (banned to minors under 18)
Premiere: September 23, 1937, Berlin

CAST

Lil Dagover (Leontine Brackwieser), Willy Fritsch (Hans Eckhard, her brother), Maria von Tasnady (Helga Franck), Claus Detlef Sierck (Erwin Brackwieser), Ernst Waldow (Dr. Kanitz), Eva Tinschmann (the cook), Bruno Harprecht (Thomas Brackwieser), Ernest Stahl-Nachbaur, Walter Janssen, Ernst Rotmund, Elisabeth Flickenschildt, Tatjana Sais, Rudolf Klein-Rogge, Hubert von Meyerinck, Anton Pointner, Eberhard Itzenplitz, Johanna Blum, Erich Walter, Hellmuth Passarge, Angelo Ferrari, Hadrian M. Netto, Maurus Blesson.

SYNOPSIS

There is no reason why Leontine Brackweiser, one of the loveliest women in Cairo, wife of a prominent bank president and mother of fifteen-year-old

Erwin, should have worries of any kind. And yet, in a street accident in the city she meets a boy who bears an incredible resemblance to her husband. His name is Jo, he is thirteen and he is the son of one Helga Franck. Is it certain that on January 10, thirteen years before, a tragic error was not made at the hospital? This doubt obsesses Leontine. Frau Franck refuses to undergo a blood test, but the one who suffers most is Erwin, who runs away from home together with Jo, and falls ill. In this moment Leontine realizes that Erwin is her son. The resemblance is explained when, later, she discovers that Jo's father was also a Brackwieser, a cousin of Leontine's husband, who called himself Franck when he emigrated.

CRITICS' COMMENTS

This film must be analyzed from different points of view. . . . It has warmth and humanity; Germans abroad; the love and joy of a mother; seemingly mixed-up children. . . . Lil Dagover as the mother does her usual expert job.

. . . The story is truly complicated, since the boy Jo really does have Brackweiser blood in his veins. But, in the words of a consultant to one of the film companies: "At the movies people want to see out-of-the-ordinary events and surprise endings." And this applies to the film at hand. It was accorded enthusiastic and well-deserved applause. The two boys stepped out onto the stage shyly to thank the audience.
F. RÖHL, *Der Film,* Berlin, September 25, 1937

Lil Dagover—a creature of marvelous femininity. Maria von Tasnady . . . so simple and warm, one could watch her forever.
K. RICHTER, *Hamburger Anzeiger,* Hamburg, September 25, 1937

A work that once again demonstrates the capability of the German film industry. . . . Lil Dagover displays her consummate skill; Willy Fritsch reveals new depths as an actor.
H. LOFFER, *Münsterischer Anzeiger,* Münster, September 27, 1937

BRIGITTE HORNEY

THERE ARE THOSE WHO BELIEVE THAT, ALL THINGS considered, the place left vacant in the German film industry by Marlene Dietrich should have been filled, not by Zarah Leander but by Brigitte Horney. Neither the intense Leander nor the gypsy-like Käthe von Nagy emanated the same erotic vibrations as Horney, whose distinctive, husky voice was highly reminiscent of the smoky, baritonal timbre of the Blue Angel. Her high cheek bones, thick black hair and dark eyes veiled in a cloud of myopia made her a unique and striking figure—a home-grown seductress with a touch of oriental mystery about her. Unlike Leander's grand-scale theatricality, Horney's acting style was spare and understated—even brusque. It was said that she could say more with her eyes than the censors would ever allow her to say.

Horney was born in the Dahlem neighborhood of Berlin on March 29, 1911, to a prominent family. Her parents were doctors, and her mother, Karen Danielsen Horney, became one of the world's best-known psychoanalysts, eventually teaching at the University of Chicago and in New York. After finishing secondary school, Brigitte, nicknamed Biggy, studied for a time at the Academy of Dramatic Arts, the entrance examinations of which were held at the Deutsches Theater in the presence of Max Reinhardt. He presented young Horney with a merit prize.

In the summer of 1930, Horney took a screen test at the UFA studios, and was given a contract for her first film, *Abschied* (Farewell), directed by Robert Siodmak from a story by Billy Wilder, two promising young talents fresh from the success of their *Menschen am Sonntag* (People on Sunday, 1929). It was hardly a demanding test of her ability—she played a frustrated sales clerk—and the film was completed in two weeks, after which she went to Würzburg, where she alternated theater rehearsals there with swimming in the Main.

UFA was impressed by her *Abschied* and offered her a one-year contract. She still didn't consider herself ready for films, however, and preferred to gain experience performing in large and small roles at the Volksbühne (People's Theater) in Berlin, where she worked at intervals until 1943. An offer from Paul Wegener induced her to return to the screen. In his *Ein Mann will nach Deutschland* (A Man Wants to Reach Germany, 1934), a film with propaganda overtones, she portrayed a wife waiting for her engineer husband to return from South America and help the Fatherland, in what was to become her characteristic style: intense, understated and highly expressive. The expert photography of Fritz Arno Wagner, one of the major figures of the Fritz Lang era of expressionism, did much to emphasize the unique beauty of this actress, as well as to enhance the dramatic effectiveness of her performance.

The following year Horney made an unusual film in which the German love of the exotic assumed almost Hollwoodian proportions. In *Liebe, Tod und Teufel* (Love, Death and the Devil, 1934), she played the part of Ruby, a woman from the waterfront area, whose heart is susceptible not to the call of romantic love but only to that of the sea. A memorable scene is the one in which she sings an indolent, sensual song that goes: "So oder ist das Leben/So oder so ist es gut/So wie das Meer ist das Leben/Ewige Ebbe und Flut" (This way or that way life goes/This way or that way, it's all the same/Life is like the sea/A sea that ebbs and flows). This tune, used as a *Leitmotiv* throughout the film, brought new fame to its composer, Theo Mackeben, and to Horney, who, in that brief, luminous and provocative scene, reminded more than a few in the audience of Dietrich.

After the success of this film, UFA eagerly offered Horney a five-year contract. But again she refused, preferring to be free to choose her own parts. She made several films with the handsome and appealing young actor Joachim Gottschalk, who died a suicide in 1941, together with his three-year-old son and his wife, the actress Meta Wolff, rather than obey Goebbels' order that he divorce her (as a Jew, she was to be sent with her son to a concentration camp). Horney's relationship with the unfortunate actor had become personal, as well as professional, and his tragic fate affected her so deeply that her periodic attacks of asthma became greatly aggravated, and her trips to Davos, Switzerland, for treatment became increasingly frequent.

In 1941 she made another propaganda film, *Feinde* (Enemies), with Willy Birgel, who had made his film debut in Horney's *Ein Mann will nach Deutschland* in 1934. In *Feinde,* a parable on Germans' need, in their hour of danger, to be on their guard at all times, Horney played the part of Hanna, a Pole with Aryan blood in her veins, ready to risk any danger in order to aid German refugees.

Horney's most memorable performance was her portrayal of an insatiable Catherine the Great of Russia in the most spectacular film produced by the Third Reich, *Münchhausen* (The Adventures of Baron Münchhausen), directed by Joseph von Backy in 1943. The film was shot in Agfacolor, and took almost two years to complete. Ten months were spent on elaborate special effects and trick photography alone. Sets and costumes of a similar opulence had not been seen since the earlier, golden years of UFA. For the banquet scene, a magnificent hall was built, in the midst of which rose up a canopy of white silk, under which a gorgeously costumed Catherine held forth. The place settings of Meissen china and the tableware of gold and siler were borrowed from museums and palaces. The troupe went to Venice to film a magnificent regatta.

Still, Horney derived little pleasure out of working on the film; all her thoughts were focused on the war and on what could come afterward.

In March 1944, she made a film directed by Gustav Ucicky, *Am Ende der Welt* (At the End of the World), in which she took over the leading role previously assigned to Hilde Krahl. The film was unquestionably born under an unlucky star (as well as under the bombardments). Horney was frequently ill during the shooting. Goebbels constantly insisted on cuts and modifications. Finally, in December of that year the film was banned in its entirety, and was not seen until after the war. The actress played Roberta Bell, daughter of a landowner who upon his death leaves her a sizeable inheritance, with which she would like to open a cabaret. But when she realizes that in order to make this dream come true, she will have to cut down the woods in which she grew up and say goodbye to her pastoral world, she abandons the project and returns to the countryside.

With the specter of Germany's defeat staring her in the face, Horney's principal thought was now to reach safety. Leaving her husband, the Russo-German cameraman Konstantin Irmen-Tschet (who would not have problems after the invasion of Germany), at the beginning of 1945 she fled to Switzerland, where it seemed as if her career was probably over. Between 1946 and 1949, however, she appeared on the stage in Zurich in Max Frisch's *Santa Cruz* and Jean-Paul Sartre's *Les Mains sales* (Dirty Hands).

With the death of her mother in America in 1952, Horney came to the United States, eventually marrying her second husband, Hans Schwarzenski, Curator for Decorative Arts at the Boston Museum for Fine Arts. Periodically, she returned to Germany for television appearances. In 1959 she appeared in Sartre's *Huit clos* (No Exit) on German TV, and in 1961 she returned to TV for a play, *Ein Stern in einer Sommernacht* (A Star on a Summer Night), in the role of an old music-hall star.

On the occasions of her sixtieth and sixty-fifth birthdays, retrospectives of her best films were held in West Berlin, and in April 1976 a film on her life was shown on German television. She lived for many years in Cambridge, Massachusetts. Toward the end of her life, she returned to Germany, where, despite illness, she was able to be on the set of a popular TV series, "The Guldenburgs," in which she played the matriarch of a German brewery dynasty. Brigitte Horney died in Hamburg on July 27, 1988, of heart failure, after a two-year battle with cancer.

In "Der grüne Domino" (The Green Domino), 1935, with Carl Ludwig Diehl (left) and Theodor Loos.

In "Stadt Anatol" (The City of Anatol), 1936.

With C. L. Diehl in "Der grüne Domino."

In "Liebe, Tod und Teufel," 1934, with Käthe von Nagy.

Savoy-Hotel 217   (1936)

Director: Gustav Ucicky

This film was remade in 1950 under the title *Mord im Savoy* (Murder at the Savoy). The director of *Savoy-Hotel 217,* Gustav Ucicky, born Gustav Klimt in Vienna on July 6, 1898, was one of the most interesting figures of the film industry of the Third Reich. At twenty-two, appointed chief cameraman of Sacha-Film in Vienna, he supervised the photography of several of the films of Mihály Kertész (who in 1929 changed his name to Michael Curtiz). In 1927 he made his debut as a director with *Die Pratermizzi* (Mizzi, the Prater Entertainer), starring Anny Ondra, followed the same year by *Café Elektrik,* with Marlene Dietrich and Willy Forst.

In 1929 Ucicky went to Berlin, where he signed a contract with UFA. A master of his craft, he directed some of the finest films to come out of Germany between 1933 and 1945. Particularly memorable were the poetic *Mutterliebe* (Mother Love, 1939), *Der Postmeister* (The Postmaster, 1940) and *Ein Leben lang* (All My Life Long, 1940), a love story with Paula Wessely and Joachim Gottschalk. Like his colleagues Max Ophüls and Erich von Stroheim, Ucicky was always particularly drawn to meticulous re-creations of Old Vienna, its sights and its stories. It is probably not by chance that after the *Anschluss* in 1938 he worked primarily in Vienna, striving until 1945 to maintain the Austrian quality of his films. He was also an excellent director of women: Renate Müller, Käthe von Nagy, Brigitte Horncy and Heidemarie Hatheyer gave some of their best performances in his films. He was less successful, however, in his propaganda films, such as the militarist *Morgenrot* (Dawn, 1933), the chauvinistic *Flüchtlinge* (Refugees, 1933) and *Heimkehr* (Homecoming, 1941). In West Germany after the war, Ucicky made a number of films, most of which were undistinguished, although always technically impeccable. He died, virtually forgotten, in Hamburg on April 27, 1961.

Story and screenplay: Gerhard Menzel
Photography: Fritz Arno Wagner
Set design: Robert Herlth and Walter Röhrig
Costumes: H. Plöberger
Music: Walter Gronostay (with choruses)
Editing: Eduard von Borsody
Production: UFA
Length: 63 minutes
Country of origin: Germany, 1936
Censor's approval: April 7, 1936 (banned to minors under 18)
Premiere: April 7, 1936, Stuttgart; April 11, 1936, Berlin
Award: Artistic Value

CAST _____

Brigitte Horney (Nastasia Andreyevna Dashenko), Hans Albers (Andrei Antonovich Volodkin), Alexander Engel (Feodor Feodorovich Dashenko), René Deltgen (Sergei Gavrilovich Shuvalov), Gusti Huber (Daria Sergeyevna Plagina), Käthe Dorsch (Anna Feodorovna Orlova), Jacob Tiedtke (Leonid Shapkin, judge), Aribert Wäscher (Pavel Pavlovich), Hans Liebelt (examining magistrate), Paul Westermeier, Carl Auen, Helmuth Begmann.

SYNOPSIS _____

It is Easter, 1911, at the Savoy-Hotel in Moscow. The beautiful and high-spirited Nastasia, who has brought only misfortune to her husband, the businessman Dashenko, as well as to Shuvalov, her previous husband, makes her way through the lobby, heading for room 217. Judge Shapkin awaits her there, but Nastasia has no time for him. She is thinking only of Andrei Antonovich Volodkin. This dashing waiter, with his flashing smile, who is engaged to the maid Anna, but also involved with the young Daria, must be hers. Nastasia knows well the little intrigues that spring up in the corridors of the Savoy. She schemes, maneuvers, listens. Furious, she goes to her room, number 217. A shot is heard, immediately followed by two more. Who killed the beautiful Nastasia Andreyevna Dashenko? Her husband? Her ex-husband? Or could it have been Andrei? Rumors fly faster than ever through the halls of the Savoy.

CRITICS' COMMENTS _____

The inner and exterior conflicts in this film revolve around what Nietzsche called "the problem of the boy in the man." The film's thesis is that the woman in general reaches full maturity at an early age, whereas the man never does, dividing his life into a series of separate episodes. . . . The role of this particular man is enacted by Hans

Albers, and the women who cluster around him, with varying degrees of success, are Brigitte Horney, Käthe Dorsch and Gusti Huber. . . . But the gleaming jewel who lights up the entire film is Brigitte Horney, who brings artistry and credibility to even the most improbable situations. Thanks to her, the film never lags. Impassioned, mistress of romantic entanglements, she gives a memorable portrayal of a beautiful woman who, despite appearances, is completely alone.

J. KLIPPEL, *Film-Kurier,*
Berlin, February 20, 1936

This film of Gustav Ucicky's reveals greater depth and refinement than any of his preceding works. Brigitte Horney plays her part with an intensity that at times is almost painful. In the final scene, her bitterness turns to hope and then to desperation in a crescendo of emotion. . . . Above all, Brigitte Horney earns our praise for her creation of a human being, with all of her contradictions; she moves through the streets and hallways of Czarist Russia as though she had been born there.

A. SIEDEL, *N.S.-Kurier,*
Stuttgart, April 9, 1936

With René Deltgen, in both photos.

Befreite Hände   (1939)

(Unfettered Hands)

Director: Hans Schweikart

With Ewald Balser (right).

Befreite Hände was a great popular success, and is still frequently revived in Germany in theaters and on television.

Story: from the novel of the same name by Erich Ebermayer
Screenplay: Erich Ebermayer and Kurt Heuser
Photography: Carl Hoffmann and Heinz Schnackertz
Set design: Ludwig Reiber and Willi Depenau
Costumes: Ruth Wagner
Music: Lothar Brühne; Beethoven's Fifth Symphony performed by the Philharmonische Staatsorchester of Hamburg, conducted by Hans Schmidt-Isserstedt
Production: Bavaria Filmkunst
Length: 99 minutes
Country of origin: Germany, 1939
Censor's approval: November 28, 1939
Premiere: December 20, 1939, Munich
Awards: Particular Artistic Value; Cultural Value

CAST _____

Brigitte Horney (Dürthen), Olga Tschechowa (Kerstin Thomas), Ewald Balser (Prof. Wolfram), Carl Raddatz (Joachim von Erken), Eduard von Winterstein (Erken, Sr.), Paul Dahlke (Thomsen), Luise Hohorst (Aunt Mathilde), Hänschen Pfaff (Little Jens), Franz Weber (Berg, the butler), Otto Brefin (the shepherd), Erna Selmer (his wife), Erika Helmke (Carla), Vera Hartegg (Josefa), Edwig Wangel (Frau Steinmann), Albert Lippert (van Daalen, the art dealer).

SYNOPSIS _____

Dürthen is a farm girl who carves figures out of wood while she watches her flock. She has real talent, but is still an amateur. One day, Kerstin, a true artisan, visits the farm, discovers the girl's talent, and invites her to go to Berlin with her. Here Dürthen meets Wolfram,

With Olga Tschechowa (left) and Carl Raddatz.

a sculptor under whom she is to study the art of woodcarving. Her work soon begins to reveal a certain maturity. Kerstin, who produces only objects of a practical nature, observes Dürthen's progress with increasing jealousy. The two women quarrel, and Dürthen leaves Kerstin's studio. Wandering through the city, she meets Joachim, a wealthy man with whom she passes several weeks in Rome. Dürthen overcomes this period of crisis and resumes her work. In Wolfram, she finds not only a teacher, but her life's companion.

CRITICS' COMMENTS _____

A compelling story, beautifully acted, this is without a doubt the finest film of the year. Brigitte Horney's performance alone would make it worth seeing. Rarely have we seen her face, that wonderful, enigmatic Sphinx mask, loosen up to such a degree, and express the myriad emotions that it does in this film. She is a joy to look at and to listen to — truly a creature blessed by fortune. Olga Tschechowa . . . alluring and womanly, gives, as always, a highly

polished performance. The premiere, under the patronage of the Minister and of the Gauleiter Adolf Wagner, was held at the Luitpold Theater before an audience that showed its approval with thunderous applause.

H. FLINK, *Münchner Neueste Nachrichten,* Munich, December 22, 1939

We like the basic idea of the film — that a natural talent will out, will overcome all the obstacles that life may put in its way, and will achieve its goal. Brigitte Horney's Dürthen has an inner intensity. . . . There are scenes in which, with just a glance and the sparest of gestures, she succeeds in communicating sorrow and despair more effectively than any other actress, even working with a far better script. . . . Even in the scenes in the workshop, where her face assumes the same impenetrability and compactness as the marble, she is still marvelously expressive. Olga Tschechowa has the difficult role of a sculptress who has sacrificed her artistic aspirations for commercial ones, and whose heart behaves like a school-

girl's, despite her better judgment.

Die Filmwelt, Berlin, April 3, 1940

The film has been a bit late in arriving in Berlin, and thus in the meantime our readers have seen the reviews from the other cities of the Reich. . . . The film tries to find the solution to the problem of the artist precisely where it is to be found: in that which we call passion. It seems to us, however, that the director has not succeeded in giving sufficient emotional depth to his characters, and here lies the dramatic weakness of the film. As Dürthen, the Frisian country girl, Brigitte Horney has perhaps her most complex part to date, and she brings out the artistic and the womanly sides of the character. . . . Olga Tschechowa is poised and perceptive in the role of the more experienced woman . . . and though playing the part of the girl's enemy in art and in love, she shows the woman's humanity as well. The two ladies could not ask for a better partner than Ewald Balser.

O. SEEBER, *Die Filmwoche,* Berlin, September 3, 1940

Das Mädchen von Fanö *(1941)*

(The Girl from Fanö)

Director: Hans Schweikart

Story: from the novel of the same
 name by Günther Weisenborn
Screenplay: Kurt Heuser
Photography: Carl Hoffmann and
 Heinz Schnackertz
Set design: Ludwig Reiber and
 R. Pfenninger
Music: Alois Melichar
Production: Bavaria-Film (Munich)
Length: 97 minutes
Country of origin: Germany, 1940
Censor's approval: December 30, 1940
 (banned to minors under 18)
Premiere: January 24, 1941, Berlin

CAST

Brigitte Horney (Patricia), Joachim
Gottschalk (Ipke), Gustav Knuth
(Frerk), Paul Wegener (the old sea-
wolf), Viktoria von Ballasko (Ipke's
wife), Fritz Hoopts (Geerd Bienert),
Charlotte Schultz, Wilhelm P. Krüger,
Paul Bildt, Karl Dannemann, Fritz
Reiff, Franz Weber, Helmuth Brasch,
Isa Vermehren, Justus Paris, Luise
Hohorst, Heddo Schulenburg.

SYNOPSIS

Pat, a girl of the Danish isle of Fanö in
the North Sea, falls desperately in love
with Ipke, a fisherman, not knowing
that he is married and the father of a
child. When she discovers the truth, she
turns her attention to Frerk, another
young fisherman, a friend of Ipke's and
his partner in business. But just when
things between the two seem to be going smoothly, the old passion between
Pat and Ipke is rekindled. Frerk
challenges Ipke to a duel at sea. Their
plan is thwarted, however, when the
boat capsizes. In that desperate moment the two men realize the strength
of their friendship; Frerk suddenly
disappears beneath the waves. Pat,
heartsick at the news, realizes that it is
Frerk she loves. Finally Frerk is found
alive, and Pat vows to take care of him
for the rest of her life.

CRITICS' COMMENTS _____

Hans Schweikart, production head of Bavaria-Film, has created a Nordic ballad told in harsh tones — the story of three men of courage and dedication, and their daily struggle with the winds and ragings of the North Sea. It must be admitted, however, that the tacked-on happy ending, with Frerk rescued, was unexpected. If one sets out to portray the demonic nature of a woman possessed by passion, he should also have the courage to bring this somber narrative to its inevitable tragic climax. . . . As interpreted by Brigitte Horney, the girl of Fanö expresses the eternal yearning for a man who cannot be hers. The film achieves an uncommon level of intensity thanks to her performance. The film was warmly applauded at last night's premiere at the Capitol.

G. SCHWARK, *Film-Kurier*,
Berlin, January 25, 1941

This is a (human) drama played out against the backdrop of a hostile island. It may sound somewhat somber, and yet the image of this wild landscape refuses to disappear from our eyes and our thoughts. The director has managed to give the film and its events the same rhythm as that of the life of the village itself, since men and the landscape there are one. . . . Brigitte Horney's performance is unadorned and straightforward; she imparts her own singular enigmatic quality to the girl Pat. Joachim Gottschalk's simple and rugged Ipke is highly appealing. Viktoria von Ballasko's controlled performance is as effective as the more flamboyant one of Paul Wegener. The enthusiastic applause showed the audience's thanks for a work that transported them for an evening to an epic world.

L. EYLUX, *Die Filmwoche*,
Berlin, February 5, 1941

Below: Horney in a storm-swept scene of "Das Mädchen von Fanö."

SYBILLE SCHMITZ

THE FILM INDUSTRY OF THE THIRD REICH DID NOT neglect the genre which had long been a German specialty, that of the fantastic and the macabre. There were some notable successes in this field, from Frank Wysbar's hallucinatory *Anna und Elisabeth* (1933) to Harry Piel's cycle of space films, from the protagonist in *Ein Unsichtbarer geht durch die Stadt* (An Invisible Man Stalks the City, 1933) to the diabolical laboratories of

Gold (1934). Now, obviously no producer would have thought of using the healthy, smiling face of Renate Müller or the soap-and-water charm of Kristina Söderbaum in a film of this kind. These otherworldly stories of mad scientists and cities of the future called for actors capable of conveying, physically as well as dramatically, the atmosphere of the fantastic and the supernatural evoked by the film. Sybille Schmitz, whose face seemed

swallowed up by her enormous dark, brooding eyes, had the ideal look for films of a surreal nature.

Schmitz was born in Düren in western Germany not far from the Belgian border on December 2, 1909, and as a girl studied drama in Cologne, under Hermine Körner. At the age of sixteen she was given a contract by Max Reinhardt for the Deutsches Theater. It wasn't long before film companies became aware of her withdrawn and somnambulistic beauty, more suited to the screen than to the stage, and in 1932 Carl Theodor Dreyer gave her the female lead in his *Vampyr*. The title forebodes a tale of sorcery and necrophilia. In the part of Léone, daughter of the lord of a castle, who is relentlessly pursued at night by a vampire, Schmitz proved to be a performer of rare dramatic intensity, passing, as in a delirium, from the smiles of a naive young girl to the snarls of a creature thirsty for blood. Perhaps on that occasion a part of the impact she made could be credited to the direction of Dreyer, master of the Danish cinema, but succeeding films proved that she possessed a dramatic strength that could excite the most impassive spectator.

In 1932 Schmitz signed a five-year contract with UFA, and made her first science-fiction film, entitled *F.P.1 antwortet nicht* (F.P.1 Doesn't Answer). It was a period in which the principal airline companies were trying to solve the problem of transoceanic flights; this was the story of an island in the middle of the Atlantic, used as a refueling station for all the aircraft flying between the Old and New Worlds. The German newspapers of the day exaggerated about the shooting of this visionary film, even writing that UFA had actually built an island where Lufthansa aircraft could land. The film, a cross between an adventure story and science fiction, was an enormous success. Schmitz's name was mentioned often by the critics, who were struck by the penetrating intensity of her glance and her vibrant, husky voice.

Goebbels did not like Schmitz (one reason why her career was not more brilliant), not so much because of her enigmatic, somewhat troubled appearance, but because of certain character traits. She was known to be an elusive person, one who kept to herself. And in effect she *was* a woman of a somewhat emotional fragility; after the war, in fact, she attempted suicide following an unsuccessful return to films, convinced that she was finished as an actress. Gustav Gründgens (whose life story has been unsympathetically portrayed by Klaus Maria Brandauer in the 1981 film *Mephisto*), despite being Generalintendant of the Berlin State Theater, had to fight Goebbels to obtain Schmitz's participation in the film *Tanz auf dem Vulkan* (Dance on the Volcano, 1938), in which, between magic tricks and comedy routines, she was seen as the mistress of the mime Deburau.*

The most interesting film interpreted by Schmitz, however, is certainly *Fährmann Maria* (Maria, the Ferryboat Pilot, 1936). In this expressionistic work, the actress—almost like a figure from Greek mythology—ferried passengers from one bank of a river to the other, pursued by apocalyptic horsemen. The power of many of the film's dramatic episodes—Maria's dance with Death, the wounded soldier's prayer—was somewhat weakened by the movie's happy ending, when Maria finds a home and love. With its customary bias, the magazine *Volk und Rasse* (People and Race) accused the film of "lacking racial awareness," because Schmitz represented a type of "foreign" beauty. To be sure, with her face she could only be cast in a certain type of role; with her unsettling glance, it would be impossible to imagine her as a wholesome German milkmaid. When not in fantasy or science fiction, she was cast as problematic women: she was George Sand in *Abschiedswalzer* (Farewell Waltz, 1934), a lovely spy in *Hotel Sacher* (1939), and an astute princess in *Trenck, der Pandur* (Trenck the Hussar, 1940).

Her most memorable performance, however, was given in *Titanic* (1943), a retelling, by directors Herbert Selpin and Werner Klinger, of the 1912 disaster in which the gigantic ocean liner sank during its maiden voyage. It was, of course, by now the era of anti-British propaganda, of such films as *Der Wolf von Glenarvon* (The Wolf of Glenarvon, 1940) and *Mein Leben für Irland* (My Life for Ireland, 1941), so *Titanic* was banned by Goebbels because of its too-realistic scenes of British and French panic and desperation. Furthermore, such scenes were not the best thing for the morale of audiences in the midst of a war. Besides, everyone knew of the tragic fate of director Selpin, hanged in prison by the S.S., in what was officially called a suicide. In *Titanic*, Schmitz played the role of Sigrid, a beautiful young Danish passenger. As the ship is about to sink, Sigrid casually discards her white ermine coat to step into the lifeboat. From the wildly tossing boat, she raises her glance on high to look one last time on the face of the courageous Petersen (the only "decent" member of the crew, a German). Her face is a mask of suffering—difficult to forget. Her expression makes it clear that she does not believe in an improbable salvation, and for this reason too the film obviously could not be shown. In a sense, Selpin had a kind of macabre final triumph: his scenes of disaster were too real to be seen by the German public.

Sybille Schmitz died on April 13, 1955, under mysterious circumstances seemingly involving an overdose of sleeping pills or the poisoning of them. Her life was the basis for Rainer Werner Fassbinder's film *Die Sehnsucht der Veronika Voss* (Eng. title, *Veronica Voss*, 1981).

*Probably the celebrated French mime Gaspard Deburau (1796– 1846), or possibly his son, Charles (1829–73).

Fährmann Maria   (1936)

(Maria, the Ferryboat Pilot)

Director: Frank Wysbar

In 1945, the director made a remake of this film in Hollywood, under the title *The Strangler of the Swamp,* with Rosemary La Planche (1941's Miss America), Robert Barrett and a youthful Blake Edwards. Although hardly the equal of the German original, it was an exceptionally well made film; but because it was a B-picture, and probably also because of the unfortunate title, it attracted little attention.

Frank Wysbar (1899–1967) was an assistant to Carl Boese and Carl Froelich until 1932, when he made his debut as a director with *Ann und Elisabeth,* the story of a girl gifted with paranormal powers. From then on, he showed a marked preference for mysterious and supernatural themes, the exception being his aviation film, *Rivalen der Luft* (Rivals of the Air), in 1934. He emigrated to the United States in 1938, changing his last name to Wisbar. During the 1940s he made a number of small-budget films for PRC (Producers Releasing Corporation). During the early days of television he

directed and hosted the weekly series *Fireside Theater.* In 1955 he returned to Germany, where he made several films on military themes, including *Hunde, wollt irh ewig leben* (Dogs, Do You Want to Live Forever?, 1959) and *Fabrik der Offiziere* (Factory for Officers, 1960). In 1962 he directed the Italian-German-Spanish coproduction *Marcia o crepa* (March or Die), about the Algerian War.

Story and Screenplay: Hans Jürgen Nierentz and Frank Wysbar
Photography: Franz Weihmayr
Set design: Bruno Lutz
Music: Herbert Windt
Editing: Lena Neumann
Production: Pallas-Film
Length: 84 minutes
Country of origin: Germany, 1936
Censor's approval: January 2, 1936
Premiere: January 7, 1936, Hildesheim
Awards: Artistic Value; Educational for the People; Educational for the Young

CAST _____

Sybille Schmitz (Maria), Aribert Mog (the man on the other shore), Peter Voss (the stranger, or Death), Karl Platen (the old boatman), Carl de Vogt (the violinist), Eduard Wenck (the mayor), Gerhard Bienert (the owner of the farm).

SYNOPSIS _____

The old boatman of an unnamed village at a river's edge dies mysteriously, in the arms of a stranger he was ferrying across, and his place is taken by a girl named Maria, who has neither home nor homeland. One night she ferries to her side of the river an injured young man, who claims that he is being pursued by the horsemen of Death. Maria looks after the youth and tries to prevent Death from carrying him away. She returns to the village, dances with Death at the festival given by the farmers to celebrate the harvest, and goes to the church to ask for God's help. But in vain: Death will not give up his victim. Maria then attracts him

With Brigitte Helm (right) in "Ein idealer Gatte" (An Ideal Husband, 1935), based on Oscar Wilde's comedy.

into the swamp, where the quicksand swallows him up. The two lovers—for she has fallen in love with the injured man—board the ferryboat and sail toward his country, which from now on will also be Maria's.

CRITICS' COMMENTS _____

The film Fährmann Maria *was given its premiere last night at the Bernward cinema in Hildesheim. Much of it was shot here, on the moors. The representatives of the Berlin press came to Hildesheim to immerse themselves in this legend of the swamp. . . . Sixty percent of the film is accompanied by a musical score. There is a spoken dialogue in 15 percent, which shows that from time to time it was necessary to counterbalance the sometimes unten-*

able irrationality of the story. . . . The cameraman's bravura technique is everywhere evident here. As a smile lights up Sybille Schmitz's face, rays of sunlight illuminate the moor that surrounds her.

W. MEINHART, *Film-Kurier,* Berlin, January 8, 1936

This is a work that stands outside all genres of film heretofore known to us; this is a legend on film. . . . The lighting of the peasant festival is reminiscent of Rembrandt; the fear visible in Maria's eyes recalls Kubin and Brueghel. Sixty percent of the film was shot at night, with marvelous results. In a dreamlike world of visions, symbols and legends, Sybille Schmitz gives the most sincere performance of her career. We lift our hats to this lady boatman, and we will-

ingly forgive two moments, probably due to a technical slip-up, when it was impossible to comprehend what she was saying. . . . A success that reaffirms the maturity of the German public.

SCHNEIDER, *Licht-Bild-Bühne,* Berlin, January 8, 1936

Omnia vincit amor. *From Kleist's* Das Käthchen von Heilbronn *to Truffaut's* L'Histoire d'Adèle H., *certain romantic themes recur in the minds of men. The tale recounted here is a medieval allegory in which Death struggles with Love. The capacity to love, expressed by self-sacrifice, and portrayed with heart-breaking intensity by Sybille Schmitz, is the principal theme of this haunting mixture of mythology and romanticism.* KRAFT WETZEL and PETER HAGEMANN, *Liebe, Tod und Technik* (Berlin, 1977)

Titanic *(1943)*

Directors: Herbert Selpin and
Werner Klingler

Much of the notoriety of this film is due to the "suicide" of its director, Herbert Selpin, who on August 1, 1942, died at the hands of Gestapo agents in the prison in which he had been confined for "verbal treason." He had been denounced by the screenwriter and Nazi fanatic Walter Zerlett-Olfenius, who had had constant quarrels with him during the shooting of *Titanic.* In April 1947, a trial was ordered on the Selpin case, during which photos were produced of the director's "suicide"—photos that Goebbels had ordered taken. Zerlett-Olfenius, sentenced to five years at hard labor, fled to Switzerland. The director Veit Harlan stated in the 1960s that the elimination of Selpin had been reported to him at the time by Wolfgang Liebeneiner, head of UFA from 1943 and an eyewitness to the arrest of Selpin. Selpin, in addition to the propaganda films *Die Reiter von Deutsch-Ostafrika* (The Riders of German East Africa, 1934) and *Carl Peters* (1941), had also directed light comedies, such as *Sergeant Berry* (1938), *Ein Mann auf Abwegen* (A Man Astray, 1940) and a kind of Western set in northern Canada, *Wasser für Canitoga* (Water for Canitoga, 1939), the last three starring Hans Albers, who shared Selpin's critical attitude toward the regime.

Story: Harald Bratt
Screenplay: Walter Zerlett-Olfenius
    and Herbert Selpin
Photography: Friedl Behn-Grund
Special effects: Ernst Kunstmann
Set design: Robert A. Dietrich, Fritz
    Lück and August Herrmann
Music: Werner Eisbrenner
Editing: Friedel Bukkow
Production: Tobis Filmkunst
Country of origin: Germany, 1943
Censor's approval: banned April 30,
    1943 (90 min.); approved
    December 1949 (86 min.) but not
    released; banned March 29, 1950,
    by the Allied Board of Censors

because of anti-British propaganda (86 min.); approved for the Soviet Zone in March of the same year (90 min.)
Premiere: February 7, 1950, Stuttgart;
    April 8, 1950, East Berlin

CAST

Sybille Schmitz (Sigrid Oole), Charlotte Thiele (Lady Astor), Kirsten Heiberg (Gloria), Monika Burg (Heidi, the manicurist), Liselotte Klinger (Anne), Hans Nielsen (First Officer Petersen), Karl Schönböck (Lord Astor), Ernest F. Fürbringer (Sir Bruce Ismay). Otto Wernicke (Captain Smith), Franz Schafheitlin (Hunderson), Sepp Rist (Jan), Theo Schall (First Officer Murdock), Theodor Loos.

SYNOPSIS

The great event of 1912 is the maiden voyage of the *Titanic.* Among those on board are a bankrupt lord, a German scholar, Sigrid Oole (a young Danish woman, believed to be an heiress), Lord Ismay, president of the White Star Line, with his mistress, Gloria, and the imposing Lord and Lady Astor. There are also poor immigrants, in steerage. The festive atmosphere on board is misleading; for Lord Ismay and his mistress, the voyage is a desperate attempt to raise the fortunes of the steamship line, while Lord and Lady Astor try to thwart their financial schemes. Ismay bribes the ship's captain, inducing him to sail toward New York along a shorter

route, but a more dangerous one, because of icebergs. The *Titanic* has to win the Blue Ribbon if the White Star Line is to keep ahead of its competition. The ship collides with an iceberg, and during the rescue operations both the cowardice and the nobility of the human spirit surface. The captain goes down with his ship, and the tribunal that has opened an inquiry to ascertain the causes of the disaster exonerates Ismay. Petersen's testimony that the latter is the person responsible for the tragedy is in vain.

CRITICS' COMMENT

The degree of boredom that Selpin and Klinger are capable of imparting to the episodes preceding the sinking of the Titanic *is truly awesome; the quarrel between the British plutocrats . . . for example, is so unimaginatively photographed, with routine shots endlessly repeated, effectively robbing their argument of any dramatic interest. . . . Until the final catastrophe, one never has the feeling, even for an instant, of really being on a ship in the middle of the Atlantic. The total insensibility with which these directors have treated their actors is clearly demonstrated by a scene in which the camera focuses on the face of Sybille Schmitz, giving this actress, so attractive and expressive in other films, the appearance of a painted cadaver.*
KRAFT WETZEL and PETER HAGEMANN,
    Zensur: Verboten deutsche Filme
    (Berlin, 1978)

ZARAH LEANDER

EVER SINCE THE LEGENDARY MARLENE DIETRICH abandoned Germany for the United States, the German film industry had been trying desperately to come up with a substitute. Zarah Stina Leander, born Hedberg, on March 15, 1907, in Karlstad, Sweden (according to the Swedish *Who's Who*), seemed just the type who might fill the void that the Blue Angel had left in the hearts of the German public. Not only did La Leander possess a deep and vibrant contralto singing voice, but she also came the homeland of another great diva of the screen, Greta Garbo. A highly astute campaign was devised to launch her as an explosive mixture

of Nordic exoticism and icy sensuality; cinemagoers would soon find in Zarah Leander, the industry fervently hoped, a new Garbo and a new Dietrich.

In her book of memoirs, *Es war so wunderbar* (It Was So Wonderful), the actress recounts the initial difficulties of her dealings with the Ministry of Propaganda, since "Goebbels was highly displeased that the leading lady of UFA should be a foreigner. . . .The fact that the mighty Third Reich could not produce its own Greta Garbo seemed to him an admission of inadequacy. He didn't like that Swedish woman, and that was that. Consequently, I was completely ignored by the higher-ups."[1] Goebbels would shortly be forced to change his mind, however: her second and third films for UFA—*Zu neuen Ufern* (Toward New Shores, 1937) and *La Habanera* (1937)—made Zarah Leander the prima donna of the German musical film; in Sweden, she might well have remained a luminary of the second magnitude.

Leander had made her debut in provincial theaters with Ernst Rolf (the Swedish Ziegfeld) in 1929. From 1930 to 1931 she worked at the Vasa-Theater and from 1931 to 1932 at the Ekmanstheater, both of them in Stockholm. Her first marriage was to the actor Nils Leander, whom she divorced in 1932 to marry Vidar Forsell, son of the celebrated John Forsell, baritone star, later director, of the Stockholm Opera. Through numerous foreign engagements, Leander had already made a name for herself as an accomplished actress and singer, and she scored a genuine triumph in Vienna in 1935, performing with Max Hansen in the operetta *Axel an der Himmelstür* (Axel at Heaven's Gate). Even Hollywood had heard of her success; it was at this same time that UFA became interested in her.

In 1936 she made her initial German-language film, *Premiere,* an Austrian production in which UFA's future star, in ornate gowns that made her appear far more matronly than she really was. She sang "Ich hab' vielleicht noch nie geliebt" (Perhaps I Have Never Yet Loved) while descending a seemingly endless staircase, her outstretched arms holding up the train of her dress. The film proved to be less successful than hoped for, but nevertheless UFA signed her to a contract, the provisions of which show just how eager the industry was to secure her services. Not only was she paid 400,000 marks for eleven months' work, a relatively high salary for the period, but 53 percent of it was paid in Swedish kronor directly to her bank in Stockholm. This was a most unusual clause, which UFA in 1942 tried to circumvent, paying her in marks, with the excuse that by now the time had come for her to become a German citizen.

Meanwhile, films such as *Zu neuen Ufern, La Habanera, Das Lied der Wüste* (The Song of the Desert), *Es war eine rauschende Ballnacht* (It Was a Wild Night at the Ball), *Der Blaufuchs* (The Blue Fox), *Heimat* (Homeland) and *Die grosse Liebe* (The Great Love) had all proved enormous box-office successes. The public went primarily to hear her sing, rather than to watch her act. (Both adults and children loved to parody her deep-toned voice, sometimes with improvised lyrics, when they left the theater.) Leander herself expressed certain reserves on her own talents as an actress, writing: "My films were primarily a pretext for my songs. I hope that it was the music and the songs of my films that attracted the public."[2] For that matter, she was almost always cast as a cabaret singer, opera diva, music hall entertainer—a woman with a confused past and a tragic present, who is rewarded by fate at the last minute. *Zu neuen Ufern,* for example, depicts the progressive physical and moral decay of Gloria Vane, an English singer who is taken advantage of by a member of the arrogant British upper class (the usual perfidious Willy Birgel) and winds up, through love, in the House of Discipline of Paramatta (Sydney), where she rebels by singing her famous "Yes, Sir!" The film's director, Detlef

Sierck (later, in the United States, Douglas Sirk) had wisely secured, for *Zu neuen Ufern,* the services of Ralph Benatzky, the noted composer of a long string of successful film scores and stage works. After the Berlin premiere at the UFA-Palast am Zoo, the star received over seventy curtain calls. *Der Angriff* (Exposé) wrote that Zarah Leander had conveyed "the tragic expression of an impassioned woman."[3]

In reality, all of the heroines whom Zarah brought to life were figures that could be utilized by the regime's propaganda machine. In *Zu neuen Ufern,* in fact, Miss Vane is brought to grief by the machinations of an English aristocrat (condemnation of the behavior of the British upper class, and confirmation of "perfidious Albion"), while in *Die grosse Liebe* the snobbish Hanna Holberg discovers, thanks to World War II, the humanity of the German people and the sense of loyalty of its soldiers, whom she decides to reward by singing for the troops in Paris.

Die grosse Liebe was the most popular film of its time in Germany; it is estimated that by 1943, close to seven million people had seen it. It was a well-deserved success for Zarah, who was seen at her best—impassioned, and, for a change, not playing her usual role of the ill-starred beauty; intense but not the *femme fatale*—besides being given the opportunity to sing two songs that would forever be associated with her: "Mein Leben für die Liebe" (My Life for Love) and "Ich weiss, es wird einmal ein Wunder geschehen" (I Know That, for Once, a Miracle Will Happen). In 1942, the year in which the film was released, the German people were thinking of one miracle only: victory over the enemies of the Reich. Moreover, the women who were left alone while their men were at the front were able to recognize themselves in the prima donna who sacrificed herself, giving up a life of comfort in order to feel closer to her Luftwaffe officer/beau. The air raid alarms and painful goodbyes in Rome and Paris were somehow softened by the strains of the waltz "Davon geht die Welt nicht unter" (The World Doesn't Die of This), which so many women—their fathers, brothers and husbands away—hummed to keep their spirits up.

It becomes apparent that all of Zarah Leander's roles have one thing in common—exoticism. Neither unaffected and reassuring like Henry Porten, nor wholesome and fun like Marika Rökk, the Swedish actress took advantage of her dual difference—she was both a star and a non-German—playing a Swede in 1937's *La Habanera,* a Hungarian in *Der Blaufuchs* (1938), an American, despite the name Maddalena dell'Orto, in *Heimat* (1938), a woman of the Sahara in *Das Lied der Wüste* (1939), and finally a South American in *Damals* (At That Time, 1943). It is no coincidence that in most of her films she plays a foreigner; there was her imperfect command of German to reckon with, and she furnished the German public with an opportunity for evasion, a momentary escape from the strictures of the Third Reich and from the war. On the Appian Way or in the office of a theatrical agent, in Puerto Rico or on a luxurious yacht, wherever Leander was it was instantly another country, a dream, flight.

During the war, however, the highest-paid star of the entire German film world could not leave. Only after her home in Dahlem, Berlin, was destroyed in 1943 by Allied bombs, was she able to flee to Sweden, after having completed, just in time, the filming of *Damals.* At about this time, Goebbels had suggested that she give up not only her Swedish citizenship but her estates in Sweden in exchange for German citizenship and a manor/estate in East Prussia. She refused. Leander returned for the film's premiere and to make some recordings, then went back to Stockholm.

At the war's end Leander had to face the hostility of Swedish audiences, both in film and theater, since all remembered her strong affiliation with the Nazi authorities. Leander defended herself by reminding them of her apolitical stance. However, it was at this time that she got her second divorce and threw herself wholeheartedly into the administration of the patrimony she had invested in a fish cannery in Lönö.

Leander returned to Germany seven years after her departure, after having tried in vain to reintegrate herself into the Swiss and Austrian film worlds. In February 1949, together with the composer Michael Jary, she managed to organize a concert tour of West Germany. She made films in the postwar period—*Gabriele, Kuba Kubana* and *Ave Maria*—but they failed to reestablish her as the top star she had been. On September 4, 1958, Leander attempted a comeback at the Raimund-Theater in Vienna in a musical entitled *Madame Scandaleuse,* written for her by Peter Kreuder. It was a success, and was greeted with equal enthusiasm in Munich, Hamburg and Berlin. Between 1961 and 1963 she appeared in it at the Haus Vaterland theater in Hamburg and the Astoria in Bremen. In 1964 she returned to Vienna in a new musical by Kreuder, *Lady aus Paris* (The Lady from Paris), and in 1968 appeared in *Wodka für die Königin* (Vodka for the Queen) in Hamburg.

From time to time she was seen on television, as in "Star unter Sternen" (A Star Under the Stars). On the occasion of her sixty-fifth birthday the program "TV Hören and Sehen" (TV Heard and Seen) presented a series on her life entitled *Mein Leben.* At the end of January 1956, Leander married her third husband, the orchestra leader Arne Hülphers. Zarah Leander died on June 23, 1981, in Stockholm, aged seventy-four.

La Habanera *(1937)*

Director: Detlef Sierck

The director of this film, Detlef Sierck (1900–1962), was one of the most interesting figures of the German film industry of the late 1930s, and one of the few directors capable of developing a personal style while obeying the laws of the regime. He had an affinity for melodrama, a genre in which he worked with notable success after leaving Germany in 1937 and, finally, emigrating to the United States in 1943, changing his name to Douglas Sirk. His first American movie was *Hitler's Madman,* that same year. Films such as *All That Heaven Allows* (1955), *Tarnished Angels* (1958) and *Imitation of Life* (1959) were praised by the most exigent critics, even those who objected to his excessive predilection for the lachrymose and sentimental.

Sierck's German films were not totally free of Party line, but they were never propagandistic. It might be said that, of German film directors, he collaborated the least with the Nazi regime. In the retrospective on the cinema of the Third Reich organized by Julian Petly for the National Film Theatre in London in March 1979, four of his Nazi-period films were shown.

With Karl Martell as Dr. Sven Nagel.

Story and screenplay: Gerhard Menzel
Photography: Franz Weihmayr
Set design: Anton Weber and Ernst Albrecht
Costumes: Annemarie Heise
Music: Lothar Brühne
Song lyrics: Detlef Sierck, Bruno Balz and Franz Baumann
Editing: Axel von Werner
Production: UFA
Length: 99 minutes
Country of origin: Germany, 1937
Censor's approval: date uncertain (banned to minors under 18)
Premiere: December 18, 1937

CAST —————————————

Zarah Leander (Astrée Sternhjelm), Julia Serda (her aunt, Ana Sternhjelm), Ferdinand Marian (Don Pedro de Avila), Karl Martell (Dr. Sven Nagel), Boris Alekin (Dr. Luis Gómez), Paul Bildt (Dr. Pardway), Edwin Jürgensen, Carl Kuhlmann, Michael Schulz-Dornburg, Rosita Alcaraz, Lisa Hellwig, Werner Fink, Karl Hannemann, Roma Bahn, Franz Arzdorf, Geza von Földessy, Günther Ballier, Hans Kettler, Max Wilhelm.

SYNOPSIS —————————————

Astrée, a young Swedish woman visiting Puerto Rico with her Aunt Ana, goes to a *corrida,* and is fascinated by the courage of the bullfighter Don Pedro in facing a ferocious animal. She falls in love with him and marries him, in order to remain in that tropical paradise. After ten years of marriage, however, Astrée, who in the meantime has had a child, has come to feel like a prisoner and gives vent to her sadness by singing the songs of her homeland to her young son. A fellow Swede, Dr. Nagel, visits her in order to warn her of the fever, whose cause he is desperately trying to determine, that is rapidly spreading throughout the country. Don Pedro, however, bent on sabotaging his research, invites him to a party, while in the meantime his henchmen destroy the vaccine that Dr. Nagel has discovered. The deed eventually costs Don Pedro his life, for he falls victim to the epidemic, whereas a brighter future awaits Astrée and her son, who return to Sweden with Nagel.

With the little Michael Schulz-Dornburg.

If the first two German films of Zarah Leander introduced us to a singing star, her new film surprises us by presenting Leander the actress. In this film as well there are scenes in which she sings . . . but for the rest she acts with warmth and naturalness, so that never for a moment do we have the impression that we are watching a singer. Perhaps the fact that she has become a convincing actress is in part due to her having finally mastered the German language. "La Habanera," the title song, recurs throughout the film to heighten the dramatic effect and to impart the mysterious atmosphere of the tropics. The film had a great success with the audience, which applauded frequently throughout the showing.

A. M. SCHMIDT,
Deutsche Filmzeitung,
Munich, December 26, 1937

Just as infinite emotions vibrate in this voice, so joy and sorrow are reflected in this face, which is comparable to a landscape upon which the sun shines or a storm rages. A splendid woman and a fine actress: Zarah Leander.

J. SPIEKERMANN,
Berliner Lokal-Anzeiger,
Berlin, January 20, 1938

If Zarah Leander is another Greta Garbo, then it can be said that her partner Karl Martell is another Clark Gable.

Leipziger Neueste Nachrichten,
Leipzig, February 10, 1938

The main attraction in this film is Zarah Leander. She moves us deeply when she smiles and when she sighs. . . . And she touches us most of all when she sings "La Habanera" in that deep voice.

W. MILTNER, *12 Urh-Blatt,*
Berlin, February 8, 1939

In a lonely mood, as Astree, she is about to sing a nostalgic song.

Heimat   *(1938)*

(Homeland)

Director: Carl Froelich

Zarah Leander's role in this film is a highly dramatic one, but one that nevertheless permits her to make full use of her musical gifts. Happy at returning home, she sings a lively number, "Eine Frau wird nur schön durch die Liebe" (A Woman Becomes Beautiful Only with Love), and the song "Kluge Frauen sagen nur vielleicht" (Clever Women Only Say Maybe). She expresses her patriotism with the popular song "Drei Sterne sah ich scheinen" (I Saw Three Stars Shining). She exhibits her operatic talents in an aria from Gluck's *Orfeo,* "Ach, ich habe sie verloren" (Ah, I Have Lost Her), and at the end of the film sings an excerpt from Bach's *St. Matthew* Passion, accompanied on the harpsichord by Paul Hörbiger. At the 1938 Venice Film Festival, *Heimat* won the cup of the Ministry of Public Instruction for best direction. Following the war, the Allied military government prohibited showing of this film in Germany.

Story: from the play of the same
name by Hermann Sudermann,
adapted by Otto Ernst Hesse and
Hans Brennert
Screenplay: Harald Braun
Photography: Franz Weihmayr
Settings: Franz Schroedter
Costumes: Manon Hahn
Music: Theo Mackeben
Editing: Gustav Lohse
Production: UFA-Froelich-Studio
& Co.
Length: 102 minutes
Country of origin: Germany, 1938
Censor's approval: May 31, 1938
Premiere: June 25, 1938, Danzig;
September 1, 1938, Berlin
Awards: National Film Prize (1938);
Artistic Value

CAST

Zarah Leander (Maddalena dell'Orto), Heinrich George (her father, Leopold von Schwartze), Ruth Hellberg (Marie, Maddalena's sister), Babsi Schultz-Reckewell (Poldi, Maddalena's daughter), Lina Carstens (Fränze), Paul Hörbiger (Franz, organist of the Immingen Cathedral), Franz Schafheitlin (bank director von Keller), Georg Alexander (Ludwig, Prince of Immingen), Leo Slezak, Hans Nielsen, Hugo Froelich.

SYNOPSIS

After an absence of many years, the celebrated opera singer Maddalena dell'Orto returns to Immingen, her native city, from which her father had driven her because of a youthful indiscretion. Maddalena, whose real name is Magda von Schwartze, was cast out when it was learned that she was to bear the child of the banker von Keller, who, after seducing her, abandoned her. Magda's father, an officer and a warm-hearted man, but one of unyielding principles, swore never to see her again. When Maddalena returns, her father demands that she keep away from the family because her sister Marie is about to be married. But the reputation of the von Schwartze family is threatened not by Maddalena but by von Keller, who involves the officer in an underhanded banking scheme. Before the police arrive, von Keller commits suicide, and Maddalena, having regained the love of her family, in the Cathedral of Immingen sings her most beautiful songs.

CRITICS' COMMENTS

The return to one's roots is an instinct passed down from father to son in one of the noblest works yet produced by our national film industry. . . Zarah Leander, suffused with patriotic feeling, and with a spare, intense style stripped of the slightest superfluous gesture, portrays a woman who has done wrong but who comes to her senses in time, who left the city of her birth but returns, in faith and good will—which her father is unable to appreciate. With this performance, La Leander makes it clear that she is our most complete actress.

P. HESSLING, *Licht-Bild-Bühne,*
Berlin, June 28, 1938

The second day of the Sixth International Festival of Cinematic Art turned out to be, socially speaking, the real opening of the manifestation. E. S. Dino Alfieri, the Minister of Popular Culture, invited the delegates of the various nations who were present at the Lido, the journalists and Fascist party dignitaries on a cruise aboard the ship Francesco Marconi. The majority of the celebrities present at the Lido, including Count Volpi and Edda Ciano-Mussolini, were present in the auditorium to see this German masterpiece with Zarah Leander, whose legend has spread to our shores. An imposing audience filled both the Palazzo del Cinema and the Hotel Excelsior. The film was warmly received, above all because of Zarah Leander, whose intense and touching performance held the spectators enthralled, right up to the final scene.

J. PFISTER, *Film-Kurier,* Berlin,
August 11, 1938 (reporting from Venice)

In the difficult role of Maddalena, Zarah Leander has given her most conclusive demonstration to date that she is an artist of international stature. What other artist would be as capable of giving a performance that is as effective in the film's lighter moments as in its more serious ones? She not only sang Gluck's Orfeo; she lived it. The film reaches its dramatic peak in the scene of Bach's St. Matthew Passion, and Zarah Leander's artistry makes it work. Heinrich George gives an outstanding performance as well. . . At the film's end, Zarah Leander, together with Heinrich George, Ruth Hellberg, Hans Nielsen and the director, Carl Froelich, were rapturously greeted by the audience.

W. LÜTHE, *Die Filmwoche,* Berlin,
September 14, 1938

With Heinrich George as the father who cannot forgive.

Es war eine rauschende Ballnacht   (1939)

(It Was a Wild Night at the Ball)

Director: Carl Froelich

Story: Georg Wittuhn and Jean Victor
Screenplay: Geza von Cziffra
Dialogue: Frank Thiess
Photography: Franz Weihmayr
Costumes: H. Ploeberger
Choreography: Sabine Ress
Music: Theo Mackeben, with added
   music by Tchaikovsky
Editing: G. Lohse
Production: Froelich-Studio Film
Length: 94 minutes
Country of origin: Germany, 1939
Censor's approval: July 18, 1939
Premiere: August 15, 1939
Awards: Particular Artistic Value;
   Cultural Value

CAST

Zarah Leander (Katharina Murakin),
Marika Rökk (Nastasja Petrovna
Yarova), Hans Stüwe (Peter Ilyich
Tchaikovsky), Leo Slezak (Prof. Max-
imilian Hunsinger), Grete Greff (Mam-
ma Yarova), Franz Stein (a doctor),
Arnim Süssengut (Prince Konstantin
Kostantinovich), Leopold von Ledebur
(a general), Maria Reisenhofer (an old
princess), Eva Immermann (a young
princess), Aribert Wäscher.

SYNOPSIS

At a ball at the Club of the Upper Ten
Thousand in Moscow, Tchaikovsky
plays a new waltz for the first time.
Nastasja Yarova, the most beautiful
dancer in all Russia, is enamored of the
composer, who that night has eyes only for Katharina Murakin, the lovely
wife of a wealthy businessman. As a
youth, Tchaikovsky had abandoned her
rather than have her share a life of hardship with him. The two resume their
relationship, heedless of the suspicions
of Katharina's husband. She decides to
have Tchaikovsky's music published.
Murakin's jealousy is placated only
when the musician presents the dancer
Nastasja as his wife. While Katharina
asks for a divorce, Tchaikovsky's star

begins to ascend; but before the two
lovers can be reunited, the composer
falls victim to cholera and dies.

CRITICS' COMMENTS

*Guiding the destiny of great men there
is always a woman. Froelich's film
stresses the importance of the woman
in a man's life. This time it is two
women. . . .The fact that they are
played by Zarah Leander and Marika
Rökk is a guarantee of a work of uncommon merit as well as unusual*

*interest. . . .The personalities of the
two actresses provide a fascinating contrast, with Leander's majestic beauty set
against Marika Rökk's piquant, ani-
mated charm. The imposing, elegant
woman, used to a life of luxury, is
counterposed with the gay and bewitching ballerina. The two actresses
manage to convey the stately and lyrical
aspects of the story, as well as its more
lighthearted ones.*

E. Jerosch,
Der Film, Berlin, pre-premiere
assessment, date uncertain

With Hans Stüwe.

There is much here that is reminiscent of Heimat — the rarefied atmosphere, the characters who are contrasted effectively and sometimes violently, the crowd scenes, the alternating of light-hearted moments with serious ones. Zarah Leander has created a Katharina of real stature, and succeeds in carrying off scenes that might not have worked were she not the actress she is. Marika Rökk . . . is her equal here . . . . The audience was highly enthusiastic, applauding in mid-scene and at the end of the film. The director and stars took many bows.

H. W. BETZ, *Der Film*, Berlin,
August 19, 1939

. . . And Zarah Leander? Is it necessary to mention again that vibrant, fascinating voice? No. But it must be said that in this film she is more beautiful than ever, and truly moving in its numerous dramatic scenes. Another outstanding feature of the film is its photography. Franz Weihmayr is a master cameraman, one who creates music for the eyes. Every shot glows with an inner light of its own, and this is truly the mark of a master!

H. E. FISCHER, *Die Filmwelt*,
Berlin, August 25, 1939

On the set of "Es war eine rauschende Ballnacht," 1939.

With Aribert Wäscher.

Die grosse Liebe   (1942)

(The Great Love)

Director: Rolf Hansen

After the war this film was prohibited by the Allied board of censorship from being shown on German territory, but was redistributed in other European countries with a brief prologue saying that, when it was shot, a depiction of life in the military had been deemed necessary. Cut from the original were the scenes where the singer and the officer take refuge in an air raid shelter and those in which Zarah Leander sings for the German troops in Paris.

Story: Alexander Lernet-Holenia
Screenplay: Peter Groll and Rolf Hansen
Photography: Franz Weihmayr
Set design: Anton Weber
Music: Michael Jary
Editing: Anna Höllering
Production: UFA
Length: 100 minutes
Country of origin: Germany, 1942
Censor's approval: June 6, 1942
Premiere: June 12, 1942, Berlin
Awards: Political and Artistic Value;
    Popular Value

CAST

Zarah Leander (Hanna Holberg), Viktor Staal (Lieutenant Paul Wendlandt), Paul Hörbiger (Rudnitzky), Grethe Weiser (Käthe, Hanna's maid), Wolfgang Preiss (Lieutenant von Etzdorf), Viktor Janson (Mocelli), Julia Serda (Mrs. Westphal), Hans Schwarz, Jr. (Alfred).

SYNOPSIS

Everyone who goes to the "Scala" in Berlin falls under the spell of the singer Hanna Holberg; the young Luftwaffe pilot, Lt. Paul Wendlandt, meets her there and is no exception. An air raid takes them by surprise, and Paul and Hanna go to her house, Paul remaining until the next morning. When he leaves, he realizes that he is in love with Hanna. The composer Rudnitzky, who also loves Hanna, watches the flowering of this relationship with increasing jealousy. During a party, Hanna and Paul announce their engagement. In the midst of the congratulations, a telegram arrives summoning Paul to duty. After his departure for the front, Hanna rejoins him in Rome, but their meeting is again interrupted by the war. Meanwhile, Hanna is working as a nurse in a military hospital, where one day Paul arrives, wounded. Firmly convinced that the war will soon end, Hanna silently takes Paul's hand in her own.

CRITICS' COMMENTS

In Zarah Leander's new film, the love and the sorrows of a music hall singer are intertwined with the destiny of an aviator in the war—a situation that sorely tests the sincerity of their sentiments! The director, with intelligence

With Viktor Staal.

and humor, avoids the danger of excessive sentimentality, and his story moves briskly from Berlin to Paris and Rome and to the African front. Zarah Leander, marvelously photographed, pours out her hopes and fears and longings in Michael Jary's songs. Paul Hörbiger, as the composer and friend of the diva, wins all hearts, except hers. The stars, present at the opening, were enthusiastically applauded.

E. KRAFT, *Die Filmwoche*, Berlin, pre-premiere assessment, date uncertain

Our era—one that tests one's fortitude, intermingles destinies and creates problems. The pressure of life, of the great struggle and of death render invalid the normal tenets of our hearts and minds. Art cannot be silent about this fact without negating itself, and for this reason this film has chosen to confront a theme of our own time. . . . *Zarah Leander gives a performance of the highest level. . . .The film reaches the hearts of its audience because its external realism is matched by an inner truth.* The lion's share of the applause at the end of the film went to Zarah Leander, who was present in the hall.

H. W. BETZ, *Der Film*, Berlin, June 13, 1942

I spoke by telephone with Göring, who complained about the OKW (Oberkommando der Wehrmacht), which protested against the new Leander film. The OKW considers itself morally insulted and insists that a Luftwaffe lieutenant should not act in this way. Göring, on the contrary, maintains, justly, that a Luftwaffe lieutenant who did not take advantage of a similar occasion would simply not be a Luftwaffe lieutenant. Göring is making fun of the sensibilities of the OKW. This is all to my benefit, because the OKW causes me all kinds of trouble in my film work. In this case, we can always point out that Göring is our top expert on Luftwaffe matters, and we can be sure of not running into any legal difficulties.

JOSEPH GOEBBELS, in *The Goebbels Diaries*, edited by L. Lechner (Garden City, NY: Doubleday, 1948)

With Viktor Staal, never without his beloved puppy.

KRISTINA SÖDERBAUM

ALL THE ARTS OF SEDUCTION OF HER COMPATRIOT Zarah Leander proved to be no match for the tranquility that the blond, apple-cheeked Kristina Söderbaum seemed to promise to the German public. Born in Djursholm, a suburb of Stockholm, on September 5, 1912, she became the embodiment of the fresh, ingenuous German *Fräulein*—modest and selfless—as well as of the strong and healthy Aryan—the fruit of Kraft durch Freude (Strength Through Joy). The eternal child-wife, she provided an image of the feminine ideal of the Third Reich in a series of films that carried a strong message of propaganda.

Söderbaum's father, Henrik, a professor of chemistry and president of the committee that awarded the Nobel Prizes, never accepted the idea of his daughter becoming a film actress. On the other hand, her aspirations had been unwittingly stimulated by her family, which on every holiday would present performances of various kinds for friends and relatives. Söderbaum waited until after her father's death before pursuing her dream. She moved to Berlin to try her luck, and began to study German under the tutelage of the actor Rudolf Klein-Rogge, who found her a part in *Onkel Bräsig* (Uncle Bräsig, 1936), a film of a patriotic nature, which attracted little attention. Kristina remained relatively unknown until 1938, when the director Veit Harlan came across some of her photographs in studio files.

This was a double stroke of luck, because at that time Harlan, one of the directors most favored by Goebbels—not only for his total "alignment," but also for the speed with which he turned out one film after another—had just divorced his second wife, Hilde Korber, a well-known actress in the theater, and had been looking for someone to play the leading role in *Jugend* (Youth, 1938). This was the story of an eighteen-year-old girl who lived in the house of her uncle, a clergyman. She fell in love with a student, with whom she had a clean and honest relationship, but they were spied upon by a puritanical vicar. After the boy's departure, the girl ran off and drowned herself. For this tale with its naturalistic overtones and its relevance to the problem of female emancipation, Söderbaum seemed made to order. It was a tragedy about a girl barely out of adolescence, living in an austere corner of western Prussia, who was terrified by her first feelings of love. A somewhat overly sentimental film, *Jugend* achieved a level of considerable dramatic intensity thanks to the solid theatrical background of its young leading lady.

The public decreed that a new star had been born—one whom the director wasted no time in making his wife, as well as his favorite actress. She spoke German with a kind of purring Swedish accent, which audiences liked, and was attractive in a simple, girl-next-door way, in contrast to her more glamorous colleagues. Within a few years she was the most popular actress on the German screen.

After filming a romantic drama, the couple Harlan-Söderbaum turned to a mystery, *Verwehte Spuren* (Covered Tracks, 1938), based on a true incident. The story took place in Paris in 1867, where Séraphine Laurence, the protagonist, was investigating the mysterious disappearance of her mother. Dr. Morot (Fritz von Dongen—who later became Philip Dorn in Hollywood) discovered the cause: Mme. Laurence had died of the plague, and her body had been hidden in order to avoid an outbreak of panic in the city. *Verwehte Spuren*'s success was as great as that of *Jugend*, due in no small measure to the first-rate script that Thea von Harbou had provided Söderbaum, enabling her to give a more controlled and understated performance. The following year she made *Das unsterbliche Herz* (The Immortal Heart), a historical film based on a play by Walter Harlan, the director's father. A work of the type encouraged by Goebbels—films about the great Germans of the past, for audiences to emulate—it boasted an exceptional cast, including Paul Wegener and Heinrich George, two celebrated figures of the German stage. Harlan hit the bull's-eye again, with even the *New York Times* praising the film extravagantly after its opening at the 86th Street Playhouse in the city's "Germantown" on October 20, 1939, commending in particular the richness of the film's settings.

Ironically enough, it was certain elements of the banal and the stereotyped in the portrayal of women in Harlan's films that were to increase his fame, and not only in Germany. The characters played by Söderbaum reflected the German ideal, as fixed by the tenets of Romantic literature: sentimental, traditional, self-sacrificing, as well as disciplined, upright and proper. As a result, audiences liked her, and her films made money.

The heroine of *Die Reise nach Tilsit* (The Journey to Tilsit, 1939), based on the story by German playwright/novelist Hermann Sudermann (1857–1928), is somewhat reminiscent of the young girl in *Jugend*. Söderbaum was ideally cast as Elske, the demure young wife of an arrogant husband who betrays her with a Polish woman, Madlyn (Anna Dammann). As is to be expected in a Nazi film of the period, the foreign woman is lustful, promiscuous and provocatively clad, while the blond Elske is old-fashioned, virtuous, and wears the

traditional folk dresses of Memel, the town on the eastern Baltic shore in which the story takes place. The film also confirms that city people are corrupt, and that the "asphalt culture" (as Goebbels called it) produces only types like Madlyn; whereas, thanks to women like Elske, the wholesome principles of German life continue to flourish. It may be that *Die Reise nach Tilsit* bore too strong a resemblance to F. W. Murnau's *Sunrise,* filmed in America in 1927 (also based on the work by Sudermann), and perhaps Söderbaum was no match for Janet Gaynor (Murnau's heroine). Nevertheless, Harlan claimed that his was a "*real* film," whereas *Sunrise* was "only a poem."[1] *Sunrise* was, indeed, all symbolism and fantasy, filmed in soft focus; Harlan's film was more down-to-earth and literal, having been shot in Memel itself.

The plot of the film—the faithful German wife looks on, helpless, at her husband's flirtation with a beautiful foreign adulteress—closely resembled the experience of Magda Goebbels, whose domestic happiness had been threatened by the Czech actress Lida Baarova. Indignant at the similarity—which was unintentional—to persons and facts well known to Berlin gossips, at the premiere of the film Frau Goebbels got up and ostentatiously left the auditorium. In any case, she could have remained, because at the end it was the wife who won out; the film actually served as a reminder that the German hearth and home were sacred. After all, hadn't the "Baarova affair" been expeditiously straightened out by sending the actress back to Czechoslovakia?

The subject of the most delicate legal case in the annals of the German film industry, *Jud Süss* (Jew Süss, 1940) was the most unfortunate episode in Söderbaum's career. Strongly anti-Semitic, the film is an attempt to convince the viewer that the Jewish race is inferior to the Aryan one, and recounts the story of an unscrupulous adventurer who, among other things, ravishes Dorothea, a German girl (Söderbaum). Desperate at having lost her honor at the hands of a Jew, the girl drowns herself. It was at this point that Söderbaum found herself pinned with the nickname Reichswasserleiche, the official drowned girl of the Reich, since in virtually every film to come she ended up drowning herself. In the role of the profaned Aryan girl, she furnished an example of how to increase anti-Jewish feeling, adding her undoubted talent to that of well-established actors such as Heinrich George, Ferdinand Marian and others (including a very young Wolfgang Staudte), in one of the most deplorable films of the Hitler regime. Furthermore, in Lion Feuchtwanger's novel, the character of Dorothea did not exist. It is clear that Harlan and Goebbels wanted to add it to the story for their own political purposes. Also invented for the film was the scene after the rape of Dorothea in which the Jews, instigated by Süss, tortured her fiancé. And in fact, after the film's release, numerous incidents of anti-Semitic violence took place; perhaps more to the point, *Jud Süss* was shown just before the Jews were rounded up to be sent to extermination camps.

As Joseph Wulf observes, rightfully: "It is not surprising that the question is still constantly raised as to whether the actors who took part in these films were responsible or not for the murder of millions of people."[2] It is known that Söderbaum was quick to secure the role for herself when she found out that Viktoria von Ballasko was being considered for it. Even though after the war Harlan wrote a book of memoirs in which he declared that his wife would have taken refuge in Sweden if she had not just given birth to their firstborn, Caspar, the question still remains: To what extent were the actors who participated in *Jew Süss* unaware of the effects that a work of that nature would produce on the German public, already growing hostile to its Jewish population?

No longer a stranger to propaganda films, Söderbaum, now directed exclusively by Harlan, appeared in one of the many films about Frederick the Great, *Der grosse König* (The Great King) in 1942. She seemed somewhat out of place, inasmuch as the film was a historical reconstruction of battles and situations that were totally "masculine." Harlan writes, in fact, that Goebbels was not happy with the insertion of a romantic interlude in a work of this kind; he praised the film, however, as soon as he saw how enthusiastically it was received by the public.

In *Die goldene Stadt* (The Golden City, 1942), Söderbaum's pink cheeks and hair as golden as the spires of Prague, where the film was shot, were captured in Agfacolor, in the second color film to be made by a German studio. She played Anna, a German country girl, whose great dream is to see Prague, the golden city that had brought her mother to perdition. She falls in love with a visiting surveyor (Paul Klinger), and flees to Prague. Unable to find him, she goes to the home of an aunt, where she is seduced by a cousin, Toni (Kurt Meisel), who disappears when he learns that she is expecting a baby, and marries a rich older woman. Even her father rejects Anna, who goes to the same swamp that had been her mother's grave, and drowns herself. The metaphor is evident: Anna deserves her fate because she abandoned her homeland: the Czechoslovak countryside. As she dies she says, "Forgive me, father, for not loving my native land as much as you did." The film surrounds Söderbaum with obviously caricatured figures—typically dissipated city dwellers—and Prague itself is shown as a place of dark alleys and labyrinths. Whereas in the play by Richard Billinger, *Der Gigant* (The Giant), it was Anna's father who died, in the film version it was apparently necessary to have the "guilty" one commit suicide, so that women contemplating abandoning their traditional role might see the destiny that awaited them.

Another film dealing with the concept of "Germanic fidelity" was *Immensee* (1943), based on Theodor Storm's classic novel of the same name, the story of a woman who marries a rich landowner to forget her unrequited love for a young musician. Once she becomes Reinhardt's wife, Elisabeth learns to love him deeply. The old flame returns, now a celebrated conductor, but she remains faithful to her husband, even after his death. Once again Söderbaum lent her blue eyes, blond hair and sturdy features to a portrayal of the 100-percent-Aryan woman, with even a brief shot of an *au naturel* swim in the lake, intended to emphasize the benefits of outdoor life. The basic message of the film was the sanctity of marriage. The beauty of the northern German landscape, captured by Agfacolor in UFA's fifth color film, did much to heighten the idyllic mood.

An excellent vehicle for Söderbaum was *Opfergang* (Sacrifice, 1943), in which she played Aels, a lover of nature and solitude. When her former lover and his new wife move into the house next door to hers, old passions are rekindled, and then dampened by the outbreak in Hamburg of an epidemic, which infects Aels and her lover. Once again Söderbaum dies; but despite the unhappy ending, the character she plays is not wholly a negative one. Romanticism and pantheism, funereal obsessions and the wish to "become one with the universe" are mingled in the character of a woman who speaks in terms of dreams and other worlds. When a rose is seen floating at the spot where her ashes have been scattered, it is clear that she has been redeemed by her love of nature.

Despite certain romantic excesses, *Opfergang* marked a step forward in Söderbaum's artistic development. Her next appearance was in a costly *Kolossal* assigned to Harlan by Goebbels when it became apparent that no hope remained for Germany. In fact, the most painful signs of the imminent collapse could be sensed precisely in such patriotic film epics as *Kolberg* (1944). The historic basis of the film is the heroic resistance of a German city besieged by the French in 1806 during the Napoleonic era. Young Maria Werner has been given the task of negotiating with the Queen of Prussia, who has been asked to help organize the resistance. The army is unwilling to fight, however, and so the citizens of Kolberg act on their own. The battle will not be won, but they will have shown that Germans do not surrender easily. When all has been lost, the mayor says to the sole survivor of the Werner family: "Yes, Maria, you have given everything you had. But not in vain. . . . Beautiful things are born from great sorrows. And when someone takes upon himself so much suffering, then he is truly a beautiful person. You are noble, Maria; you have done your duty; you were not afraid to die. You have won, too, Maria—you, too." Söderbaum

was not totally convincing in this part, particularly in the poorly written scene in which she goes to negotiate with the Queen. On the other hand, even if she had been more persuasive, who was going to believe that the Reich could save itself by a few heroic deeds? On January 10, 1945, a print of the film was dropped by parachute into the German Atlantic fortress at La Rochelle, France, where an audience of bewildered soldiers watched the premiere of the last of UFA's super-productions.

After the war, Kristina Söderbaum received offers of work in Italy, in Sweden and also in Germany, all of which she refused until Veit Harlan was allowed to resume his career as well. A trial against him in the spring of 1949 ended in his acquittal, but on December 12 of the same year there was a second trial, in the British Zone of occupied Germany. In April 1950 there was a third, and this time, too, Harlan was acquitted, based on the fact that during the Hitler era he had, as a young director, been in need of work. After 1950 the couple returned to films, but the success of earlier years eluded them. In the fall of 1955 Söderbaum converted to Catholicism, together with her children, Caspar and Kristian; her husband remained an Evangelical Protestant until his death in 1964. Since 1966, Söderbaum has devoted much of her time to photography. She died on February 12, 2001.

Söderbaum in "Der grosse König," 1942.

Das unsterbliche Herz   *(1939)*

(The Immortal Heart)

Director: Veit Harlan

The Allied Military Government banned the showing of this film in Germany, not because Söderbaum is seen nude for an instant under a fur robe as she tries to arouse the passion of her husband, but because it was decided that the work contained strongly chauvinistic elements.

Story: from the play by Walter Harlan, *Das Nürnbergisch Ei* (The Nuremberg Egg)

Screenplay: Werner Eplinius and Walter Harlan
Photography: Bruno Mondi
Music: Alois Melichar
Production: Tobis
Length: 108 minutes
Country of origin: Germany, 1939
Censor's approval: January 26, 1939 (banned to minors under 18)
Premiere: January 31, 1939, Nuremberg; February 14, 1939, Berlin
Award: Artistic Value

With Heinrich George on the cover of "Film-Kurier," advertising a 1944 film, "Kolberg."

SYNOPSIS ——————————

The geographer Martin Behaim (1459–1506) is shipwrecked during a voyage for research. He cannot even determine his location because all the pendulum clocks on board have stopped. His friend Peter Henlein, a gifted inventor and friend of master painter Albrecht Dürer, wants to invent a new type of clock, but first has to think about his young wife Ev, who has lost her head over the young apprentice Konrad, accused of adultery by Henlein. Konrad accidentally shoots the inventor, who is struck in the heart by a special double bullet that Henlein himself invented. The doctor is able to remove only half of it. Dying, Henlein testifies in court on behalf of Behaim, accused of having endangered the lives of others. Having succeeded in inventing the water-clock, Henlein dies, blessing the love between Ev and Konrad.

CRITICS' COMMENTS ——————

The premiere took place in the presence of and under the patronage of the Gauleiter Julius Streicher at the UFA-Palast in Nuremberg. Two hundred journalists, representatives of the radio, and winners of the Tobis Prize were present in the auditorium. Harlan's direction is extraordinary. . . .Kristina Söderbaum is particularly affecting in the difficult part of Ev. . . . At the end, the Gauleiter spoke to the audience of how the film came to be made, and what it means to Germany, and to Nuremberg in particular. He complimented the artists present in the theater on their achievement. In conclusion, he paid homage to the Führer, whose support made the production of the film possible. During the reception offered to the press. . . a representative of the Nuremberg Clockmakers' League presented precious clocks to Veit Harlan and Heinrich George as souvenirs of German craftsmanship.

A. SCHNEIDER, *Die Filmwoche*, Berlin, February 8, 1939

There are those who say that nothing exists in this film except one great actor: Heinrich George! Nevertheless, although it would be difficult indeed to equal the expressive power and the scenic presence of this artist, we must mention Kristina Söderbaum, who gives a moving performance as the young wife, Ev. Perhaps, however, she has emphasized more the tragi-comic aspects of the union between a man and woman so different in their habits and needs than she has their inner, psychological differences.

I. MARTINI, *Deutsche Filmzeigung*, Munich, February 12, 1939

Kristina Söderbaum has a part that permits her to display the full range of her dramatic skill, particularly in the gripping confrontation scene with her husband. As Ev, the wife, she is warmly appealing and bewitchingly attractive, but also capable of vehemently attacking the blind idealism of her husband. The Tobis company can be proud of the reception that this exceptional film was awarded at the UFA-Palast in Berlin.

A. HOLLER, *Film-Kurier*, Berlin, February 15, 1939

Jud Süss   (1940)

(Jew Süss)

Director: Veit Harlan

Anti-Semitic films such as this one were intended to justify the total persecution of the Jews, initiated only gradually by Hitler after his coming to power. It was not by chance that the first anti-Semitic films were made between 1939 and 1940, the years of mass deportations and of the beginning of the "final solution." Jews were presented as ridiculous, and reduced to subhuman caricatures, as in H. H. Zerlett's *Robert und Bertram* (1939), E. Waschneck's *Die Rothschilds* (1940) and F. Hippler's "documentary" *Der ewige Jude* (The Eternal Jew, 1940). Goebbels considered these films sufficiently important to issue special instructions to the press. On April 26, 1940, in fact, he announced: "The publicity campaigns relative to *Jud Süss* and *Die Rothschilds* must not refer to them as 'anti-Semitic films.'"

To call the film cursed may be going a bit far; nevertheless, a number of its leading actors subsequently met with tragedy. Ferdinand Marian, persecuted by guilt at having appeared in the film, committed suicide, smashing his automobile into a tree; in 1950, his wife was found drowned in a canal in Hamburg;

The scene of the ritual slaughter.

Ferdinand Marian attempting to undermine Dorothea's Aryan purity.

Heinrich George died in 1946 in the Russian-controlled concentration camp at Sachsenhausen; Werner Krauss was blacklisted. Inasmuch as the film was an avowedly political one, most critics analyzed the work as a whole, paying scant attention to the actors' performances. A few critics, however, commented on Söderbaum's affecting portrayal of Dorothea. A few prints of this film managed to escape destruction. It is known for certain that there is one at Fort d'Ivry, outside of Paris, in an army photography and motion picture building. The National Center for Jewish Film at Brandeis University acquired a print from the German government in 1988, and is opposed to allowing this, and other anti-Semitic films, to be shown to the public, only permitting scholars to see them after a panel has reviewed their applications. Protests from the Jewish community prevented the film's being shown at the Valencia Film Festival in 1978.

Story: from the novel of the same name by Lion Feuchtwanger

Screenplay: Ludwig Metzger, Eberhard Wolfgang Möller and Veit Harlan
Photography: Bruno Mondi
Music: Wolfgang Zeller
Production: Terra
Length: 98 minutes
Country of origin: Germany, 1940
Censor's approval: August 6, 1940 (banned to minors under 14)
Premiere: August 24, 1940, Venice
Awards: Particular Political and Artistic Value

CAST _____

Kristina Söderbaum (Dorothea Sturm), Ferdinand Marian (Süss Oppenheimer), Werner Krauss (Rabbi Löw), Eugen Klöpfer (Councilor Sturm), Malte Jäger (Court Scribe Faber), Hilde von Stolz (the duchess), Albert Florath (Roeder), Theodor Loos (von Remchingen), Walter Werner, Charlotte Schulz, Anny Seitz, Erna Morena, Jakob Tiedtke, Else Elster, Emil Hess, Ursula Deinert, Erich Dunskus, and others.

SYNOPSIS _____

Süss Oppenheimer comes from Frank-furt to the Duchy of Württemberg, quickly ingratiating himself with the Duke, Karl Alexander. The Duke confides his economic problems to Süss, who agrees to furnish him sufficient funds to continue his dissolute life at court, in return for the right to collect taxes in the Duchy. Although Rabbi Löw disapproves of him, Süss's power grows. Aided by his secretary, Levi, he abducts Dorothea, the lovely daughter of Councilor Sturm, and rapes her. Meanwhile, Faber, Dorothea's fiancé, who has been organizing a revolt against Süss, is tortured in a cellar. The girl manages to escape, and drowns herself. Süss is tried and condemned to death. He is locked in an iron cage, which lifts him up to the scaffold. As the Jews evacuate the city, a passerby warns: "May the citizens of other states never forget this lesson."

CRITICS' COMMENTS _____

In this film I show primordial Judaism, as it was then and as it has remained until today, substantially unchanged. In contrast to international Judaism, there

The virtuoso star of the German stage and screen, Werner Krauss, as the defeated rabbi.

is only the Jew Süss, the elegant court financial adviser, the treacherous schemer; in short: the disguised Jew.

VEIT HARLAN, *Der Film*, Berlin, January 20, 1940

During the Week of Italian and German Film in Venice last August, this great motion picture was written about and discussed at length. At the UFA-Palast in Berlin, Minister Goebbels personally congratulated the director and the actors for having shown in this epic film how relevant for us today are the shadows of the past. The direction rises at times to a demonic pitch. . . . Kristina Söderbaum, natural and moving, gives one of her finest performances. Werner Krauss, in a multiple

role, is remarkable in his portrayal of several different Jewish characters. The effect upon the audience of this dramatic achievement of our national film industry was attested to by its thunderous applause.

H. E. FISCHER, *Die Filmwelt*, Berlin, October 4, 1940

The overall reaction to this film can be conveyed by overheard remarks such as: "It makes you want to go and wash your hands." Reports from Leipzig, Breslau, Oppeln, Salzburg, Potsdam, Troppau, etc., state that when parents and teachers were asked whether children should be permitted to see the film, they said no, that the negative effects of the work could be extremely

harmful to their psyches. . . . One scene in particular remains in the mind—apart from that of the rape—the one in which the Jews enter Stuttgart, with all of their belongings. In Berlin, for example, the audience yelled, "Throw the Jews out of the Kurfürstendamm! Kick all the Jews out of Germany, every last one of them!" The prevailing opinion among the audience was that the Duke is as guilty as the Jew Süss, and that his death is a just punishment, which unfortunately arrives too late to teach him the necessary attitude to adopt toward Süss, and Jews in general.

Report of the S.D. (Sicherheitsdienst, the S.S.'s security division), November 26, 1940, Federal Archive of Koblenz

Der grosse König   *(1942)*

(The Great King)

Director: Veit Harlan

Otto Gebühr (right), as the defeated Frederick, weeps on the breast of Herbert Hübner.

Goebbels declared this motion picture to be a Film of the Nation, a highly coveted award. In his diary he notes: "Harlan's film is an excellent example of political education, because it shows the solitude in which the Führer lives and works today." Behind the figure of the "great king"—wise, alone, plagued by destiny—many Germans may have perceived that of Hitler. Particularly telling is the scene in which Frederick, after the Peace of Hubertusburg, inspects the town. In the midst of the ruins, new life has sprung up; in the midst of the dust and the corpses he sees men busy tilling the soil, beginning again. If one thinks of the year in which the film was made, *Der grosse König* seems more a prophetic work than a consolatory one, even if Goebbels did write, in regard to Harlan's film: "If we succeed in overcoming these difficulties, they will have served to strengthen the nation's capability of resistance. . .proving Nietzsche's words that that which does not destroy us, strengthens us."

Story and screenplay: Veit Harlan
Photography: Bruno Mondi
Music: Hans-Otto Borgmann
Production: Tobis
Length: 118 minutes
Country of origin: Germany, 1942

Censor's approval: February 28, 1942
Premiere: date uncertain
Awards: Film of the Nation; Particular Artistic Value; Cultural Value; Popular Value; Formative for the People; Suited for the Young

CAST

Otto Gebühr (Frederick II, "the Great"), Kristina Söderbaum (Luise), Gustav Frölich (Marshall Treskow), Hans Nielsen (Niehoff), Paul Wegener (General Czernitscheff), Paul Henckels (Grenadier Spiller), Elisabeth Flickenschildt (his wife), Kurt Meisel (Alfons), Hilde Körber, Claus Detlev Sierck, Claus Clausen, Herbert Hübner, and others.

SYNOPSIS

The scene is Prussia, after the battle of Kunersdorf. Half of the Prussian army has fallen in battle; the entourage of the King considers the situation hopeless and presses for peace at any cost. Frederick manages to escape an attempt on his life and to win the Battle of Torgau. A brief alliance agreed upon with the Russians lasts until the new Czar is assassinated. Meanwhile, the Prussian army again wins a decisive battle against the Austrians. The king returns to Kunersdorf, where he meets Luise, the miller's daughter and wife of Treskow, who will not be decorated despite having performed an act of heroism. He has, in fact, violated the military code. The great King and the young girl exchange brief, but eloquent, words. Frederick knows that now his life can be dedicated only to Prussia.

CRITICS' COMMENTS

It could also have been called The King Alone, *since Harlan shows us the Prussian king between the Battles of Kunersdorf and Schweidnitz as the most solitary man in the world, who not only has to be harsh with himself, but also with those whom he loves and respects....In the many scenes between Frederick and Luise we noted how much Söderbaum has matured of late....She is extraordinary, especially in the scene of the bivouac at night, when she raises her lantern on high to illuminate the face of the unknown horseman. Even when not uttering a word, in her amazement at having discovered the king in person, how lovely and touching she is in her portrayal of the humble girl from Kunersdorf!*

H. KOCH, *Film-Kurier,*
Berlin, March 17, 1942

This film portrait of Frederick during the second half of the Seven Years' War brings us from the darkness to the light, from catastrophe to victory. His great destiny is also reflected in that of the miller's daughter, played by Kristina Söderbaum, more radiant than ever.

The actress is particularly touching when, alone with her baby, she meets the great king and speaks to him, with an informality to which he is unaccustomed, words that speak to his heart, just as Kristina's eyes speak to our hearts, engulfing us in a sea of blue.

N. LIND, *Die Filmwoche,*
March 25, 1942

Kristina Söderbaum is simply not convincing here. Her role itself seems artificial. In this film she is merely an appendage to her man—a lovely decoration put there to supply the love interest that the public demands.

F. COURTADE and P. CADARS,
Histoire du cinéma nazi
(Paris, 1973)

The great king (Gebühr) with the lovely miller's daughter (Kristina Söderbaum).

LUISE ULLRICH

WHEN LUISE ULLRICH BEGAN HER SCREEN CAREER, the German film industry needed someone exactly like her. Neither a great beauty nor a great actress, she looked out from the screen offering her audience comfort and reassurance. Blond, but not flashy, slender (nothing Valkyrian about her), with dark eyes under pencil-thin brows, La Ullrich seemed made for domestic dramas played out in well-bred silence. The parts she played tell the story: a wife who supports her penniless painter husband in *Versprich mir nichts!* (Promise Me Nothing!, 1937), the willing prisoner of a man desperately in love with her in *Ich liebe Dich* (I Love You, 1938), an exemplary mother in *Annelie* (1941), a weak and lonely creature in *Nora* (1944). The actress brought to life a gallery of resigned and uncomplaining creatures, reflecting the feminine ideal of the era.

Ullrich was born Aloisa Ullrich in Vienna on October 31, 1911, daughter of a count and major in the Austro-Hungarian army. Perhaps it was growing up in a household of strict discipline and repression that gave her that well-bred manner that made her the ideal interpreter of so many stories of women living out lives of renunciation. She attended secondary school and at the same time took acting classes at the Vienna Theater-Akademie, until, still in her teens, she was offered a two-year contract with the city's Volkstheater.

Ullrich's first success was in the part of Marieschen in German playwright/novelist Hermann Sudermann's *Heimat* (Homeland). In the fall of 1932, Ullrich appeared with Werner Krauss in Richard Billinger's *Rauhnacht* (Brawly Night) at the Lessing-Theater in Berlin. One night, film actor/director Luis Trenker happened to see the play. He was in the midst of writing the screenplay for *Der Rebell* (The Rebel), and had not yet found a leading lady for the film. The young Viennese actress seemed suitable to him, and he offered her the opportunity to make her film debut in the part of Erika, the Bavarian fiancée of a patriot who fights to free the Tyrol from Napoleon's troops. In *Der Rebell* (1932), Ullrich had little to do except cast beseeching glances at her hero (Trenker, naturally), as she skipped from rock to rock, and burst into tears at regular intervals. In the "Trenker-Filme," the stars were the glistening Alpine peaks and the former mountain guide—yes, Trenker, whose film image was "like that of John Wayne"[1]— who had taken to writing, directing and starring in his own, enormously popular mountain-climbing epics.

In *Leise flehen meine Lieder* (titled *Schubert's Unfinished Symphony* in England and the United States,

1933), directed by the equally multifaceted Willi Forst, Ullrich was eclipsed this time by the lovely blond Hungarian Marthe Eggerth, the soprano star of this musical film based on the life of Franz Schubert (played by Hans Jaray). Another Viennese story finally gave her an opportunity to reveal her worth as an actress: Max Ophüls' adaptation of Arthur Schnitzler's play *Liebelei* (Flirtation, 1933), in which she played Mizzi Schlager, a sensitive girl in love with an officer. The protagonist of the film was Magda Schneider (mother of late actress Romy Schneider), who gave a memorable performance as the tragic Christina in this screen classic. Continuing along the line of screen adaptations of literary and theatrical works, always a popular genre with German filmmakers, in 1934 UFA produced *Regine,* based on Swiss novelist Gottfried Keller's famous love story, and in 1935 *Viktoria,* from a novel by Norway's Knut Hamsun. Both were with Ullrich, who again proved to be an actress of uncommon skill and intelligence.

In 1937, Wolfgang Liebeneiner, directing his first film, *Versprich mir nichts!,* chose her for the part of a would-be painter. Liebeneiner, an exceptionally gifted artist, turned out a work of such brilliance that Goebbels, who had a particular admiration for formally well crafted films, appointed him head of the Terra film company, one of the four major German production houses.

But Ullrich's finest performance is considered to be her portrayal of the title role in *Annelie: Die Geschichte eines Lebens* (Annelie: The Story of a Life), an intimate film, one that grossed 6½ million marks for UFA—an enormous sum for the time. Its success can be explained in part because it was a woman's film, and because in 1941, when it was released, German audiences were primarily women, eager to see the story of a life so similar to their own. In a torrent of dramatic images— two wars and countless births and deaths pass in review—the actress brought to vivid life every scene in which she appeared. The propagandistic value of that life, dedicated to duty and to the Fatherland, was naturally obvious at times, but there were also truly touching moments, as when Annelie, addressing her son, who is about to leave for the front, says: "Im Leben übersteht man alles. Es ist nicht leicht, aber mit der Zeit lernt man's" (In this life one survives everything. It's not easy, but with time you learn). Which reflected the morale of German mothers at that moment, who were reminded of the necessity to give to their country what was dearest to them.

Ullrich as an aging Annelie.

With *Nora,* it is difficult not to conclude that once again the actress is portraying a character who is meant primarily as a symbol. Although the film is based on Henrik Ibsen's great Norwegian drama *A Doll's House* — in which at the end Nora leaves her home forever, slamming the door behind her — here the sense of that feminine rebellion is completely distorted. If we looked for the famous door-slamming in director Harald Braun's *Nora,* we would be wasting our time; the dominant theme here is the sanctity of marriage. In addition, some anti-Semitic touches can be noted in the figure of Brack, the perfidious blackmailer of Nora and her husband, played by the same actor (Carl Kuhlmann) who had been Nathan Rothschild in the anti-Semitic film *Die Rothschilds* (1940). With a classic stock of melodramatic exclamations — "I cannot escape my destiny!" "I made a mistake and I must pay!" — Nora seems to be modeled on the archetype of the woman who has learned to atone for sins that exist only in the mind of the one who condemns her.

In the postwar period, Ullrich continued to perform, appearing in Rainer Werner Fassbinder's television series "Acht Stunden sind kein Tag" (Eight Hours Are Not a Day), opposite Werner Finck, as a dynamic and impertinent grandmother. During the same period, she published a book of memoirs, *Komm auf die Schaukel, Luise: Balance eines Lebens* (Come onto the Swing, Luise: Appraisal of a Life), which takes its place alongside a little volume on her trips to South America, *Sehnsucht, wohin führst Du mich?* (Nostalgia, Where Are You Leading Me?), published in 1943. In addition, she published a novel, *Ricarda,* in 1954, and some short stories, one of which, *Einen Augenblick ohne Theater* (A Moment Without Theater), appeared in the collection *The 56 Best Short Stories in the World.* In 1942 she married Wulf Diether, Count of Castell-Rüdenhausen and director of the airport Munich-Riem. She died in Munich on January 22, 1985.

With the irresistible "grand seigneur" Adolf Wohlbrück (later Anton Walbrook).

Regine *(1934)*

Director: Erich Waschneck

Story: from a story of the same name
  by Gottfried Keller*
Screenplay: Erich Waschneck
Photography: Werner Brandes
Set design: Hans Sohnle and Otto
  Erdmann
Music: Clemens Schmalstich
Editing: Wolfgang Bagier
Production: Fanal-Film-Produktion
Length: 95 minutes
Country of origin: Germany, 1934
Censor's approval: November 20, 1934
  (banned to minors under 18)
Premiere: January 7, 1935
Award: Artistic Value

CAST

Luise Ullrich (Regine), Adolf Wohl-
brück (engineer Frank Reynold), Olga
Tschechowa (actress Floris Bell), Ekke-
hard Arendt (Merlin, a friend of Floris
Bell's), Hans Junkermann (Prof.
Gisevius, Frank's uncle), Eduard von
Winterstein (Keller, Regine's father),
Hans Adalbert Schlettow (Robert,
Regine's brother), Julia Serda-
Junkermann (Frau von Steckler), Olga
Engel (Frau Sendig).

SYNOPSIS

The young German-American Frank
Reynold returns to Germany after an
absence of ten years. On the ship bringing him back he meets Floris Bell, a
lovely and well-known actress, who
falls in love with him. She is not the
type that he is looking for, however,
after so many years of hard work; she is
too spoiled and capricious. In a village
in Bavaria, where Frank is spending a
few days' vacation, he falls in love with
Regine, a pretty country girl who works
as a domestic in the city; he has her
educated and he marries her, after having turned her into a woman of great
class. During a long absence of Frank's,
Regine becomes friendly with three
frivolous society women, who induce

*Director Waschneck had made a previous
  version of Keller's story, with the same
  title, *Regine,* starring Lee Perry, in 1928.

Adolf Wohlbrück kisses the barefoot beauty.

With her bridegroom, Adolf Wohlbrück.

When the husband's away . . . (two scenes from "Regine").

her to sit for a semi-nude painting by a fashionable lady painter, and to accept the attentions of a Brazilian diplomat. When her husband returns from his trip, Regine entreats him never to leave her alone again, telling him nothing, however, of having hidden a man in her bedroom for a night. It turns out that this person was her brother, wanted by the police for having killed their alcoholic father. Embittered, Regine commits suicide by turning on the gas, wearing the dress she wore on the day of her engagement.

CRITICS' COMMENTS _____

The principal reason for the success of this film is the performance of Luise Ullrich, one of the finest she has given so far. We would like to point out specific moments, but there is not one of her scenes that does not deserve to be mentioned. When she cannot comprehend the degree of her own happiness . . . when she takes her first timid steps into a society all too eager to laugh at her awkwardness . . . when, safely in the privacy of her own home, she kicks her too-tight shoes into the air . . . one would gladly see the entire film over again. But wait! There is one scene that must be considered the best of all: when, shaken by a series of strange events, she cries to her husband: "Don't ever leave me alone again!" . . . Waschneck has dedicated this film, from the first scene to the last, to his actress . . . and La Ullrich has deserved it.

G.H., *Film-Kurier*,
Berlin, January 8, 1935

The film has a rhythm of andante sostenuto, with a majestic and moving crescendo finale! . . . Luise Ullrich is touching as the inexperienced, awkward young girl confronted with a corrupt, big-city world; she is exceptional when she shares her brother's anguish, trying desperately to invent excuses. . . . Adolf Wohlbrück . . . is terse and incisive.

H. WEIGEL, *Licht-Bild-Bühne*,
Berlin, January 8, 1935

This is a forceful work, of noble intentions, particularly in those sections where it succeeds in avoiding the clichés commonly found in sentimental films. Even though the character of Regine is weak, Luise Ullrich is admirable as she passes from the old-fashioned German country girl . . . to the drawing-room beauty who seems to have forgotten the wholesome values of her former rustic life.

W. SELLMER, *Die Filmzeitung*,
Munich, January 10, 1935

With Adolf Wohlbrück.

Annelie: Die Geschichte eines Lebens   *(1941)*

(Annelie: The Story of a Life)

Director: Josef von Baky

For her performance in this film Luise Ullrich was awarded the Volpi Cup for best actress at the Venice Biennale film festival in 1941. By a decree of the Allied Military Government, following the war the film was banned in Germany.

Story: from the play of the same
    name by Walter Lieck
Screenplay: Thea von Harbou
Photography: Werner Krien
Costumes: Manon Hahn
Music: Georg Haentzschel
Editing: Walter Wischniewsky
Production: UFA
Length: 99 minutes
Country of origin: Germany, 1941
Censor's approval: August 2, 1941
Premiere: September 9, 1941, Venice
Awards: Particular Political and
    Artistic Value; Value to the People

CAST

Luise Ullrich (Annelie Dörensen), Werner Krauss (her father), Käthe Haack (her mother), Carl Ludwig Diehl (Martin Laborius), Albert Hehn (John Pants-Harding), Johannes Schütz (one of Annelie's children), Ilse Fürstenberg (the maid), Eduard von Winterstein (the doctor), Josefine Dora.

SYNOPSIS

Five minutes after the arrival of the New Year 1881, Annelie, daughter of Councilor Dörensen, came into the world. From her earliest days, she always arrives, everywhere, a quarter of an hour late. She meets and marries Dr. Martin Laborius, who leaves for the front in 1914, as World War I begins. Annelie volunteers as a Red Cross nurse. She finds her husband (as always, too late) in a military hospital near the battlefield, only to have him die in her arms, leaving her with three young sons. In 1941, Annelie celebrates her sixtieth birthday. Her grandchildren surround her, and her oldest son, a captain at the front, telephones his best

wishes. Annelie, content and serene, rests in her rocking chair. She closes her eyes, and her whole life passes before her. She has done as Martin told her to in his last words: she has always accepted her destiny with humility, charity and gratitude. Satisfied with her life, she passes from sleep to death.

CRITICS' COMMENTS

Reports from Venice inform us that the film has exceeded all expectations. No praise, oral or written, could convey the impression that the film has on the audience. . . . The director has had superior talents to work with, particularly his marvelous protagonist, Luise Ullrich, who portrays with exemplary simplicity the figure of Annelie, the girl who is always late. The scene of the fantastic conversation between little Annelie and the great doctor will

With Carl Ludwig Diehl, the man of Annelie's life.

remain a classic example of the art of film acting. Luise Ullrich towers over all the others from the first scene to the last. The film was meant for her, for her temperament and for her figure as well. At the end of the film, the audience remained in total silence for a few seconds; then there was a torrent of applause. Luise Ullrich, Carl Ludwig Diehl and the director were called back on stage repeatedly.

G. Herzberg, *Film-Kurier*, Berlin, September 10, 1941

An unusually warm applause greeted this film and its gifted cast. This film was made, not with the hands and the head, but with the heart. . . . Annelie is Luise Ullrich, as impetuous and likeable in her youth as she is wise and confident in old age. She seemed to change her voice, in its tone and in its very inflections, in each stage of the woman's life. The script itself almost seemed prepared as a vehicle to display the formidable talent of this artist. At the Berlin premiere, the enthusiasm of the audience was not inferior to that of the Venice Biennale.

H.J. Wille, *Filmwelt*, Berlin, September 14, 1941

Annelie covers a period of time that goes from 1880 to the Hitler era — literally from the cradle to the grave. Luise Ullrich gives a magnificent portrayal of feminine discipline and feminine submission. The Reich's Censor's Office awarded the film for "particular political and artistic value."

K. Kreimeier, "Das Kino als Ideologiefabrik," *Kinemathek*, Berlin, November 1971

From the left: Ilse Fürstenberg, Werner Krauss, Eduard von Winterstein and Josefine Dora.

HEIDEMARIE HATHEYER

HEIDEMARIE HATHEYER WAS BORN ON APRIL 8, 1919, in Villach, a small city in eastern Austria. Following World War II, her name came to special public attention, when the censorship committee of the Allied Military Government declared her guilty of indirect complicity in the mass exterminations in Germany and placed her on the "black list" of the film world. In 1941, in fact, the actress had been the star of *Ich klage an!* (I Accuse!), a film that subsequently acquired an unhappy notoriety because of its subject matter: it advocated the necessity of euthanasia for the incurably ill. It was certainly not an ordinary film; the trial scene alone, in which the argument for and against euthanasia is debated, lasts 126 minutes—more than two hours of continuous dialogue! During the so-called "trial of the doctors" by an Allied court in Nuremberg, Hatheyer declared that she had accepted the part of an incurably ill woman only at the insistence of the director, Wolfgang Liebeneiner, who had told her that the public should become aware of the problem of euthanasia. If she is remembered today, it is—unfortunately—because of that lugubrious *Ich klage an!*

Nevertheless, Hatheyer was an actress of talent, who proved herself highly effective in a wide variety of roles. If we glance at just two of her roles—Hanna Heyt, the hopelessly ill woman in *Ich klage an!*, and Wally, the fierce little mountain girl in *Die Geierwally* (Wally of the Vultures, 1940)—it is sufficient to show her versatility. What's more, Hatheyer remained primarily a stage actress, even after her film successes. She had begun in Vienna, in a small cabaret, the "Literatur am Naschmarkt," and then gone on to appear with Zarah Leander, in the part of an old Negro woman in the operetta *Axel vor der Himmelstür* (Axel at Heaven's Gate), for over two hundred performances. She played small parts at the Theater an der Wien from 1936 to 1937, when Otto Falckenberg offered her a three-year contract at the Kammerspiele theater in Munich, where she followed in the footsteps of such great names as Elisabeth Bergner, Käthe Gold, Heinz Rühmann and Ferdinand Marian. The role that brought her to the attention of the Munich public was that of Anuschka in Richard Billinger's *Der Gigant* (The Giant). She was given starring roles in Friedrich von Schiller's *Kabale und Liebe* (Intrigue and Love) and George Bernard Shaw's *Saint Joan,* and in 1942 signed a contract to appear with Gustav Gründgens at the Berliner Staatstheater.

Hatheyer's film debut had taken place in 1937, when Luis Trenker chose her to play opposite him in *Der Berg ruft* (The Mountain Calls), an Alpine film about the Italian guide Antonio Correi and the first ascent of the Matterhorn. Normally in Trenker's films—written, produced, directed and starred in by him—any actor, no matter how talented, disappeared into the background. Not so for Hatheyer, however, who was immediately noticed by the Tobis company, which offered her a contract for 10,000 marks a film. Before and during the war the actress made *Die Geierwally, Frau Sixta* (1938), *Der grosse Schatten* (The Big Shadow, 1942), and *Die Nacht in Venedig* (The Night in Venice, 1942).

In the postwar period, Heidemarie Hatheyer returned to the theater, again with Gründgens, in Düsseldorf and Berlin. She appeared, later, principally at the Schauspielhaus in Zurich and the Burgtheater in Vienna, where, in 1960, she scored a notable success in a revival of Austrian playwright Franz Grillparzer's *Medea.* In 1968 she was the protagonist in a memorable production of Bertolt Brecht's *Mother Courage* in Düsseldorf. On the screen, she was seen in: *Wohin die Züge fahren* (Where the Trains Go), *Begegnungen mit Werther* (Encounters with Werther), *Dieser Mann gehört mir* (This Man Is Mine), *Vom Teufel gejagt* (Hunted by the Devil), *Das letzte Rezept* (The Last Receipt), *Mein Herz darfst du nicht fragen* (You Cannot Ask for My Heart), and *Glücksritter* (The Fortunate Horseman)—a film that marked the first screen appearance of her fourteen-year-old daughter, Regine Feldhüter. Hatheyer was also in *Ruf der Wildgänse* (Call of the Wild Geese), again with her daughter Regine, who played her mother as a girl. Hatheyer also worked occasionally in television. In 1977 she appeared in the series "Auf dem Chimborazo" (On the Chimborazo), by Tankred Dorst.

In 1952, Heidemarie Hatheyer in a second marriage wed journalist Curt Reiss, author of an entertaining book on the golden age of the German film that has sold 330,000 copies, and in which his ample chapter on Heidemarie begins, "Her like had not been seen on the German screen since the great days of naturalism."[1]

In October 1961, Hatheyer was awarded the Josef-Kainz-Medaille, a medal named after the great classical actor Josef Kainz,* and in 1967 the Grillparzer-Ring—two prestigious awards given by the state for distinguished contributions to German theater. She died on May 11, 1990.

*Born in Wieselburg, Hungary, Kainz lived from 1858 to 1910.

Die Geierwally   *(1940)*

(Wally of the Vultures)

Director: Hans Steinhoff

In 1921 the German director E. A. Dupont (1891–1956) had already directed a legendary *Die Geierwally,* starring Henny Porten, with Wilhelm Dieterle and Eugen Klöpfer, and with photography by Karl Freund, Fritz Lang's favorite cameraman. Hans Steinhoff, one of the major directors of the Third Reich—who made *Hitlerjunge Quex* (Hitler Youth Quex, 1933), *Der alte und der junge König* (The Old and the Young Kings, 1935), and *Robert Koch, der Bekämpfer des Todes* (Robert Koch, Crusader Against Death, 1939) —in order to measure up to Dupont, secured the services of Richard Angst, favorite cameraman of Arnold Fanck, one of the creators of the German "outdoor film." Angst's photographic skill was particularly evident in another

Steinhoff film, *Rembrandt* (1942), based on the life of the Dutch painter, in which the cameraman enhanced the evocative aura of the film's stunning sets. Germany's leading art forger was released from prison to re-create the masterpieces used in the film.

Steinhoff's insistence on authenticity bordered on the maniacal. For the costumes of *Die Geierwally,* he sought the assistance of the curator of the People's Museum of Innsbruck, and recruited most of his cast from among the inhabitants of the Ötz Valley. When Hatheyer, at seven o'clock one morning, requested glycerine eyedrops for a scene in which she had to quarrel with her father, he hurled so many insults at her that she had no problem in crying real tears. When the film was finished, the

actress checked into a clinic to recuperate from eight months spent filming this monumental mountain drama among the Alpine peaks, threatened by the vultures' pointed teeth.

Story: from the novel of the same
    name by Wilhelmine von Hillern
Screenplay: Jacob Geis and
    Alexander Lix
Photography: Richard Angst
Music: Nico Dostal
Production: UFA
Length: 104 minutes
Country of origin: Germany, 1940
Censor's approval: August 2, 1940
    (banned to minors under 18)
Premiere: August 12, 1940
Awards: Artistic Value;
    Value to the People

Wally follows her father's coffin.

Die Geierwally

With Winnie Markus.

CAST

Heidemarie Hatheyer (Wally), Winnie Markus (Afra), Sepp Rist (Joseph), Eduard Köck (Fender), Leopold Esterle (Vinzenz).

SYNOPSIS

Life is hard for those who live in the Tyrol. Wally, a farmer's daughter, rebels against her father, who wants her to marry Vinzenz, rich and heir to a farm. She runs away, taking refuge in a cabin at the edge of the glacier, while in the valley there are those who try to steal her property. Her heart beats for Joseph, who saved her life during a fight with a vulture, when she incautiously tried to take its chick from the nest. Joseph is as proud as Wally. One day she confesses her love to him, adding that she suspects he already has a mistress (in reality, it is his illegitimate daughter). To make her stop talking, he kisses her. They are interrupted by Vinzenz, who attempts to kill his rival. But danger is averted, and the two lovers fall into each other's arms.

CRITICS' COMMENTS

Hans Steinhoff, director of the new film, combed the fields and meadows of the valley of Ötz, near Sölden, together with his production manager, Gerhard Staab, to find not only themes but also characteristic faces among the inhabitants of the region. While pursuing his head-hunting activity, he came across a mountain boy, Franzel Grüner, who hadn't the slightest regard for the camera, acting or film art in general. He recognized only Steinhoff's authority. In addition to this little rogue, another young villager, Alois Kneisel, was invited by Steinhoff to participate in a scene in the inn. Authenticity at any cost! The boy turned out to be a formidable yodeler; whenever he got bored during rehearsals, he would break out into song: "Yo-del-o-di-o! What's the use of rehearsing? / Herr Steinhoff is going to begin / As soon as he finds a mountain / Covered with gentian!" Knowing Steinhoff as we do, however, it is certain that he is seeking something more than mere authenticity. As film lovers, we wish him every success.

J. R. GEORGE, *Film-Kurier*, Berlin, pre-premiere, November 22, 1939

Terrified, Wally hears strange voices.

There is no star in this film — not even the mountains. Whereas up till now, in mountain films they have assumed an epic dimension, here their role is merely that of a majestic backdrop. "I deliberately tried to keep them from dominating," Steinhoff declared. "The destinies of the characters must be read in their own faces. The story itself must be the main thing." And yet there is a star — the vulture. . . . It appears only briefly, yet it has a great tragic role. In a certain sense it is a symbol of the fierceness of the mountains, and of the boundless freedom that Wally seeks. . . . Before shooting a scene with the strange bird-star, his "manager," a certain Herr Boek, must first be consulted. He takes care of it, grooms it and prepares it for each shot. They were lucky indeed to find Herr Boek; he is the only person who understands the psyche of the vulture.

T. RIEGLER, *Filmwelt*, Berlin, pre-premiere, March 1, 1940

To the great and unforgettable artistic achievements of German film we must now add Die Geierwally. *We fervently hope that the young actress Heide Hatheyer will maintain in the future the promise that she has shown in this film; that the exceptional talent shown by this member of the new film generation will continue to develop and flourish. On the face of the actress, passion blazes like a flame. Her eyes can reflect a hard, almost sinister arrogance, and in the next moment a wonderful sweetness and timidity. Her mouth can tighten into a bitter grimace, when she must defend herself against the world's harshness, and then soften into the warmest of smiles. . . . For her own good and for that of the German screen we fervently hope that she will be able to cultivate, unhurriedly and judiciously, this talent. At the Berlin premiere there was an ovation for the director and the players.*

H. E. FISCHER, *Die Filmwelt*, Berlin, September 27, 1940

Ich klage an! *(1941)*

(I Accuse!)

Director: Wolfgang Liebeneiner

The trial scene. At the center, Christian Kayssler.

This film won the Prize of the Nation at the Venice Film Festival in 1941. By a decree of the Allied Military Government following the war, the showing of *Ich klage an!* in Germany was banned.

Story: from the novel *Sendung und Gewissen* (Mission and Conscience) by Helmuth Hanger and an idea of Harald Bratt
Screenplay: Eberhard Frowein and Harald Bratt
Photography: Friedl Behn-Grund
Music: Norbert Schultze and Franz von Klepacki
Production: Tobis
Length: 125 minutes
Country of origin: Germany, 1941
Censor's approval: August 15, 1941
Premiere: August 29, 1941
Awards: Great Artistic Value; Educational Value

CAST

Heidemarie Hatheyer (Hanna Heyt), Paul Hartmann (Dr. Paul Heyt, her husband), Mathias Wieman (Dr. Lang), Harald Paulsen (a friend), Charlotte Thiele (Bertha, the maid), Christian Kayssler, Bernhard Goetzke, Werner Pledath, Ott Graf, Franz Schafheitlin, Franz Weber, Karin Evans, Erich Ponto, Just Scheu and others.

SYNOPSIS

While playing the piano, Hanna Heyt notices that her hands are not responding properly. Dr. Lang, a friend of the family, examines her and realizes that the young woman is gravely ill; she has multiple sclerosis, an incurable illness that kills slowly. Paul Heyt cannot bear to see his wife suffering; one day he gives her a poison to drink, and she dies a painless death. Lang and Bertha, the maid, are horrified when they learn that Hanna was killed by her husband, who is to be tried for murder. The rest of the film is the lengthy trial scene, in which the various arguments for and against euthanasia are discussed.

CRITICS' COMMENTS

Men suffer when they have to watch without being able to help; this is perhaps the most painful aspect of the doctor's profession. . . .In this film we witness one man's struggle against circumstances beyond his control. There have been few films up to now that have obliged the spectator to deal with a problem of such magnitude. . . . Heidemarie Hatheyer lives up to the promise shown in her earlier films. Her Hanna Heyt conveys movingly everything that a young woman feels when she hears the terrible word "incurable." Without histrionics or obvious gestures, but simply the look in her eyes, she conveys the progress of the disease, the gradual weakening of the body, the final acceptance of the inevitable.

H. W. Betz, Der Film,
Berlin, August 30, 1941

It is the doctor's sacred duty to prolong life and to combat death. But here it is precisely a doctor who is faced with the question of breaking the moral laws of his profession, when his heart and his common sense tell him that it would be inhuman to prolong his wife's suffering rather than shorten it. This is the theme of the new film from Tobis, and a masterpiece of German artistry. . . .We recall the scene in which Paul Hartmann peers into his microscope in the vain hope of finding a last-minute sign of recovery. We think of Heidemarie Hatheyer's death scene, so poignantly enacted as to make it all the more painful.

G. Sawatski, Die Filmwelt,
Berlin, October 1, 1941

All available reports show that the film has aroused great interest throughout the Reich. The film has for the most part been received and discussed favorably. In many cities where the film has not yet arrived, even the simplest people speak of it as a work to be seen. It raises two problems. Its principal theme is death on request in cases of the incurably ill. The second question is whether it is necessary to put an end to a life that is no longer worth living. The majority of the German people accept the film's argument. . .but with certain reservations. . . .The attitude of the church. . .is one of total refusal. . . . Catholic priests have visited the homes of their parishioners, urging them not to see the film. . . .In general, the practice of euthanasia is approved, if it is decided upon by a committee of several physicians, and with the consent of the incurable patient and his family.
Report of the S.D. (Sicherheitsdienst, the S.S.'s security division), January 15, 1942, Federal Archive of Koblenz

. . .one of the best of the Third Reich propaganda films, because in the first two-thirds it tries to show at least a semblance of objectivity.
P. Kochenrath, *Der Film im Dritten Reich* (Cologne, 1963)

With Paul Hartmann.

Der grosse Schatten (1942)

(The Big Shadow)

Director: Paul Verhoeven

Story and screenplay: Harald Bratt
Photography: Richard Angst
Set design: Otto Erdmann and
    Franz Fürst
Music: Hans-Otto Borgmann
Editing: Johanna Rosinsky
Production: Tobis
Length: 97 minutes
Country of origin: Germany, 1942
Censor's approval: date uncertain
    (banned to minors under 18)
Premiere: August 25, 1942, Munich;
    September 23, 1942, Berlin

CAST

Heinrich George (Conrad Schroeter),
Heidemarie Hatheyer (Gisela Ahrens),
Will Quadflieg (Robert Jürgensen),
Marina von Ditmar (Inge, Schroeter's
daughter), Ernest Schröder (Dr. Martin
Scholz), Ernst Stahl-Nachbaur (man-
ager of the provincial theater), Hans
Hermann Schaufuss (the Inspector),
Friedrich Maurer (Nolte, the theater
clerk), Hans Mierendorff, Ilka Thimm,
Hans Meyer-Hanno, Winnie Markus,
Walter Werner, Hubert von Meyerinck,
Elsa Wagner, Paul Verhoeven, Erich
Fiedler, Berta Drews and others.

SYNOPSIS

A young Robert Jürgensen, while having a relationship with the actress
Gisela Ahrens, also dallies with the
young, star-struck daughter of Conrad
Schroeter, an actor colleague who is also
the manager of both Robert and Gisela.
Robert seduces the infatuated girl, but
leaves and forgets her when Gisela tells
him that she is carrying his child. While
Gisela and Robert follow wherever
their careers take them, Inge, the young
daughter of Schroeter, continues to
hope that Robert will return to her one
day. When Gisela and Robert find that
they are cast in the same drama with
Schroeter, whom they recognize as their
ex-manager, Robert also remembers
that Schroeter is the father of the girl he
seduced. When Inge learns that Gisela
and Robert are now married, and that
Robert is lost to her forever, she commits suicide. Fate has it that Schroeter,
who plays the title role in the drama
they are enacting, *The Judge of Zalamea* (*El Alcalde de Zalamea* by Spanish
playwright Calderón de la Barca), is
confronting Jürgensen in a similar situation in the play, when he is told of his
daughter's death, and the reason for her
suicide. Overcome by grief, and obsess-
ed with the role he has to play, he assaults Robert as the destroyer of his
happiness. Schroeter is taken to a men-
tal institution, but on his release it is
Gisela who helps him to forget and
who persuades him to return to his
work. There is a suggestion that his
future will be with Gisela, who in the
German synopsis is identified as "the
September Love of a great actor."

CRITICS' COMMENTS

*Der grosse Schatten is a film of the
world of actors, a film that takes art
and artists seriously and without the
cheap romanticism with which novels
and films about actors are so often
burdened. . . . The script contains a
great number of strong scenes in which
the actors, under the direction of Paul
Verhoeven, can fully demonstrate their
talent. Heinrich George finds compelling expression for the human and
artistic greatness of the actor. . . .
Heidemarie Hatheyer succeeds in ex-
pressing also what is hard to under-
stand in her part. . . . For the viewers
this film is a moving experience.*
    G. HERZBERG, *Film-Kurier*,
    Berlin, September 14, 1942

*Heidemarie Hatheyer plays the young
actress with an intensity, a moving, artistically convincing interpretation that
in each nuance of tone and in each gesture leads from artifice to truth. Will
Quadflieg as a young actor gives this
ambiguous part interesting human
contours.*
    H. HENSELEIT, *Film-Kurier*,
    Berlin, October 24, 1942

Marina von Ditmar with Heinrich George.

LILIAN HARVEY

LILIAN HARVEY WAS ONE OF THE BRIGHTEST STARS IN the UFA firmament. Small and slender, with big blue eyes and blond curls, she was worlds apart from the full-figured Henny Porten or the voluptuous Zarah Leander; compared to them, she was an elf. She was born on January 19, 1906, in the London suburb of Muswell Hill, as Lilian Muriel Helen Pape. When she was eight, her parents moved to Berlin. When World War I broke out, fearing for her safety, they sent her to Switzerland, where she went to school in Solothurn. At war's end she returned to Berlin, where she studied dance at the school of the celebrated Mary Zimmermann. Thus, although in looks she was British, in upbringing and education she was German, and Germans always considered her one of their own.

At sixteen Lilian joined the Emil-Schwarz-Revue, a Viennese dance company, with which she toured the major German cities, as well as Budapest, Prague and Vienna. It was in the latter city, at the Ronacher Theater, that she was noticed by the film director Richard Eichberg. She made her motion-picture debut in his *Der Fluch* (The Curse) in 1925, and made eleven more films in Vienna in quick succession. The perfect soubrette, she was given the title role in *Die keusche Susanne* (Chaste Susanne, 1926), a film version of the operetta of the same name, adapted for the screen by a German composer who wrote under the name Jean Gilbert. The film made her famous, and marked her first appearance with Willy Fritsch, who would be her partner in thirteen more films. She soon became the most popular interpreter of that curious genre, the silent-film operetta. With the coming of sound and the screen musical, it was not surprising that she became a bigger star than ever.

Harvey was trilingual, and in the early days of sound made French- and English-language versions of her films, with separate casts and such prestigious leading men as Laurence Olivier and Charles Boyer. Intelligent, a good actress and singer, and an excellent dancer, she was a versatile performer. However, given her special combination of doll-like features, dainty figure and youthful ebullience, she was inevitably cast as "the girl next door," flirtatious but virtuous, and just what millions of German mothers considered the ideal daughter-in-law.

It was not long before Harvey attracted the attention of Erich Pommer, impresario, producer and shrewd judge of talent, who gave her the lead in his *Liebeswalzer* (Waltz of Love, 1930), directed by Wilhelm Thiele (filmed the same year in England as *The Love Waltz*,

with Harvey and John Batten). In this musical classic—ranked by many critics as one of the two finest sound films of the 1929–30 season—Harvey played the Princess Eva von Lauenberg, courted, as usual, by Willy Fritsch, who serenaded her with "Du bist die süsseste Mädel der Welt" (You Are the Sweetest Girl in the World). *Liebeswalzer* was a worldwide success, even in Japan, where audiences packed the Nagasaki Theater in Tokyo to hear "You are the sweetest geisha in the world."

Harvey had an even greater success the same year in another charming musical, also directed by Thiele, *Die drei von der Tankstelle* (The Three from the Filling Station), filmed in French as *Le Chemin du Paradis* (The Road to Paradise). Now signed to a UFA contract by Pommer, who for box-office reasons insisted that she always play opposite Willy Fritsch (the public believed that they were romantically involved in real life as well, whereas Fritsch was married to the actress Dinah Grace), Harvey, in the role of Lilian Crossman, gave the quintessential Harvey performance—singing prettily, smiling

Lilian Harvey, the sweetest star of UFA.

In "Glückskinder," 1936.

with her eyes closed, wrinkling her nose and displaying all the mannerisms that had made her the sweetheart of the German screen, as well as everyone's ideal fiancée.

It is difficult to say why on October 1, 1937, the Reich's Board of Censors decided to ban the film. It may have been because the director, Thiele, had inserted into this operetta world the too-realistic story of three penniless friends whose lives were sustained mainly on hope. (At the time the film was made, there were three million unemployed in Germany.) Also, the regime disliked films that made fun of German daily life or depicted certain aspects of it in too graphic a manner. Perhaps the real reason for the banning was that it had become common to ban films, older ones, in whose production Jews had figured prominently; Pommer and Thiele were Jewish.

In 1931 *Der Kongress tanzt* (The Congress Dances) assembled some of the biggest names of the German film-operetta genre: director Erik Charell (who left shortly afterward for Hollywood), the couple Harvey-Fritsch and the best available scriptwriters. Set in Vienna at the time of the celebrated Congress of 1814–15, which was meant to end Napoleon's career, the film offered Harvey one of her most memorable parts, that of the little glove-maker dazzled by Czar Alexander I of Russia. This was the part of her lifetime, and she made the most of it. She will always be remembered for the enchanting scene in which she sings the waltz "Das gibt's nur einmal, das kommt nie wieder" (This Happens Once in a Lifetime, and Never Again), as her carriage makes its way through the narrow streets of old Vienna.

This was the first film directed by Charell, whose career up until that time had been in the theater. Under his expert guidance, Harvey gave a scintillating performance, and, inevitably, Hollywood beckoned. UFA resigned themselves to losing her to Darryl F. Zanuck and his Fox (not yet Twentieth-Century) studios.

Her American debut film was *My Weakness* (1933), about a servant girl's romance with a handsome young man (Lew Ayres). The film was no great shakes, but U.S. critics called her "ebullient" and "entrancing." This was followed by *My Lips Betray* (1933), a highly unfunny (despite a screenplay by S. N. Behrman) operetta-like tale of a poor working girl and a king in disguise (John Boles); *I Am Suzanne* (1934), undeservedly forgotten, a charming tale of a young dancer in love with a puppeteer (Gene Raymond); and *Let's Live Tonight* (1935), with Tullio Carminati—her last Hollywood film. Fox had another musical planned for her, *George White's Scandals,* but she quit the production at the last minute, and the studio gave her part to another lovely blonde, a young band singer who had never made a film before: Alice Faye. Harvey also made two films in England: *The Only Girl* (1933) and *Invitation to the Waltz* (1935).

The American public liked Harvey, despite the mostly mediocre material given her. But she realized that in Hollywood there were a number of beautiful and talented blondes—Ginger Rogers, Jean Harlow, Carole Lombard—to compete with, so in 1935 she returned to UFA, where she knew her reign would be unchallenged.

Harvey returned to a Germany that had changed radically during her two-year absence. Fewer musicals were being made, and more emphasis was being given to propaganda films. She was cast in *Schwarze Rosen* (Red Roses, 1935), which told of Finland's struggle for freedom against Czarist Russia, and, in spite of the inclusion of several pleasing musical numbers, the film stressed propaganda more than entertainment, with Willy Birgel as the treacherous Bolshevik governor. In 1937, however, she was given a plum—a real musical, one created expressly for her, and which would display her talents as a singer and dancer to the fullest—*Fanny Elssler.* She

had six beautifully choreographed and opulently staged production numbers, with a corps de ballet of ninety ballerinas and fifty-six male dancers. This was the most lavish of all Harvey vehicles, and she rose to the occasion, equaling, if not surpassing, her sparkling performance in *Der Kongress tanzt.*

In *Sieben Ohrfeigen* (Seven Slaps, 1937), and in *Frau am Steuer* (Woman at the Wheel, 1939), Lilian again appeared opposite Willy Fritsch. In the former, she delivered hearty slaps to the poor man, who played a gentleman fleeced by the world of high finance; in the latter, she abandoned the role of the super-efficient secretary of the Donau-Bank for the more comfortable one of a housewife. But the years were passing, and Harvey's porcelain features seemed less fresh and luminous than before; she was no longer the same singing and dancing doll of the days of the first "100-percent all-talking pictures."

In 1938 she made *Castelli in aria* (Castles in the Air) in Italy, directed by Augusto Genina and co-starring Vittorio De Sica, a real fiasco, which made it clear that her days as a little blond ray of sunshine were numbered. In *Capriccio,* also made in 1938, she had a few amusing moments disguised as a man, but the fact is that during the Hitler period she never made a film comparable in quality to *Die drei von der Tankstelle.* Her films were popular because they were lighthearted and undemanding, and because they had songs, dances and Willy Fritsch. Now they were becoming flimsier and more predictable, and her star was beginning to dim. One looks in vain in these later films for the verve and gaiety of Christel, Susanne or the Princess Trullalà.

During the war, Harvey went to France, and in order to finance two 1940 films made there, *Sérénade,* with Louis Jouvet, and *Miquette,* she sold her jewels and her castle in Tetélen, Hungary. From France she went to Spain, then to South America, then to the United States. There were no film offers in Los Angeles, and she worked for a time as a nurse there. Finally, her old friend Noël Coward came to her rescue and offered her a leading role in his stage comedy *Blithe Spirit,* in which she toured for several months.

Harvey returned to Germany in 1951, but her attempts at a comeback were failures. She married the Danish impresario Valeur Larsen on February 7, 1953, and left him in May 1954. She published a book of memoirs, *Es war nur ein Traum* (It Was Only a Dream) in 1956. Retiring to the French Riviera, she returned to Germany for a stage appearance in the 1960s. She died at her villa, "Asmodée," in Antibes, France, on July 27, 1968, her old friend the celebrated dancer Serge Lifar having taken care of her affectionately during her last days.

Glückskinder   *(1936)*

(Fortune's Children)

Director: Paul Martin

Harvey's director in this film, Paul Martin (1899–1967), Hungarian-born and said to be her lover, is considered to have been one of the few specialists in German light comedy during the Nazi regime. He had the knack of turning out films about ordinary people and the sentiments that were dear to their hearts, without ever lapsing into "kitsch." Originally a medical student, he worked as an actor in silent films, then turned to editing, and in 1931 worked as technical assistant to Charell on *Der Kongress tanzt.* A year later he was an assistant director, and in 1933 UFA sent him to the United States to study its fast-moving, wisecracking comedies about reporters and madcap heiresses. Apparently he did not learn enough. *Glückskinder* is a shameless copy of Frank Capra's *It Happened One Night* (1934), but Martin isn't Capra, and Harvey and Fritsch do not possess the verve of Claudette Colbert and Clark Gable.

Story and screenplay: R. A. Stemmle,
    Paul Martin and Curt Goetz
Photography: Konstantin Irmen-Tschet
Set design: Erich Kettelhut
Music: Peter Kreuder
Editing: Karl-Otto Bartning
Production: UFA
Length: 94 minutes
Country of origin: Germany, 1936
Censor's approval: September 17, 1936
    (banned to minors under 18)
Premiere: August 19, 1936
Award: Artistic Value

CAST ─────────────────────

Lilian Harvey (Ann Garden), Willy Fritsch (Gil Taylor), Oskar Sima (Mr. Jackson), Paul Kemp (Frank Black), Albert Florath, Paul Bildt, Otto Stoeckel, Fred Goebel, Paul Rehkopf, Kurt Seifert, Carl Merznicht, Walter Steinweg, Max Hiller, Hermann Meyer-Falkow, Arno Ebert.

With Willy Fritsch.

SYNOPSIS ─────────────

Blond-haired Ann wanders aimlessly through the streets of Manhattan, risking being jailed for vagrancy. She hasn't reckoned with the reporter Gil Taylor, however, who tells the judge that Ann is his future wife. Gil then begins to wonder if, by chance, Ann might not be the missing niece of Mr. Jackson, the oil magnate. Before she can protest, she is kidnapped. She suggests to Mr. Jackson that he play along, and that perhaps in this way he will find the real niece. Ann and Mr. Jackson go to the opera, followed by Gil; suddenly a fire alarm goes off. An enormous man grabs Ann; Gil runs after him. After a wild chase, everything works out: Gil can keep his Ann, and Jackson recovers his niece.

CRITICS' COMMENTS ──────

. . . another victory for the talking film. The bursts of laughter heard at the Gloria-Palast bear this out. The film is a mad dash from one improbable and hilarious situation to another, to the rhythm of sparkling, fast-paced dialogue. In the part of the high-spirited heroine,

Lilian Harvey gives a sprightly and amusing performance. Where she really lights up the screen, however, is when she is given an opportunity to dance. La Harvey also reveals an unexpected gift for broad, slapstick comedy; we would like to see her do more of it. As for Willy Fritsch—well, just the sight of him puts us in a good mood. The editing of Karl-Otto Bartning deserves special mention, in particular the scene in which Lilian imitates Mickey Mouse. The audience laughed heartily throughout, and at the end awarded an ovation to the stars, who were present.
    A. SCHNEIDER, *Licht-Bild-Bühne,*
        Berlin, September 19, 1936

A film bursting with charm, humor and music. What a lovely, delightful and bewitching creature this Harvey is!
    R. THIERY, *Berliner Lokal-Anzeiger,*
        Berlin, September 19, 1936

Polished performances, an amusing script, tricky dialogue that requires skilled performers. The film is over before we know it. Glückskinder will give an hour of pleasure to millions of filmgoers.
    Berliner Tageblatt, Berlin,
        September 20, 1936

With Jean Galland in the French version of "Schwarze Rosen," 1935.

With Jean Galland and Jean Worms in the same film.

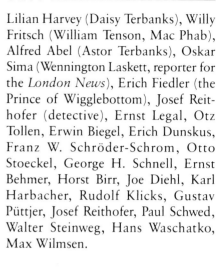

CAST

Lilian Harvey (Daisy Terbanks), Willy Fritsch (William Tenson, Mac Phab), Alfred Abel (Astor Terbanks), Oskar Sima (Wennington Laskett, reporter for the *London News*), Erich Fiedler (the Prince of Wigglebottom), Josef Reithofer (detective), Ernst Legal, Otz Tollen, Erwin Biegel, Erich Dunskus, Franz W. Schröder-Schrom, Otto Stoeckel, George H. Schnell, Ernst Behmer, Horst Birr, Joe Diehl, Karl Harbacher, Rudolf Klicks, Gustav Püttjer, Josef Reithofer, Paul Schwed, Walter Steinweg, Hans Waschatko, Max Wilmsen.

SYNOPSIS

In the most recent stock market crash, young William Tenson has lost all of his savings: seven pounds! Foaming with rage, he protests to the banker Terbanks, insisting that it is nothing less than robbery. He promises to get even; for every pound lost, he will deliver a good slap to the president of the bank, and furthermore, in public! Terbanks' lovely daughter Daisy tries to reason with him, but meanwhile William has already slapped her father six times. Daisy then decides to marry William in Scotland's Gretna Green. After the ceremony, she lands a resounding slap on her bridegroom's cheek. The family honor is saved. William has gotten the lesson he deserved, but he has also gotten the love of Daisy.

With her leading men in "Schwarze Rosen": from the left, Willy Birgel (German), Esmond Knight (English), Jean Galland (French).

Sieben Ohrfeigen (1937)

(Seven Slaps)

Director: Paul Martin

Story and screenplay: B. E. Lüthge, Paul Martin and Curt Goetz
Photography: Konstantin Irmen-Tschet
Set design: Erich Kettelhut
Costumes: Manon Hahn

Music: Friedrich Schröder
Editing: Karl-Otto Bartning
Production: UFA
Length: 98 minutes
Country of origin: Germany, 1937
Censor's approval: July 16, 1937
Premiere: August 3, 1937
Award: Artistic Value

CRITICS' COMMENTS

Lilian Harvey. . . plays a girl who is as strong-willed as she is delightful. Hers is a thoroughly winning performance. Willy Fritsch passes effortlessly from the comic to the romantic. . . . Paul Martin shows that he has acquired the proper light-comedy touch, and that he has rid himself of the slight trace of heavy-handedness that characterized his earlier films. The audience showed its appreciation of this highly entertaining film by its hearty applause.
F. HENSELEIT, *Licht-Bild-Bühne*, Berlin, August 4, 1937

Here we go abroad again, but this time it's Merry England. There's another reporter, too, and an important one, but not important enough to challenge the power of the press. But Lilian and Willy always seem to be so favored by fortune! Fritsch...is his usual highly amusing self. Lilian Harvey is not seen at her best, however. She should be given parts in which she can display her musical talents, as in Schwarze Rosen, *for example....Martin's expert touch is noted particularly in the grand-scale scenes—at the stadium, in the cabaret, on the street. The background music is at times too intrusive.*

H. SPIELHOFER, *Deutsche Filmzeitung,* Munich, August 8, 1937

It's incredible how much you can squeeze out of the slightest of plot premises, if you know the right way to squeeze it! This film has obviously been closely patterned after the American comedies, and is full of sight gags and wisecracks. Willy Fritsch is delightful as the impetuous hero, and Lilian Harvey is, as always, warm, feminine and lovable. She should always be like this, and forget about more grand-scale histrionics. She is especially effective in her little soliloquy in which she decides to put William in his place.

F. RÖHL, *Der Film,* Berlin, August 12, 1937

Fanny Elssler   (1937)

Director: Paul Martin

At the time of this film there were two famous Willys in Germany: Willy Fritsch (1901–73) and Willy Birgel (1892–1973).* Both attractive, their screen personalities could not have been more different. Fritsch always played the part of the lighthearted, amusing, pleasure-loving young man; Birgel, on the other hand, was more the *grand seigneur*: reflective, laconic, and just a touch sinister. The public liked to imagine the two Willys fighting over the hand of the "blond dream," as Lilian was called. Birgel's thwarted passion for Harvey was displayed at its height in *Schwarze Rosen*. Here as in no other film Birgel, as the Bolshevik governor, was given the opportunity to show his specialty—contained passion, coupled with fiery glances. While the happy-go-lucky Fritsch drove around (in real life) in a convertible with the license plate 1A–1111 (see photo in the Introduction; Harvey had an identical model, even to the license plate, except that hers was cream color), one could only imagine Birgel on horseback, particularly after his masterful performance in . . . *reitet für Deutschland* (Riding for Germany, 1941), a film directed by Arthur Maria Rabenalt about the famous horseman Freiherr von Lingen, who though severely injured in World War I became a great rider again and won a major victory for Germany.

*Translator's note: There was also Willi Forst (1903–80), both actor and director.

Story and screenplay: Eva Leidmann and Paul Martin
Photography: Konstantin Irmen-Tschet
Music: Kurt Schröder
Production: UFA
Length: 83 minutes
Country of origin: Germany, 1937
Censor's approval: October 26, 1937
Premiere: November 4, 1937, Berlin
Award: Artistic Value

CAST

Lilian Harvey (Fanny Elssler), Willy Birgel (Councilor Friedrich Gentz), Rolf Moebius (the Duke of Reichstadt), Paul Hoffmann (Metternich), Liselotte Schaak (Therese Elssler), Walter Werner (the Maestro), Ernst Sattler, Ernst Karchow, Hubert von Meyerinck, Werner Kepich, Erwin Biegel, Hubert I. Stowitts, Johannes Bergfeld, Angelo Ferrari, André Saint-Germain, Kurt Lenz, Ruth Nimbach, Anna von Palen, Paul Rehkopf, Bruno Ziener.

SYNOPSIS

The lovely ballerina Fanny Elssler has all of Vienna at her feet. Prince Metternich asks her to keep an eye on the young Duke of Reichstadt, the son of Napoleon; for the Prince, nothing is more to be feared than a rebirth of the French empire. Fanny rejects the idea of involving herself in this kind of espionage. But, as fate will have it, she and the Duke meet; she hasn't the faintest idea of the true identity of Lieutenant Franz von Mödling, but she is dazzled by his gallant ways. The two fall in love. Metternich discovers their bond and suspects a plot. Fanny must leave Vienna for Paris, where the lovers meet again. Napoleon's son dreams of leading the Bonapartists to victory, but his plan fails. He is obliged to return to Vienna, where he dies. Fanny, in Paris, goes on to greater artistic heights.

The scriptwriters obviously intended the film primarily as a vehicle for Lilian Harvey, and so Fanny Elssler and her private life are given considerably more attention than the figure of Metternich. In other words, romance wins out over history. . .This film has shown us a new and more exciting Lilian Harvey, who at the premiere was called back to the stage more than twenty times—a tribute that was only fitting in view of her extraordinary talent both as dancer and actress. The film is a great personal success for her.

P. ICKES, *Die Filmwoche*,
Berlin, November 17, 1937

It is a blessing for Lilian Harvey that she is given so many opportunities to dance, because here she is unequaled. For the film, however, it is somewhat less of a blessing. It is hardly proper to utilize the political events of Europe during the era of the Duke of Reichstadt solely as a means to tell the story of a ballerina. The Americans can rearrange the facts of history because they have little sense of it. In any event, the dance numbers could not be bettered, nor could the splendid performance of Lilian Harvey.

H. SPIELHOFER, *Der Deutsche Film*,
Berlin, December 1937

With Jean Galland in "Schwarze Rosen."

With Erich Fiedler in "Seven Slaps."

RENATE MÜLLER

MANY OF THE MOST FAMOUS GERMAN STARS OF THE silent period disappeared with the advent of sound, clearing the way for a raft of younger players, none of whom was more notable than Renate Müller. She was born in Munich on April 26, 1907, into an uncommonly cultivated family. Her mother, a German born in South America, was a painter, and her father, a historian and philosopher, was editor-in-chief of the *Münchner Zeitung* (Munich News). Renate's early years were spent between the Bavarian capital and the Müllers' summer home in Emmering, some fifty miles from Munich, where she read everything from Schopenhauer to Nietzsche — as well as the French classics.

In 1924 Müller's father was transferred to Berlin, at that time the center of cultural life of Germany and, in fact, of all Europe. The war years were past, and inflation was easing; and Berliners were eager to enjoy themselves. Renate, who thought of becoming an opera singer, succeeded in enrolling in Max Reinhardt's Academy of Dramatic Art, thanks to influential friends of her father's. Her teachers, in particular Berthold Heldt, the actor Lothar Müthel and the director G. W. Pabst, immediately recognized her talent. On March 31, 1925, the academic year of the Reinhardt-Schule ended; on June 1, the young actress was awarded a summer contract in the mountains with the Harzer Bergtheater, directed by Pabst.

After several months in the provinces, Renate was engaged by the prestigious Lessing Theater in Berlin. Her first role was that of a lady of the court in French playwright Edmond Rostand's *L'Aiglon* (The Eaglet). Within two weeks she was also playing the part of the ballerina Fanny Elssler in the same play. This was followed by successful performances with the Jung Bühne, a young actors group, under the guidance of director Joe Sherman, which presented the works of little-known playwrights.

Renate did not remain unknown for long; she was singled out, in fact, by the vitriolic Berlin critic Alfred Kerr, who, at the end of the 1920s, wrote in the *Berliner Tageblatt* (Berlin Daily News): "Remember the name: Müller." Whether or not this remark was made ironically (in Germany the name Müller is as common as Smith is in the United States), the young actress was indeed remembered by many. While many of her co-workers in the Junge Bühne found themselves unemployed for entire seasons, Renate performed steadily, albeit in lightweight comedies. On a couple of occasions she played opposite Johannes Riemann, and the two spoke of one

day doing films, without taking the idea too seriously. From time to time she was assigned a tragic role, as in Georg Kaiser's *Zweimal Olivier* (Twice Olivier), where she appeared with Alessandro Moissi, a celebrated actor from Trieste, and in Frank Wedekind's *Franziska*.

During the years of the change-over from silent to sound films, Müller was appearing with the Berlin Stadttheater, where she played the part of a prostitute in a short-lived play, *Harte Bandagen* (Heavy Bandages), that would later be adapted for the screen. In 1928 she signed her first film contract. In that year Reinhold Schünzel was seeking the right actress for his film *Peter, der Matrose* (Peter the Sailor), in which he was to play the title role. With his practiced eye, he was quick to intuit that Müller was a likely bet for success in films. And he was right: she established a name for herself with her first film. In 1929 she played in *Teure Heimat* (Beloved Homeland), directed by Carl Wilhelm and produced by Erich Engel. The following year, George Asagaroff awarded her the leading role in *Revolte im Erziehungshaus* (Revolt in the Reformatory), opposite future director Veit Harlan. The film, inspired by a socialist work, was banned for several months by the censors, who realized later that it had been so watered down from the original that it was merely a harmless costume drama; it was okayed for release.

In August 1930, the actress appeared in *Der Sohn der Weissen Berge* (The Son of Mont-Blanc), produced by Itala Film and directed by Mario Bonnard. It was a typical Luis Trenker mountain epic, unfolding against snowy Alpine peaks, replete with purifying ascents and breathtaking photography. Barely eight weeks after the premiere of this film, she appeared again on screens throughout Germany in *Liebling der Götter* (Darling of the Gods), a made-to-order vehicle for Emil Jannings. It was not easy playing opposite the celebrated actor, whose last partner had been Marlene Dietrich, and in a part that really called for an older actress, but Müller proved that she could hold her own alongside Jannings and Olga Tschechowa.

Die Privatsekretärin (The Private Secretary, 1931) gave Müller her best role, and is the film for which she will always be remembered. Its story line seemed to mirror the lives of the countless Fräulein Müllers who could be seen walking down the Kurfürstendamm after a day's work at the office. In the little secretary-typist who takes the train for Berlin every morning and whose only assets are a pair of shapely legs, every German secretary, private or not, could recognize herself. French and

Renate Müller greets the New Year, 1934.

English versions of this delightful comedy were also filmed, and Goffredo Alessandrini directed an Italian version that was received in Italy with as much enthusiasm as the original: *La segretaria privata,* with Elsa Merlini and Nino Besozzi. The film's message was a simple but heartening one: fortune can smile on *any* Fräulein Müller.

After this success, Renate was naturally much sought-after. After filming *La canzone d'amore* (The Song of Love, 1931) at the Cines studio in Rome, she appeared in Reinhold Schünzel's light comedy *Der kleine Seitensprung*

(The Little Escapade, 1931), another success. By now she was one of UFA's leading moneymakers. Busy filming *Saison in Kairo* (Season in Cairo) in 1933, Müller had not realized what was taking place in Germany. The film world (and not only that world) had changed; everywhere there was an air of gloom.

Goebbels, who had a high opinion of the actress "artistically," and who found her a sufficiently Germanic type, decided to organize her private life by pairing her off with Hitler. Through various pretexts, however, she succeeded in avoiding the many tête-à-têtes with the Führer planned by the Propaganda Minister. Irritated by her obstinance, Goebbels had her followed, eventually discovering that one of the most talented and popular actresses in German films was refusing invitations to the Chancellory of the Reich in order to be with a Jewish actor. The latter, not wishing to compromise Renate's career, emigrated to London, where she would join him whenever she was not working. However, there were the obstacles of her ongoing contract with UFA and of being constantly followed by the Gestapo, so that going abroad was no easy matter—not even for a Müller.

To the censorship of films was now being added the censorship of actors' private lives; we have already seen the case of Henny Porten, married to a Jew—as, indeed, so was actor Hans Albers. Fortunately, both of them were too popular for Goebbels to put on his list of those proscribed from the film world. Notwithstanding the precariousness of Müller's situation, UFA wanted to take advantage of the great popularity of their star, and cast her in *Walzerkrieg* (War of the Waltzes, 1933), directed by Ludwig Berger, he, too, a pupil of Max Reinhardt, and also a Jew—still another example of the cynicism with which Goebbels on the one hand preached the most rigorous observance of the policy of Aryanization, and on the other permitted Berger (and not only Berger) to work undisturbed in the Babelsberg studios. *Walzerkrieg* was another film-operetta, glowing with Viennese *Gemütlichkeit* and as sparkling as

a sip of Grinzing wine. Müller played the part of Kati Lanner, the vivacious fiancée of a drummer (the ubiquitous Willy Fritsch). The melodies of Mozart and Strauss evoked memories of lighthearted days in the old Austro-Hungarian capital—a world far indeed from Müller's own lonely and miserable existence at that time.

In 1935 Willi Forst cast her in *Allotria,* a scintillating comedy released in 1936 with sets and costumes modeled after French director Jacques Feyder's *Crainquebille* (1922). Ironically, the more depressed the actress became because of her personal problems, the more roles of carefree, romantic young things she was given. At the beginning of 1937, Goebbels began bringing more pressure to bear on Müller: he insisted that she make at least one propaganda film. Even though her contract specified that she was to be given script approval, she let herself be convinced to film *Togger* (1937), a film of blatantly propagandistic nature that turned out to be a fiasco. Müller played the role of Hanna, a journalist who, together with a colleague (Mathias Wieman), fights to preserve freedom of the press threatened by Jewish/Bolshevik conspiracies.

Depressed and painfully thin, Müller checked into a clinic for treatment of a simple knee injury at the beginning of October. On October 10, 1937, her death was officially announced. Her biographers appear to agree in the supposition that the actress committed suicide by throwing herself from a third-floor window of the clinic, but her death seems rather inexplicable, given the fact that she was scheduled to be discharged two weeks after her admission to the hospital. After Müller's death, all sorts of rumors sprang up: that she was a slave to morphine, that she was an alcoholic, that she had become mentally unbalanced. These were false charges that Goebbels had circulated, in order to smear the reputation of an actress beloved by the public, and who, even dead, continued to be a thorn in the side of the regime. In any event, it was obvious to everyone that even if Müller had really committed suicide—and not been thrown from the hospital window—it was the desperate gesture of a sensitive woman who, constantly shadowed by the Gestapo and frustrated in her personal life, had no more desire to live.

Müller's brief career had been peopled with smiling, buoyant characters—the private secretary, the mime, the musician: a parade of delightful, high-spirited figures who finally no longer corresponded to an existence the tiniest detail of which was known to Hitler's police. Müller's death was a tragic example of the ever-widening discrepancy between film and real life, something that Goebbels was seeking to gloss over in his office in the Wilhelmplatz. At the cemetery in Berlin, Renate Müller's friends wept when scriptwriter Thea von Harbou and another friend, novelist/poet Max Barthel, read her funeral eulogy.

Die Privatsekretärin   *(1931)*

(The Private Secretary)

Director: Wilhelm Thiele

In 1931, an Italian version of this film was made, directed by Goffredo Alessandrini and entitled *La segretaria privata,* with Elsa Merlini (Elsa), Nino Besozzi (Berri, the banker), Sergio Tofano (Otello, the porter) and Cesare Zoppetti (Chief of Personnel). A French version, *Dactylo,* was made, with Marie Glory, as well as an English one, *Sunshine Susie,* starring Müller herself.

Story: from the novel of the same name by W. von Szomahazy
Screenplay: Franz Schulz
Photography: Otto Heller and Reimar Kuntze
Music: Paul Abraham
Production: Greenbaum-Film
Length: 85 minutes
Country of origin: Germany, 1931
Censor's approval: January 15, 1931
(banned to minors under 18)
Premiere: January 16, 1931

CAST

Renate Müller (Susanne), Hermann Thimig (Courths-Mahler, her boss), Felix Bressart (a co-worker of Susanne's), Ludwig Stoessel (Chief of Personnel), Gertrud Wolle.

SYNOPSIS

Susanne, an attractive young girl from the provinces, arrives in Berlin and finds a room in a boarding house for working girls. She wants to become a secretary. Despite all the initial discouragements, she eventually finds a job in a bank, thanks primarily to her shapely legs. One evening she works overtime, and the bank manager himself, whom she mistakes for just another employee, invites her to supper. He falls in love with the little typist, and after a hasty courtship, asks her to marry him.

CRITICS' COMMENTS

Die Privatsekretärin is the title of a popular and elegantly made sound film that seeks to destroy, in an extraordinarily cunning fashion, the class consciousness — if any still remains — of the female proletariat who are employed in offices. In the film, an attractive girl arrives in Berlin and gets a room in a working girls' boarding house. There she is told not to expect anything special; if she is lucky enough to land a job, she will not earn more than eighty marks a month. Perhaps at Christmas the office manager will even give her a signed photo of himself. In any case, this pretty thing will have none of that. She calls her fellow trainees "dummies" and announces to them that something wonderful will happen to her; and then the film proceeds to show us how she manages to obtain this "something wonderful." . . .

The private secretary shows off two good reasons for her success.

A lot of frantic activity ensues, the purpose of which is to show how incredibly kind and charming bosses are, and that all that a poor little typist has to do is to make eyes at him to get ahead in this world and work as little as possible. And to make sure that everyone understands this, the fadeout kiss is followed by a montage of the heads of fifty girls, all smiling — see, this is not an exception, this can happen to you, too! Why do you want to organize? What's the use of politics and struggle? What counts is to have good legs, to be cute! This is the real solution to the "social question"!

There is no point in even replying to such cinematographic lies when we have before us the squalid reality of the pitiful condition of our white-collar workers. Hundreds of thousands of them know all too well just how amusing and full of golden opportunities it is sitting behind a typewriter. It is also known that managers often expect more from their secretaries than merely stenography and the ability to type. And marriage? That only happens in the movies and to Frau Courths-Mahler. There is slight consolation in the fact that a certain number of politically indifferent . . . "white-collar ladies" have found the film false, and have even spoken of an "offense to their political honor."
H. LÜDECKE, *Arbeiterbühne und Film,*
Vol. 3 (Berlin, 1931)

In reality, times were so bad that even the most highly qualified specialists, if they were fired, had little hope of finding another position. For that reason, most of the "success story" films indicated luck rather than ability as the real source of brilliant careers. There were a host of films with titles such as Das Geld liegt auf der Strasse *(There's Money Lying in the Street),* Morgen geht's uns gut *(Tomorrow We'll Be All Right) and* Es wird schon wieder besser *(Everything Will Be All Right Again).* And, preposterous as these films were, they were eagerly devoured by the public, as long as they delivered what their titles promised. The Germans must have been at the point of total desperation to accept the concept of luck as an instrument of success — a concept completely foreign to their traditional way of thinking. In all these films, those favored by fortune were the lowest-grade clerical workers and the poorest of the lower middle class. Typical of this genre, which reached its artistic peak with the adroit comedies of Erich Engel, was Die Privatsekretärin, *a stylish and enormously popular film that attested to Wilhelm Thiele's skill at telling seductive lies.*
S. KRACAUER,
From Caligari to Hitler
(Princeton, NJ: Princeton University Press, 1947)

With Adolf Wohlbrück, in "Die englische Heirat" (The English Marriage), 1934.

Viktor und Viktoria   *(1933)*

(Victor and Victoria)

Director: Reinhold Schünzel

With Hermann Thimig.

This film, which has more in common with the musical comedy genre than the film-operetta, is a typical product of the early Nazi regime, when works that were not totally conformist could still circulate. *Viktor und Viktoria*, in fact, continues the irreverent tradition of the Weimar sketches. The numerous disguises, the overall fast pace, the risqué dialogue, the scenes of the London music hall, with the gymnastic routine of the twelve chorus girls shot from overhead all combined to produce a

work on a level never again achieved by German *Revuefilme*. Director Reinhold Schünzel (1886–1954), disliked by the regime as a *Halbjude,* or "half-Jew," but highly paid by UFA since he was one of the few specialists in light comedies, is also remembered for *Der Roman eines Dienstmädchens* (The Story of a Chambermaid, 1921), which brought prominence to Liane Haid, and *Amphitryon* (1935), an imaginative musical version of the classic myth, with Willy Fritsch in the title role. In 1938 he went

to Hollywood, where he directed films for M-G-M, and subsequently became a successful character actor.

Story and screenplay: Reinhold Schünzel
Photography: Konstantin Irmen-Tschet
Set design: Benno von Arendt and Arthur Günther
Choreography: Sabine Ress
Music: Franz Doelle
Song lyrics: Bruno Balz
Editing: Arnfried Heyne

From the left: Heinz Rühmann, Adolf Wohlbrück, Müller and Jenny Jugo in "Allotria," 1936.

Production: UFA
Length: 102 minutes
Country of origin: Germany, 1933
Censor's approval: December 22, 1933
Premiere: December 28, 1933
Award: Artistic Value

CAST

Renate Müller (Susanne), Hermann Thimig (Viktor Hempel), Adolf Wohlbrück (Robert Lohr), Hilde Hildebrand (Elinor), Fritz Odemar (Douglas), Aribert Wäscher (F. A. Punkertin), Friedel Pisetta (Lilian), Karl Harbacher, Raffles Bill, Herbert Paulmüller, Jakob Sinn, Ewald Wenck, Gertrud Wolle.

SYNOPSIS

In order not to lose a night club engagement when indisposed, the impersonator Viktor Hempel asks the attractive singer Susanne to take his place in the show "Mister Viktoria, the Impersonator of Women." The debut of the girl in tails, impersonating a man who impersonates a woman, is hugely successful. A tour abroad follows, during which Susanne continues to appear in male disguise whenever the two appear in public. In London, "Mister Viktoria" is a sensation. In the audience are Elinor and her escort, Robert. Robert falls in love with the artist at first sight, but is disappointed when, instead of Viktoria, he is introduced to Viktor. Curious, he finds out the secret of the girl disguised as a man-as-girl. No longer capable of keeping up the masquerade, Susanne leaves the theater, followed by Robert. They go back to the music hall, because Susanne does not want to leave her partner in a dilemma. Viktor, however, continues to score huge successes as "Mister Viktoria."

CRITICS' COMMENTS

A delightful film musical. We haven't seen Renate Müller so radiant and high-spirited since the days of Die Privatsekretärin. *The audience, kept in a state of euphoria from beginning to end, showed its appreciation with enthusiastic applause.*
8-Uhr-Abendblatt, Berlin, December 29, 1933

This time director Schünzel . . . has handed us a most agreeable surprise.

Together with the gifted composer Franz Doelle and the cameraman Irmen-Tschet, he has formed an inspired triumvirate. . . . Photography, sound and acting are on a level rarely encountered. Renate Müller is an old discovery of Schünzel's, but here he has rediscovered her. No longer confined to the role of the poor little working girl, she has been, as the literal meaning of her name indicates, reborn. The dance sequences are beautifully done. With an impeccable performance by Hermann Thimig, a new Renate Müller and a delightful musical score, this film will be in demand not only by German theaters, but by those of all Europe.
Film-Kurier, Berlin, December 29, 1933

There is only one word for Viktor und Viktoria: *victory! Our congratulations to Reinhold Schünzel, who proves himself to be a master of light comedy. The audience roared with laughter countless times. And so will you, if you go to see the film. . . . It is Renate Müller's finest film to date; we cannot praise her too highly!*
P. STETTNER, Licht-Bild-Bühne, Berlin, December 30, 1933

GRETHE WEISER

IT COULD BE SAID OF GRETHE WEISER, ONE OF THE rare comic actresses of the Nazi screen, that she raised the use of Berlin street slang to the realm of dramatic art. Unrivaled in her mastery of street chatter and the local patois, and of infusing life into characters and situations that were written into the script solely to provide an excuse for clever quips or virtuoso word play, Weiser was launched by the industry as the "typical Berliner."

Actually, she was born in Hannover, had spent her adolescence in Dresden, and had been making films for almost ten years before the director Erich Waschneck opened the doors of the gilded world of the *Revuefilm* to her with *Die göttliche Jette* (The Divine Jette), in 1937. In this historic musical, pervaded by a subtle irony seldom if ever found in films of the era, Grethe, in the part of the singer Jette Schönborn, parodies La Dietrich during an audition, and succeeds—thanks to an influential friend (Kurt Meisel)—in becoming the star of the show *Berlin, wie es Euch gefällt* (Berlin the Way You Like It), singing "Ich bin die Frau der tausend Männer" (I'm the Woman of a Thousand Men). When the film was released, the *Illustrierter Film-Kurier* of Berlin wrote: "Little Jette Schönborn has become the 'divine Jette,' Berlin's darling." Waschneck, who had already directed Grethe in *Eskapade* (1936), knew that she was the only actress on the scene who could do full justice to the film, which was a great success with critics and the public.

Forthright but never coarse, droll and good-natured, Weiser was the embodiment of the "Berlin style," with her insinuating, allusive delivery of songs such as "Im Küsse der Berlinerin, da liegt so was Gewisses drin" (In the Kiss of the Berlin Woman, There's a Certain Something). Her attractive face and figure were usually hidden by silly hats or shapeless maid's uniforms. Her biographer Hans Borgelt tells how, during the shooting of *Die göttliche Jette,* "Waschneck had adopted the old moviemakers' custom of giving a ten-pfennig coin to each member of the troupe who came up with a useful idea. Grethe's take added up to several marks daily. She liked the film, to the point where she ended up identifying totally with the heroine."[1] In the musical *Ehe in Dosen* (Marriage in Small Doses, 1939), Grethe played the part of a soubrette, Mausi Blanke, star of the night club "Silbermotte" (Silver Moth), where she performs a series of comic routines and songs such as the bawdy "Das Etwas einer klugen Frau" (That Certain Something That a Clever Woman Has), wearing tight-fitting gowns slit up the sides, since her legs were always her best feature.

She then went back to the kind of parts with which she had begun her film career: the comic sidekick of the heroine, or the knowing maidservant. We remember her in *Die grosse Liebe* (The Great Love, 1942), in which she plays Käthe, the cantankerous spinster who works for Zarah Leander. There are perhaps moments when her comic effects become too broad, as in the scenes where she has to take her mistress's enormous boxer out for a walk. But she is delightful in the scene when the tenants of her building offer her a precious cup of coffee in the air raid shelter, during a bombardment. She drinks it with a smile of satisfaction, but when she finds out that it was *her* coffee that they were using, she mutters, in her purest Berlin dialect: "Det war 'ne gute idee!" (What a great idea *that* was!), the smile vanishing instantly.

Grethe Weiser died with her husband in a car accident in Bad Tölz, Bavaria, on October 2, 1970.

With Paul Hoffmann (above) and Franz Zimmermann (below) in "Meine Freundin Barbara," 1937.

Meine Freundin Barbara   (1937)

(My Girlfriend Barbara)

Director: Fritz Kirchhoff

Story: from the play of the same
    name by Willy Kollo
Screenplay: Willy Kollo and Fritz
    Kirchhoff
Photography: Georg Bruckbauer
Music: Willy Kollo
Production: Fanal-Film
Editing: Milo Harbich
Length: 82 minutes
Country of origin: Germany, 1937
Censor's approval: October 29, 1937
    (banned to minors under 18)
Premiere: December 17, 1937

CAST

Grethe Weiser (Barbara), Franz Zim-
mermann (her lover), Paul Hoffmann
(the university professor), Elisabeth
Ried (his wife), Jakob Tiedtke, Arthur
Schröder, Hans Leibelt, Ingeborg von
Kusserow, Wilhelm P. Krüger, Ellen
Bang, Manny Ziener, Günther Ballier,
Luise Morland, Gudrun Ady, Angelo
Ferrari.

SYNOPSIS

Barbara works as an usherette in a
neighborhood movie house, patronized
primarily by young couples, who go to
see old silent films. One day, she sees a
woman whom she knows come in with
a handsome man who is not her husband. Barbara realizes that a marriage
is in jeopardy, and does her best to
break up the couple. But the young
man, who has, earlier, barely escaped
being caught *in flagrante* by the lady's
husband, a dour university professor,
falls in love with Barbara and helps her
become a singing star. She marries him,
and the young rogue whom she discovered carrying on in a movie theater
becomes a devoted husband.

CRITICS' COMMENTS

*From first to last the screenplay seems
created just for Grethe Weiser. She is
the absolute mistress of comic speech.
With her loquaciousness she can do*
*anything—she ties up loose ends, pat-
ches things up for a couple about to
break up, helps to put a factory back on
its feet through new chemical discove-
ries, and ends up marrying the boss's
son. . . . It's a merry-go-round of
dialogues, monologues and jokes that,
thanks to Grethe, is immensely enjoyable. Who loves whom? Who writes
to whom? Our friend Barbara does
everything, singing the song that the
young ladies (and, we're sure, all the
young men) will be singing.*
    C. R. MARTIUS, *Der Film,*
        Berlin, December 18, 1937

*Our Barbara is such a conscientious
young lady that it's not easy to unders-
tand why everything goes wrong for her
in the first part of the film. . . . Grethe
Weiser, who handles a really difficult
part with enormous humor and charm,
gets tough not only with her personal
adversaries but with those in the audience who misbehave. (She also
charges fifty pfennigs each for programs, and the Reich Committee on
Price Controls should certainly look into that!) One would like to ask her how
such a tiny young woman could have a
voice of that size, but she never seems to*
*sit still long enough. Every film in
which she appears is bursting with action, rhythm and humor. . . . This film
was not made by [Hans] Albers, but it
follows his formula: everything for the
star. Someone should put Weiser and
Albers in the same film, just once.
When the film was over, there was
great applause for Weiser, who didn't
show up until nine, since she is current-
ly completing a theatrical engagement.*
    G. HERZBERG, *Film-Kurier,*
        Berlin, December 18, 1937

*An enjoyable comedy, in which the
story is definitely not the main thing.
This film owes everything to the talent
and personality of Grethe Weiser, who
dominates it from the first to the last
shot. . . . The plot is merely a pretext to
allow Grethe to delight the public with
a series of situations and comic lines
that never miss their mark; the audience laughs almost continually. Franz
Zimmermann and Paul Hoffmann
thanked the audience for having
decreed the success of the film, and La
Weiser, too, made an appearance at the
end of the evening.*
    F. HENSELEIT, *Licht-Bild-Bühne,*
        Berlin, December 18, 1937

With (from the left) Paul Hoffmann, Elisabeth Ried and Franz Zimmermann.

MARIANNE HOPPE

Of all the actresses of the Nazi period in German film, the one who seems most modern to us, the most distant from the acting styles of a Henny Porten or a Kristina Söderbaum, is Marianne Hoppe, Catholic, born in Rostock, a Baltic seaport, on April 26, 1911. After attending the Königin Luise academy and a business school in Berlin, at seventeen she was accepted at the dramatic arts school of the Deutsches Theater, then directed by Max Reinhardt; at the same time, she studied drama with the actress Lucie Höflich.

In 1928 Hoppe made her debut at the Bühne der Jugend, or Young People's Theater Group, in Berlin, and from 1928 to 1930 was seen at the Deutsches Theater itself, where she appeared in such lightweight roles as a page in Shakespeare's *Romeo and Juliet.* With her androgynous face and boyish figure, she was often given masculine parts, as in *Schwarzer Jäger Johanna* (Black Hunter Johanna, 1934), a patriotic film in which a girl manages to enroll in the Prussian Freikorps by passing herself off as a boy. She worked in Frankfurt am Main from 1930 to 1932, when she joined the Kammerspiele in Munich. There she would remain for several years, gaining valuable experience under the director, Otto Falckenberg.

Hoppe's first screen appearance was in 1933 in a historical film, *Judas von Tirol* (Judas of the Tyrol), under the direction of Franz Osten. In 1933, she also appeared in the patriotic film *Heideschulmeister Uwe Karsten* (Schoolmaster Uwe Karsten). With her portrait of Elke in *Der Schimmelreiter* (The Rider of the White Steed), a film adaptation of Theodor Storm's well-known 1888 novella, the following year, she took her place among the leading actresses of the German screen.

Among her most fondly remembered pictures are *Der Herrscher* (The Rulers, 1937), *Capriolen* (Caprices, 1938), *Kongo-Express* (1939) and *Auf Wiedersehen, Franziska!* (1941). She was at her best in serious parts, as, for example, in the two melodramas directed by Helmut Käutner, *Auf Wiedersehen, Franziska!* and *Romanze in Moll* (Romance in a Minor Key, 1943), vehicles that enabled her to display the full range of her dramatic ability.

Although romantic tragedy was where she was most at home, Hoppe was occasionally tempted by stories with an exotic or an American flavor. *Capriolen* and *Kongo-Express,* for example, are worlds apart from Käutner's carefully crafted, sentimental dramas. In the former film, Hoppe plays the daredevil aviatrix Mabel Atkinson, slim and smiling in her close-fitting flying suit and helmet. In *Kongo-Express,* she is Renate Brinkmann, who decides to leave her woebegone, alcoholic fiancé for an upright and generous German named Viktor. Although the picture takes place in Africa, it was shot entirely in Germany. African foliage was planted alongside a stretch of a small railway line between the north German cities of Hannover and Celle, and an ancient cow-catcher locomotive was pressed into service to film a journey from Shikapa to Kisongo.

On June 22, 1936, Marianne Hoppe married the actor-director Gustav Gründgens, who had recently been named Staatsschauspieler (State Actor); although they were to form a fortunate artistic partnership, both in films and on the stage. Hoppe gave one of her finest film performances in the role of Effi Briest,* a weak but proud creature, in *Der Schritt vom Wege* (The False Step, 1939), directed by Gründgens.

Shortly after their marriage, the Gründgens' happiness was to be disturbed by writer Thomas Mann's son, Klaus, a homosexual, like Gründgens. In order to marry Hoppe, Gründgens had had to divorce his first wife, Erika, Klaus's sister. This of course meant abandoning the Mann family, and Klaus is believed to have loved Gründgens. Klaus in 1936 published the novel *Mephisto,* depicting Gründgens, as the central figure, unfavorably.

The siege of Berlin surprised Hoppe in her house in Grunewald at the outskirts of the city. After Germany's surrender, she worked in a refugee camp near the Lehrt Railroad Station. In 1946 she divorced Gründgens and, together with their son, Benedikt, left Berlin for Bavaria. (Gründgens would die on October 7, 1963, in Manila on a round-the-world acting tour.)

After the war, Hoppe appeared in the theater in the role of Elektra in Jean-Paul Sartre's *Les Mouches* (The Flies). From 1947 until 1955, she performed frequently at the Schauspielhaus in Düsseldorf, of which Gründgens was director. In 1961 she made her debut on the long-running television detective series "Der Kommissar" (The Commissioner). In 1965 she was appointed a permanent member of West Germany's Akademie der Künste. She gave a particularly memorable performance as the mother in Tankred Dorst's play *Chimborazo* at its premiere in Berlin in 1975. Her favorite amusement: playing *Skat,* a German card game not unlike Bridge.

Effi Briest is the title of a well-known short novel by one of Germany's foremost novelists, Theodor Fontane (1819–98).

Auf Wiedersehen, Franziska! *(1941)*

(Till We Meet Again, Franziska!)

Director: Helmut Käutner

This film was banned after the war by a decree of the Allied Military Government. In 1957, Wolfgang Liebeneiner directed a remake entitled *Franziska,* with Ruth Leuwerik and Carlos Thompson. Defined by French writer/journalist Georges Sadoul as "the only true talent to manifest itself in . . . Goebbels' reign,"[1] director Helmut Käutner, born in Düsseldorf on March 25, 1908, has been considered one of the major figures of pre- and postwar German film and theater. After working as a cabaret actor and scriptwriter,

in 1939 he directed his first picture, *Kitty und die Weltkonferenz* (Kitty and the World Conference), which was followed by *Anuschka* (1942), *Wir machen Musik* (We Make Music, 1942), *Unter den Brücken* (Under the Bridges, 1944) and *Grosse Freiheit Nr. 7* (Great Freedom No. 7, 1945)—the last two banned by the censors as too realistic.

His specialty was the romantic melodrama, with tormented, neurotic heroines, the whole veiled in a kind of Max Ophüls-like irony. In the early 1950s Käutner somehow began to lose

his touch, although his *Der Hauptmann von Köpenick* (The Captain from Köpenick, 1956) was well received by critics. He went to Hollywood, and in 1958 made two disappointing pictures for Universal, *The Restless Years* and *Stranger in My Arms.* Returning to Germany, he continued to work in films and theater. From the mid-1960s, he worked mostly for German television. Käutner died at seventy-two on April 22, 1980, in Castellina in Chianti, outside Siena, Italy, where he spent his last years in solitude.

With Hans Söhnker, as her globetrotting husband in the film.

While her husband is at the front.

Story and screenplay: Helmut
   Käutner and Curt J. Braun
Photography: Jan Roth
Set design: W. A. Hermann
Music: Michael Jary
Costumes: Margot Hielscher
Editing: Helmuth Schoennebeck
Production: UFA
Length: 100 minutes
Country of origin: Germany, 1941
Censor's approval: April 18, 1941
   (banned to minors under 18)
Premiere: April 24, 1941, Munich;
   May 6, 1941, Berlin
Award: Artistic Value

CAST _____

Marianne Hoppe (Franziska Thie-
mann), Hans Söhnker (Michael
Reisiger), Fritz Odemar (Professor
Thiemann), Rudolf Fernau (Dr. Chris-
toph Leitner), Hermann Speelmans
(Buck Standing), Margot Hielscher
(Helen Philips), Herbert Hübner (Ted
Simmond), Josefine Dora (Frau
Schöpf), Frieda Richard (Kathrin),
Klaus Pohl (the mailman).

SYNOPSIS _____

Wherever a good story is breaking
somewhere in the world, Michael

Reisiger is on the spot with his camera,
to film it for the newsreels. One day he
meets Franziska Thiemann, the attractive daughter of a professor, and an artisan who makes toys. They share one
night of love. At the train station,
Michael tells her to forget him. Reflecting, however, he thinks that she might
be the woman of his life, and adds: "Auf
wiedersehen, Franziska!" They see each
other briefly between trips. Michael
finds out that Franziska is expecting a
baby; he returns home and marries her.
He stays at home for a time, and then is
ordered to cover a rebellion in
Shanghai. His best friend is killed by a
grenade, but before dying tells him to
return to the Fatherland. Arriving in
Germany, Michael is drafted: World
War II has broken out. Franziska puts
aside all thoughts of divorce, and once
again awaits his return.

CRITICS' COMMENTS _____

*The story itself is well chosen. The
scriptwriters have taken the most
hackneyed of themes — love — and by
showing us its most commonplace
aspects, and how they can enter the
lives of any one of us at any time, they
have made a film that touches the*
heart. . . . Marianne Hoppe brings
Franziska to life so eloquently that we
too can share her emotions — the joy of
a new love, the subsequent uncertainty,
the loneliness, the desire to strengthen
the character of the man she loves. The
intensity of her performance will not
soon be forgotten. Hans Söhnker is her
partner, selfish as only a man can be.
. . . The audience at the Berlin premiere
showed its enthusiasm with frequent
applause during the film and numerous
curtain calls at the end for the actors
and the director.*

   G. HERZBERG, *Film-Kurier,*
   May 7, 1941

*A few years ago, when we first began to
notice photos of Marianne Hoppe in
the lobbies of movie theaters, it seemed
even then that that fresh, likable, im-
mature face promised something more
than merely photogenic features. With
her deeply felt performance in this film
she has fulfilled that promise. It is evident that the actress, whose disciplined
portrayal rests on a solid technique acquired through years of experience in
the theater, benefits here from her collaboration with the brilliant, cynical,
restless Helmut Käutner. . . . With an
admirable economy of facial gestures
and vocal inflections, Hoppe gives a
controlled and unforgettably moving
performance.*

   K. ECKHARDT, *Der Film,*
   Berlin, August 8, 1942

To tell the truth, Auf Wiedersehen,
Franziska! *is no better than the photographed love-story magazines that
flood our newsstands, in which women
wait for the adventure-loving husbands
to return home. It also contains a couple of touches reminiscent of the
patriotic films of the period: the praising of the amateur artisan (Franziska
makes wooden toys), and the longing
for the far-off homeland. [However,]
Helmut Käutner managed to give a bit
of credibility even to the most banal
scenes, such as Franziska and Michael's
first meeting.*

   F. COURTADE and P. CADARS,
   Histoire du cinéma nazi
   (Paris, 1973)

Romanze in Moll   *(1943)*

(Romance in a Minor Key)

Director: Helmut Käutner

With Paul Dahlke.

This film won first prize at the Stockholm Film Festival in 1943. Käutner has taken his story from the short story *Les Bijoux* (The Jewels) by de Maupassant, an author disliked by the Nazi censors. Even though Madeleine pays for her sin of adultery with death, Goebbels found the film "defeatist," probably because Hoppe had brought great humanity to her character, making her highly sympathetic and deserving of compassion rather than condemnation.

Story: from an idea of Willy Clever
Screenplay: Willy Clever and Helmut Käutner
Photography: Georg Bruckbauer
Set design: Otto Herdmann and F. F. Fürst
Music: Lothar Brühne and Werner Eisbrenner
Editing: Anneliese Sponholz
Production: UFA
Length: 100 minutes
Country of origin: Germany, 1943
Censor's approval: January 28, 1943 (banned to minors under 18)
Premiere: June 25, 1943

CAST

Marianne Hoppe (Madeleine), Paul Dahlke (her husband), Ferdinand Marian (Michael), Siegfried Breuer (Viktor), Elisabeth Flickenschildt (the wife of the doorman), Ernst Legal (the deaf man), Hans Stiebner (the fat man), Karl Günther (the jeweler), Anja Elkoff (the singer), Eric Helgar, Karl Platen, Hugo Flink, Walter Lieck, Klaus Pohl, Leo Peukert, Maria Loja and others.

SYNOPSIS

Madeleine must have believed that she could find happiness in a solid, bourgeois marriage to a prosaic civil servant. But she learns that you cannot dictate to your heart, when, in front of a jewelry store window, she meets Michael, a composer, and becomes his mistress. He later gives her a pearl necklace, because she has inspired him to compose the musical "romance" of the title. Michael proceeds to fulfill her dreams of success and security, introducing her into the *haut monde.* A friend of Michael's, a co-worker of Madeleine's husband, threatens to reveal the truth of her double life, and begins blackmailing her. Either she gives herself to him or he will expose her. She goes to the premiere performance of the new composition, and finds it being sung by Michael's new favorite. Crushed, she flees the auditorium and, returning home, takes poison.

With Paul Dahlke, as the unsuspecting husband.

ILSE WERNER

Ilse Werner was born in Batavia (today Jakarta, capital of Indonesia) on July 11, 1918, daughter of a Dutch exporter, O.E.G. Still, and Lilly Werner of Frankfurt am Main. At the age of ten Ilse returned from Java to Germany, where she attended school in Frankfurt. From 1936 to 1937 she studied at Max Reinhardt's school of dramatic arts in Vienna, and made her successful stage debut in German playwright Max Dauthendey's *Glück* (Happiness) with the Josefstädter Bühne in that city in 1937. UFA immediately invited her to Berlin. Among her first films, in 1938, was *Die unruhigen Mädchen* (The Restless Girls), but Werner gained true popularity with *Wunschkonzert* (Request Concert, 1940), a picture that brought tears to the eyes of millions, in which she was the personification of the faithful German girl.

Werner was also famous throughout Germany for her virtuoso whistling, as she was for her singing. Her recordings of current popular songs were bestsellers. One of her most fondly remembered musical vehicles was *Wir machen Musik* (We Make Music, 1942), with the dashing Viktor de Kowa and Grethe Weiser. In 1943, along with Hans Albers and Brigitte Horney, she appeared in the popular *Münchhausen* (The Adventures of Baron Münchhausen).

Werner managed her career shrewdly, alternating appearances in films, theater, radio and cabaret. In 1948 she married the American journalist John de Forest and settled in California, returning briefly to Germany to film *Die gestörte Hochzeitsnacht* (The Troubled Wedding Night). The marriage lasted until 1953, when she decided to resume her German career. In 1954, she married Josef Niessen, conductor of the dance orchestra of the Bayerische Rundfunk (Bavarian Radio). In 1960 her song "Baciare" (To Kiss) was a great success throughout Europe. A frequent guest on German television, in 1967 she starred in a popular TV series, "Eine Frau mit Pfiff" (A Woman with a Whistle), built around her and her songs. Her long-standing desire to appear in a Broadway musical was realized in 1970, when she played

With Erika von Thellmann (left) in "Bal paré" (Full-dress Ball), 1940.

With Carl Raddatz in "Wunschkonzert," 1940.

the role of Anna in the German version of *The King and I*.

From September to December 1973 she toured Germany and Switzerland in a play directed by Marie Becker. In the 1970s she worked extensively as moderator and host of several television programs, including a Cologne-based talk show later, in 1982. As late as 1989, she appeared in a German TV series, "Rivalen der Rennbahn" (Rivals of the Race Track). Divorced from her second husband, conductor Josef Niessen, she lives today in Lübeck, near the Baltic. Werner's hobbies are sports, reading, music, travel—and cats.

Like so many other film divas, Werner couldn't resist the temptation to publish her memoirs. Even as early as 1941 a slim volume appeared entitled *Ich über mich* (I on Myself). She published, among other books, *So wird's nie wieder sein* (It Will Never Again Be the Same) in 1981.

Wunschkonzert *(1940)*

(Request Concert)

Director: Eduard von Borsody

This film revolves around a highly popular German radio program, "Wunschkonzert," which was broadcast every Saturday, and which played music requested by members of the armed forces. More than half of the scenes were filmed in the broadcasting studios. Weiss-Ferdl sings "Ich bin kein Intellektueller" (I'm Not an Intellectual), a number doubtless enjoyed by the average Nazi; Eugen Jochum conducts the overture to *The Marriage of Figaro*; and Marika Rökk performs her most popular successes. Intended to cheer up the women at home who were thinking of their men at the front, the film is similar to *Die grosse Liebe* and *Auf Wiedersehen, Franziska!* in its theme of the faithful woman who waits.

Story and screenplay: Felix Lützkendorf
    and Eduard von Borsody
Photography: Franz Weihmayr
Set design: Alfred Bütow and
    Heinrich Beisenherz
Music: Werner Bochmann
Editing: Elisabeth Neumann
Production: Cine-Allianz-Film, UFA
Length: 104 minutes
Country of origin: Germany, 1940
Censor's approval: December 21,
    1940
Premiere: December 30, 1940, Berlin
Awards: Political Value; Artistic Value;
    Value to the People; Suited for
    the Young

CAST

Ilse Werner (Inge Wagner), Carl Raddatz (Herbert Koch), Joachim Brennecke (Lt. Helmut Winkler), Ida Wüst (Frau Eichhorn), Hedwig Bleibtreu (Frau Wagner), Heinz Goedecke (Heinz Goedecke), H. A. Schlettow (Kramer), H. H. Schaufuss (Hemmer), E. Aulinger (Frau Schwarzkopf), W. Althaus (Captain Freiberg), O. Ballhaus (First Officer), W. Bechmann (the waiter), V. Complojer (Frau Hammer),

The best medicine is love (with Joachim Brennecke).

A. Florath (the doctor), V. Hartegg (Frau Friedrich), in the request concert: Marika Rökk, Paul Hörbiger, Heinz Rühmann, Hans Brausewetter, Josef Sieber, Weiss-Ferdl, Wilhelm Strienz, Albert Bräu.

SYNOPSIS

Berlin, the 1936 Olympic Games. Young Inge Wagner meets Lieutenant Herbert Koch; their friendship blossoms into love. Koch is ordered to Spain on a secret mission. He is forbidden to tell anyone of his departure. In 1939, war breaks out. Inge is still living in her provincial town. Her parents give a farewell party for Lt. Helmut Winkler, a childhood friend of hers. He would like to be her fiancé, but she cannot forget Koch, even though she has had no news of him. Winkler is sent to a post in the North Sea, where his commander is Koch. The two become friends. One day, Inge hears on the "Wunschkonzert": "Captain Koch would like to hear the Olympic Games fanfare, in memory of Berlin." Inge gets Koch's address from the radio station, and leaves for Frankfurt, where the two meet. Winkler has been injured and is in the hospital. Koch, who brought him there, discovers a photo of Inge among his papers. Winkler tells him that she is his fiancée. When Koch goes to visit Winkler, he finds Inge there. Winkler then admits that he is not engaged to her, and from his hospital bed he wishes the couple love and happiness.

A director who chooses to make a film centering around the "Wunschkonzert" has to be courageous indeed, inasmuch as he has to come up with something that will match the enormous appeal of the program itself. . . . Slim and lovely, Ilse Werner typifies the German girl of today. We have never seen her so likeable, so full of courage and the joy of living. Her partner, Carl Raddatz, is his usual winning self. We are taken into the radio station itself, where Heinz Goedecke, the program's producer, introduces us to Marika Rökk, Paul Hörbiger, Albert Bräu and the Seemans trio, composed of Heinz Rühmann, Hans Brausewetter and Josef Sieber. . . . Present at the premiere were Dr. Goebbels and his wife; the film's director, von Borsody, in the center box; and next to the general director of UFA, Ludwig Klitsch, sat Goedecke. There was hearty applause at the end for the film and for the actors, who greeted the public.

G. SCHWARK, *Film-Kurier,*
Berlin, January 2, 1941

We all realize the importance of the request concerts broadcast by German radio; they are a kind of bridge between the homeland and the front. This is a film of war and a film for the people, reflecting our times; but most of all it is a film that entertains. It is the story of two young people who love each other and who are willing to wait, and of the tricks that fate and war play on them. . . . Ilse Werner and Carl Raddatz are warm and appealing in their steadfastness in the face of endless obstacles. . . . The millions of radio listeners in the cities and towns, we are certain, will be no less enthusiastic in their response to this film than the Berlin audience was at its premiere.

A. SCHMIDT, *Deutsche Filmzeitung,*
Munich, January 12, 1941

Die schwedische Nachtigall (1941)

(The Swedish Nightingale)

Director: Peter Paul Brauer

Story: from the play *Gastspiel in Kopenhagen* (On Tour in Copenhagen) by Friedrich Forster-Burggraf
Screenplay: Gert von Klass and Per Schwenzen
Photography: Ewald Daub
Music: Franz Grothe
Production: Terra
Length: 97 minutes
Country of origin: Germany, 1941
Censor's approval: April 4, 1941
Premiere: April 9, 1941, Berlin
Award: Artistic Value.

CAST ————

Ilse Werner (Jenny Lind), Karl Ludwig Diehl (Count Rantzan), Joachim Gottschalk (Hans Christian Andersen), Emil Hess (Thorwaldsen), Aribert Wäscher (the impresario Perr Upän), Hans Leibelt (director of the theater), Hans Hermann Schaufuss (conductor of the orchestra), Ernst Sattler (Axel Lind, Jenny's father), Volker von Collande (Olaf Larsson, Jenny's fiancé) and others.

SYNOPSIS ——————

Hans Christian Andersen, the celebrated author of fairy tales, meets and falls in love with a young woman with a marvelous voice: Jenny Lind. At the recommendation of Count Rantzan,

With Heinrich George in "Hochzeit auf Bärenhof" (Wedding at Bärenhof), 1942.

she is invited to sing at the Stockholm Opera, and becomes the Count's mistress. He proposes marriage to her, on the condition that she give up her career. In Rome, where Andersen is living, his friend Thorwaldsen tells him of the situation. Andersen rushes back to Copenhagen to join Jenny. She has already learned, however, that passion can kill a person's artistic talent. Once more, Jenny renounces love so that genius may flower.

CRITICS' COMMENTS ───────

How much poetry there is in the life of this artist! Interpreted by the lovely Ilse Werner, Jenny Lind sacrifices . . . [love for art]. In the conflict between bourgeois marriage and artistic independence, in this film it is the latter that wins out. . . . Acting and direction combine in a single theme — that art lives on, even after love has died. Had this not been her choice, how different the life of this woman would have been — and how much poorer the world of music. Werner's performance is wonderfully touching.

P. ICKES, *Die Filmwoche,*
Berlin, April 10, 1941

Do you remember Andersen's fable of the Chinese emperor and the nightingale that wanted to stay with its master but decided to fly away in order to bring joy and love to all men? . . . It is a sweet, sad tale, and it is also the tale of the "Swedish nightingale." Ilse Werner is the heroine of this delicate, muted film; the soprano Erna Berger lends her exquisite voice to the sound track. Werner gives a restrained and graceful performance, free of theatrics. . . . The audience was warmly appreciative. The German screen has been enriched with another polished and artistic work.

H.-W. BETZ, *Der Film,*
Berlin, April 12, 1941

With Joachim Gottschalk and Ilse Werner in the leading parts, this Terra production reaches moments of almost unbearable pathos, especially because it was Gottschalk's last film before his suicide. His performance as the hopelessly-in-love Andersen is one of the milestones of German screen art.

DAVID S. HULL, *Film in the Third Reich: A Study of the German Cinema 1933–1945* (University of California Press, 1969)

With Aribert Wäscher in "Die schwedische Nachtigall," 1941.

PAULA WESSELY

T HERE ARE CERTAIN FACES ON THE SCREEN THAT seem to have an "alien" quality; they are unrelated to us, they have nothing to do with our world—Zarah Leander had such a face. And there are faces that we find reassuring, that we are at home with, such as that of Paula Wessely. Her features were neither regular nor particularly pretty, but when she smiled, heedless of wrinkles or lack of beauty, she reminded you of a sister or a childhood friend, of a woman you'd seen a thousand times. Although not blessed with what was considered to be a photogenic face (it was too wide, the features too heavy), Wessely was able to overcome this deficiency, offering to the camera the face of a genuine, one-hundred-percent actress, whose small blue eyes could convey an enormous range of emotions.

Paula Wessely was born in Vienna on January 20, 1907, the daughter of a butcher in the district of Fünfhaus and an ex-ballerina of the Hofoper, or Court

As Leopoldine in "Maskerade," 1934.

Opera. Her father's sister, Josephine Wessely, had been a fairly well known actress at the Vienna Burgtheater, and as a little girl Paula dreamed of following in her footsteps. Behind the cash register in her father's butcher shop, she would scrutinize the facial types and gestures of the customers, the way they looked and carried themselves, often becoming so absorbed in her study that she would forget to give them their change.

On the advice of her teacher, Madeleine Gutwenger, Paula enrolled in the courses in dramatic art given by the former Hungarian actress Valerie Gray, with whom her aunt Josephine had also studied, and during lengthy sessions at Demel's pastry shop, she and Fräulein Gutwenger chose the selections she would use to audition with, at Vienna's Theater-Akademie. She was accepted at the school, and was permitted to attend Max Reinhardt's seminar. In 1924, she performed at the Deutsches Volkstheater in Vienna, and on May 28, 1926, her name appeared for the first time in the playbill of the Stadttheater, where she was featured in a play of German playwright/novelist Hermann Sudermann's. The first parts she was given made use of her gifts for comedy. In both French playwright Victorien Sardou's *Cyprienne* and his compatriot Sacha Guitry's *L'Accroche-coeur* (The Kiss Curl, or Love Lock) she played a coquettish young serving maid. But her voice, of unusual range and flexibility, could find the right inflections for serious drama or light comedy, and was in surprising contrast to her solid physical aspect.

In 1926 Wessely performed at the Neues Deutsches Theater in Prague; in 1927 she returned to the Neues Deutsches Volkstheater in Vienna, where she remained for two years; and in 1929 she joined Vienna's Theater in der Josefstadt, appearing there regularly until 1945. It was there that she had her greatest personal success to date, in German master playwright Gerhart Hauptmann's *Rose Bernd*, which she also performed in Berlin in 1932. She made regular appearances with the Deutsches Theater in Berlin from 1934 to 1945.

In the meantime the actress had gotten away from the roles of flirtatious and superficial *demi-mondaines*, thanks to the close personal and artistic rapport she had established with Reinhardt. Her performances as Gretchen in his production of Goethe's *Faust* in Salzburg in 1935, and as George Bernard Shaw's *Saint Joan (Die heilige Johanna)*, brought to Berlin by the Deutsches Theater in 1936 during the period of the Olympic Games, are considered to be the greatest achievements of her artistic career.

As her stage career became increasingly successful, Wessely began to receive film scripts, which she regularly rejected, until Willi Forst and Walter Reisch submitted to her a screenplay that was irresistibly appealing to her Viennese temperament: *Maskerade,* a story of old Vienna, in which she would play the part of a naive young companion to a noblewoman and would speak in her native dialect. *Maskerade* (1934) was an enormous success, taking its place as one of the classics of the German-speaking screen, and it made Wessely a star overnight. She had entered the world of film with the fixed intention of not absenting herself from the stage for too long; as things turned out, it was a world in which she was to remain. She followed up this success in 1935 with *Episode,* directed by Reisch. That same year, she married the actor Attila Hörbiger, who would be her frequent screen partner in years to come.

The Nazi regime put to use Wessely's physical type—unglamorous, almost plain, the average middle-class German woman, someone whom audiences could easily identify with—by casting her in one of the most blatant of all German propaganda films, Gustav Ucicky's *Heimkehr* (Homecoming, 1941). A classic example of the genre, it has achieved a certain notoriety through its inclusion in a number of postwar documentaries on Nazi Germany.

More numerous and more typical in Wessely's career, however, were her portrayals of straightforward romantic heroines, free of artifice—which reflected her true nature. From the young princess Marie Luise of *So endete eine Liebe* (Thus Ended a Love, 1934) to the sculptress Valerie Gärtner of *Episode,* from the Hungarian country lass of *Die Julika* (1936) to the aspiring actress of *Die ganz grossen Torheiten* (The Very Greatest Follies, 1937), Wessely created a gallery of healthy, uncomplicated, diligent women, imparting to them her characteristic air of the typical likable Viennese girl with a fondness for *Sachertorte* and whipped cream. The affection that the Austro-German public had—and continues to have—for her can be ascribed to Wessely's air of being a down-to-earth, "normal" person, as well as to her consummate professional skill—for which, among other prizes, she has been awarded the Max-Reinhardt-Ring (1949), the Josef-Kainz-Medaille (1960), and the Goldmedaille der Stadt Wien (1967). In addition, she has been an honorary member of the Akademie für Musik und Darstellende Kunst (...Performing Art) of Vienna since 1957, as well as a special member of the Akademie der Künste of Berlin.

During World War II, Wessely worked in Vienna as long as it was possible, and then withdrew to her home in nearby Grinzing with her husband. Their three daughters, Elisabeth, Christiane and Maresa, have also become actresses. The eldest, Elisabeth Orth, in 1975 published a biography of her *parents, Märchen ihres Lebens: Meine Eltern Paula Wessely und Attila Hörbiger* (Tales of Their Lives: My Parents...). She died on May 13, 2000.

With Attila Hörbiger, her companion in art and in life.

Maskerade   *(1934)*

Director: Willi Forst

The screenplay of *Maskerade* is said to have been based on a famous scandal, an event that actually took place in Vienna at the beginning of the century. The film was awarded the gold medal of the National Fascist Confederation of Professionals and Artists for "best story" at the 1935 Venice Film Festival. With Tobis, *Maskerade* was produced by Austria's Sascha film company, which, after the Anschluss, in 1938, was transformed into Wien-Film. The Nazi regime appointed as its head the director Karl Hartl, who remained there (reluctantly) until 1954.

Story and screenplay: Willi Forst and
  Walter Reisch
Photography: Franz Planer
Set design: Carl Stepanek
Orchestra: the Vienna Philharmonic
Production: Tobis-Sascha
  Filmindustrie
Length: 103 minutes
Country of origin: Austria, 1934
Censor's approval: July 14, 1934
  (banned to minors under 18)
Premiere: August 21, 1934, Berlin
Award: Artistic Value

CAST

Paula Wessely (Leopoldine Dur), Adolf Wohlbrück (Heideneck), Olga Tschechowa (Anita Keller), Hilde von Stolz (Gerda Harrandt), Peter Petersen (Anita's husband), Walter Janssen (Paul Harrandt, a surgeon), Julia Serda (the princess), Hans Moser (the gardener), Paul Hörbiger.

SYNOPSIS

Vienna, 1905. At a ball, the womanizing painter Heidenick meets Gerda, the frivolous wife of a surgeon, Paul Harrandt, and asks her to pose for him. She hesitates, but gives in, and poses nude, except for a chinchilla muff and a mask over her eyes. By mistake, the portrait is reproduced on the front page of a magazine, giving rise to scandal and curiosity; everyone wants to know the identity of the masked beauty. It could be Anita, the fiancé of the surgeon's brother and the painter's former lover. Harrandt, who suspects the truth, confronts the painter, who, to get out of a tight spot, invents a name, Leopoldine Dur, which happens to be the name of an honest young woman who is the companion of a noblewoman. The girl falls in love with Heideneck, who returns her affection, but Anita tells her that he has merely used her, and then shoots him in a jealous rage. Leopoldine manages to call Harrandt, who operates on Heideneck and saves his life. At the scene of the crime, the doctor finds a pistol that is then identified as having belonged to Anita, and concludes that she is the woman in the painting. Heideneck marries Leopoldine.

CRITICS' COMMENTS

Willi Forst has re-created the Vienna of 1905, and the title Maskerade *is a fitting one, because he has artfully transformed a story that otherwise could easily have seemed false and artificial. . . .* Maskerade *is also notable for the performance of Paula Wessely. The sequence in which the handsome painter takes her to the tavern and she feels the first tingling of the sparkling wine and the first stirrings for her companion, in the most controlled and* delicate crescendo, would in itself be sufficient to indicate the presence of an actress of singular talent.

MARIO GROMO, La Stampa,
Turin, August 7, 1934

The main thing is that Willi Forst, the director of Leise flehen meine Lieder,* has here, in my opinion, made a film of similar quality, rendering that unique Viennese atmosphere — dissolute and disturbing — of those years of genteel decay, when the capital displayed its festive smile, along with glimpses of its flagging strength, in a Klimt-like decadence, garlanding motifs of death with flowers. . . . We will not soon

forget those eyes of [Wessely's], questioning, supplicating, in which a teardrop appears, limpid and innocent as a drop of dew; those eyes, eternally gazing upward, that seek at least a little of the enormous faith that they offer.

MARCO RAMPERTI,
L'Illustrazione italiana,
Milan, August 12, 1934

A film of a world in masks, of Viennese decadence, of the world of Schnitzler . . . the fabled city, where one is never bored. The way Hollywood, with its Stroheims and Sternbergs, loves to present it — three-quarter time, a weary elegance, profligate pseudo-friends,

born actors these Viennese. . . . Paula Wessely . . . the shining light of this film . . . has portrayed anxiety and love superbly. She sings, dances and moves like a creature from an enchanted world, and yet she emanates warmth and charm and genuine humanity.

E. LANGENBECK, Film-Kurier,
Berlin, August 22, 1934

*First line of a poem, "Ständchen," by Ludwig Rellstab (1799–1860). The poem was set as a Lied (song) by Franz Schubert. The first line might be translated: "Softly, my songs implore you."

Heimkehr   (1941)

(Homecoming)

Director: Gustav Ucicky

This film was presented in 1941 at the Venice Film Festival, which took place regularly, even though films were restricted to those coming from Axis or neutral countries. As its plot makes clear, the film is a textbook example of deep-dyed German nationalism. In the scene in the prison, for example, Marie tries to raise the spirits of her downcast companions with the following speech: "Friends, we'll go home again, I know we will. Why shouldn't we? Anything is possible, and our going home isn't just possible — it's certain. Back in Germany, they know what's happened; no one has forgotten us. On the contrary . . . they want news about us. . . . Think of how it will be, just think! When everything around us will be German, and when we enter a store, we won't hear Yiddish or Polish being spoken, but only German! And not only the village, but everything in it will be German! We'll be in the heart of Germany. Just think about it, friends! Why shouldn't it be that way? And if we can't live a German life, at least

A prisoner, but not without hope, in "Heimkehr."

From the left: Berta Drews, Franz Pfandler, Paula Wessely, Peter Petersen and Otto Wernicke.

we can die a German death. And even dead we'll a true part of Germany!"

Story and screenplay: Gerhard Menzel
Photography: Günther Anders
Set design: Walter Röhrig
Music: Willy Schmidt-Gentner
Editing: Rudolf Schaad
Off-screen narration: Alfred Norkus
Production: Wien-Film
Length: 96 minutes
Country of origin: Austria, 1941
Censor's approval: August 24, 1941
Premiere: October 10, 1941, Vienna;
    October 21, 1941, Berlin
Award: Film of the Nation

CAST —————————————
Paula Wessely (Marie), Peter Petersen (her father, Dr. Thomas), Attila Hörbiger (Ludwig Launhart, Marie's fiancé), Ruth Hellberg (Martha), Carl Raddatz (Dr. Fritz Mutius), Otto Wernicke (Old Manz), Elsa Wagner (Schmid, the midwife), Eduard Köck (her husband), Franz Pfandler (Balthasar Manz), Gerhild Weber (Josepha Manz), Oskar Friml (Werner Fütterer), Karl Michalek (Hermann Erhardt), Berta Drews (Elfriede).

SYNOPSIS —————————————
A village in Poland, the spring of 1939. The Poles are suspicious and hostile to the German-speaking minority living in their midst. The trouble begins when Marie, the heroine, and her friends go to the movies (to see Jeanette MacDonald and Nelson Eddy in *Maytime*). The film is preceded by a newsreel praising the Polish army. When the Polish national anthem is heard on the sound track, everyone in the audience rises, except the three Germans. They are thrown out of the theater, and Marie's fiancé is beaten, later dying of his wounds when the local hospital refuses to admit him. By the beginning of summer, anti-German reprisals have increased, and when war breaks out in September, the Germans are locked in a cellar, where the Poles plan to machine-gun them. A courageous German grabs the gun, and the bullets miss their target. Suddenly the Germans bomb the town. The prisoners escape and make their way back to Germany, and safety.

CRITICS' COMMENTS —————————————
The destinies of German men and women in the late summer of 1939, as depicted in this notable motion picture, bring us face to face with great historical decisions. Germany has never had imperialistic aims; it does, however, uphold the right to life of the German people, and their physical and spiritual security.. What we are being reproached for today by those who dominate the Channel and the Atlantic dates back to the decades preceding September 1, 1939—the brutal desire of the plutocratic democracies to annihilate Germany and the German people, to murder them and destroy them. The episodes described in the film stand for hundreds of thousands of similar episodes.

(anonymous)
Völkischer Beobachter,
October 25, 1941

Thousands of Germans have returned to our great Reich since those days of September 1939. It was a unique event in the history of our country, and now Gustav Ucicky has re-created it in an inspiring film. . . . The most human of our actresses, Paula Wessely, is the central figure of the drama. . . . The scene in which she learns of the death of her fiancé, and the one where she finds the strength to go on, are unforgettable. . . . It is through the intensity of her performance that this retelling of a German Passion becomes an indelible experience.

D. O. KOCH,
Die Filmwelt,
October 29, 1941

KÄTHE VON NAGY

IT IS PARADOXICAL THAT IN KÄTHE VON NAGY, ONE OF the most popular stars of the Nazi screen, there is not a trace of anything Germanic or Nordic. Born on April 4, 1909, in Szabadka, a small Hungarian city annexed to Yugoslavia after World War I, she had the dark skin of a gypsy and pitch-black eyes that radiated sensuality. Her father was the director of a bank in Palics, where he also possessed considerable property.

The daughter of affluent and tranquil parents, Käthe grew up in a normal, bourgeois household, one that in no way seemed to predestine her for screen stardom. After studying French and German—two languages that would prove to be extremely useful to her—in a school run by nuns in St. Christiania (Frohsdorf), the adolescent Käthe did not know exactly what she wanted to do in life. Seeing, however, that literature was her greatest joy, she decided that she would write short stories. Szabadka somehow did not seem the most suitable place to make a name for oneself in this field, and so, at the age of fifteen, Käthe ran away to Budapest, where she registered under a false name at the Hotel Ragusa, one of the most elegant of the Hungarian capital. Her father put the police on her trail, however, and it wasn't long before she found herself back in her home town. Her irate father offered to give Katinka a job in his office taking care of the correspondence in German, but, after seeing the bright lights of Budapest, she knew now that what she wanted was to be an actress. Strong-willed and eager, she managed to persuade her father to let her try her luck in Berlin. Months went by without the faintest hope of a job. Käthe spent a year waiting in the outer offices of all the film companies, big and small, to no avail. Tired of going up and down staircases and taking down worthless phone numbers, von Nagy returned to Budapest to take a job answering correspondence for the Hungarian newspaper *Pester Hirlop*.

In an era in which solidly built women were in vogue, who would ever have film-contracted someone like Käthe, with a figure as slim as a poplar tree, and those restless, searching eyes? Nevertheless, Constantin J. David finally gave her a supporting part in *Männer vor der Ehe* (Men Before Marriage, 1927), produced by the Deulig company. David, a Corsican, would direct her in a number of films, and would eventually become her husband. Von Nagy began her gradual transformation from a willful and capricious girl to a shrewd, painstaking performer, capable of exploiting to the maximum her role of the little hellion, all rolling eyes and provocative gestures.

In the era of the transition to sound, von Nagy made good pictures and some not-so-good ones, including *Die Durchgängerin* (The Runaway Girl, 1928), produced by Joe May, and *Republik der Backfische* (Teenagers' Republic, 1928), the film that made her widely known to the public, which liked her good-humored personality and devilish little face in the role of a girl who leads a band of young women to found a new state. For her first sound film, *Der Andere* (The Other One, 1930), she was chosen by Robert Wiene to play opposite Fritz Kortner and Heinrich George. In this film, based on the phenomenon of the split personality, and considered an important contribution to the genre of the cinema of introspection, she revealed unsuspected depths in her portrayal of the understanding fiancée of a public minister who led a double life.

Actually, von Nagy had had an earlier brush with sound in Mario Camerini's classic Italian film *Rotaie* (Rails, 1929), shot at the very end of the silent era, and to which a musical sound track was later added. The picture, produced by the Sacia company of Milan, tells the delicate story of a young working-class couple who, tired of unending and hopeless poverty, decide to commit suicide. The bottle of poison, however, falls from the window of the shabby hotel room they have rented, and they go out into the street. At the railroad station, the husband (Maurizio D'Ancora, who was later to become more famous as a member of the Gucci family fashion dynasty) finds a wallet stuffed with bills, and for a while the newly rich couple leads an unreal life of drawing rooms on the Oriental Express and evening clothes. They soon realize, however, that this life is not for them, and so they go back to the factory and resume their everyday existence. This role of the factory girl who lives like a queen for a brief moment was the first really dramatic part ever given von Nagy, and she was surprisingly effective in it. However, she would soon return to films of a routine nature, usually typecast as a little minx.

The actress herself has related that, at first, sound films were a torture for her; the sound technicians constantly had to ask her to stop fiddling nervously with her pearl necklace while they were recording. Once she mastered the technique, she was kept busy with one comedy after another, playing variations on the role that had become associated with her. Many of these films were made in both German and French versions. Among the most successful were *Ronny* (1931); an elegantly staged musical titled *Der Sieger* (The Victor, 1932), with Hans Albers in his habitual role as the bon vivant, in

Willy Fritsch   Käthe von Nagy

With Willy Fritsch in "Prinzessin Turandot," 1934.

which von Nagy played Helene, the daughter of a wealthy American banker; *Ich bei Tag, Du bei Nacht* (I by Day, You by Night, 1932) and *Prinzessin Turandot* (1934). In the first and last two of these her partner was Willy Fritsch, the exuberant star of film operetta, whose usual co-stars were Lilian Harvey and von Nagy.

There were a few more serious films in the midst of all these lightweight, escapist pictures, one of the best being *Flüchtlinge* (Refugees, 1933). Her role was less important than that of her co-star, Hans Albers, whose thunderous acting style would have put anyone in the shade; nevertheless she delivered a controlled and affecting performance. She displayed her dramatic gifts again in *La Route impériale* (The Imperial Road, 1935), shot in France, the story of a woman struggling to save the life of the man she loves.

By 1937 von Nagy had become one of the most popular stars of the German screen, although she had been living in Paris for two years with her second husband, Jacques Fattini. In 1938 she appeared with Fritsch again in *Am seidenen Faden* (By a Silken Thread). That same year she returned to Italy to make *Unsere kleine Frau* (Our Little Wife) at Cinecittà in Rome, for the Tobis company, which had an Italian branch, Germania Film. The premiere of the film was held on board the American cruiser *Milwaukee,* anchored in the Bay of Naples, where both von Nagy and the picture were well received. The success was repeated at the Berlin premiere in November.

Although von Nagy made a number of serious films with directors such as Wiene, L'Herbier and Camerini, she was most at home in light comedies, films with music such as *Prinzessin Turandot* and stories with "exotic" backgrounds like *Liebe, Tod und Teufel* (Love, Death and the Devil, 1934, after Robert Louis Stevenson's "The Bottle Imp"). She was at her best as the spoiled and capricious little flirt with the provocative, saucy smile — a type for which her Teutonic colleagues of the period had little inclination.

Käthe von Nagy died in 1973.

With the actor Charbonnier in the French version of "Einmal eine grosse Dame sein" (To Be a Great Lady Just Once), 1934.

With Viktor de Kowa in "Der junge Baron Neuhaus," 1934.

Flüchtlinge *(1933)*

(Refugees)

Director: Gustav Ucicky

With Hans Albers (center) and future director Veit Harlan.

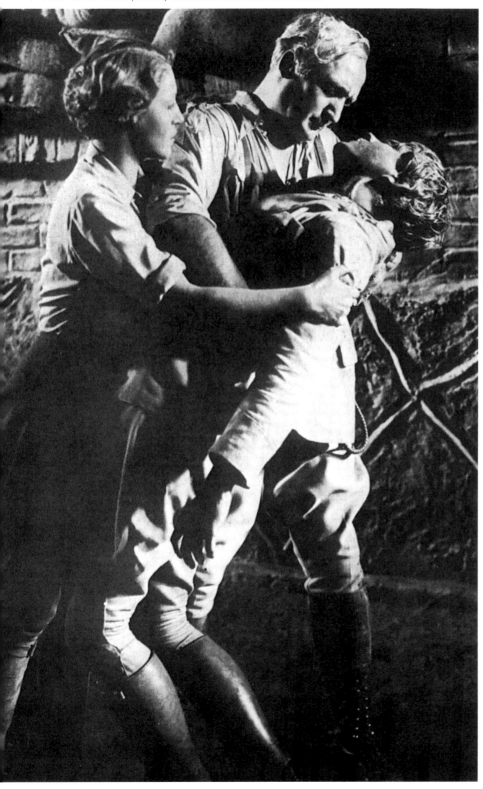

At the ceremony in which *Flüchtlinge* was awarded the prize as the best film of the year, the name of Hans Albers was never mentioned, because he had just married the Jewish actress Hansi Burg in Switzerland. Goebbels considered *Flüchtlinge* the hoped-for "new film," which would reflect the ideals of the "national revolution." A French version, *Au bout du monde* (To the End of the World), was made the same year, with von Nagy and Pierre Blanchar in Albers' role. The film was presented at the second Venice Film Festival in 1934.

Story and screenplay: from the novel of the same name by Gerhard Menzel, adapted for the screen by Menzel
Photography: Fritz Arno Wagner
Set design: Robert Herlth and Walter Röhrig
Music: Herbert Windt and Ernst Erich Buder
Editing: Eduard von Borsody
Production: UFA
Length: 88 minutes
Country of origin: Germany, 1933
Censor's approval: December 1, 1933
Premiere: December 8, 1933
Awards: National Cinematographic Prize (1933); Particular Artistic Value (1934)

CAST

Käthe von Nagy (Kristja), Hans Albers (Arneth), Eugen Klöpfer (Laudy), Ida Wüst (German refugee), Walter Herrmann (German delegate), Karl Rainer (Peter), Franziska Kinz (a pregnant woman), Veit Harlan (Mannlinger), Hans Adalbert Schlettow (the Siberian), Friedrich Gnass (a Hussar), Karl Meixner, Fritz Genschow, Hans Hermann Schaufuss, Josef Dahmen, Rudolf Biebrach, Carsta Löck.

SYNOPSIS

In 1928, during the Chinese civil wars, in a region of Manchuria a group of

With Albers (left) and Harlan.

Europeans, mainly Germans, try to flee from the violence of the armed bands. Not the least of their problems is to get the train on which they are traveling to the border, and salvation. Their leader, a German who is a voluntary exile from his country, gives courage to the group, falls in love with one of them, Kristja, and manages to steal a train and get the refugees to safety in Harbin.

CRITICS' COMMENTS ───

This film will demonstrate to serious film-lovers throughout the world the level of German film today. . . . Superficiality is the death of art. . . . If the spirit of the world is permissive, the spirit of Germany is implacable, and is concerned with things other than business and money. This film depicts, in a symbolic fashion, German youth, German feelings and Germany's destiny. Käthe von Nagy is the victorious heroine of a drama based on actual happenings. She gives a moving portrayal of Kristja, her fears and her courage. *The highest praise goes to Hans Albers, a multiform artist who proves that he has far more to offer than a well-muscled physique. Together with the public, we congratulate him on the degree of artistic maturity he has achieved.*

H.U., *Licht-Bild-Bühne,*
Berlin, December 1933

This tragic world fired by hatred, struggle, desperation and blood has been graphically re-created. The crowd scenes, the battles, the assault on the railroad station, the commandeering of the train, the desperate preparations, and then the flight, all are magnificent. . . . Hans Albers as Arneth, heroic and smiling, is magnificent. Käthe von Nagy, in a role far removed from her usual one of the carefree little coquette, gives an understated and expressive performance as Kristja.

Orazio Bernardinelli,
Il Messaggero, Rome,
August 4, 1934

The Teutonic fondness for the Kolossal *reappears in* Flüchtlinge, *where the normally genteel Ucicky is called upon to re-create the bloodbath in the ruins of Harbin, in Manchuria. He does surprisingly well, depicting the horrors of war, of hunger and thirst with the same sure hand that he displayed in the light and poetic* Der unsterbliche Lump *(The Immortal Ragamuffin, 1929). We must admit, however, that it is not clear just what this enormous roaring monster of a film is aiming at, if not as a satire of the League of Nations. The best moments in the film are Ucicky's occasional evocative touches — the railroad station at dawn, the exhausted horse at the well of putrified water.*

Corrado Pavolini,
Scenario, Rome,
September 1934

Prinzessin Turandot (1934)

(Princess Turandot)

Director: Gerhard Lamprecht

The author of this film's screenplay was Thea von Harbou (1888–1954). She and Vicki Baum were the most prolific and creative of German women screenwriters. Her romantic nature, which tended toward flights into the fantastic and the otherworldly, influenced directors like Fritz Lang (to whom she was married until 1934, when she divorced him, choosing to remain with the Nazis), F. W. Murnau, Joe May and E. A. Dupont. Von Harbou also tried her hand at directing, with *Elisabeth und der Narr* (Elisabeth and the Jester, 1934) and *Hanneles Himmelfahrt* (Hannele's Ascent to Heaven, 1934), but she preferred to return to screenwriting, continuing along the line of the romantic and the bizarre that had produced the screenplays of such films as *Das Testament des Dr. Mabuse* (1922), *Die Nibelungen* (1924) and *M* (1931), all of which she wrote in collaboration with Lang.

Story: from the opera by Giacomo Puccini
Screenplay: Thea von Harbou
Photography: Fritz Arno Wagner
Set design: Robert Herlth and Walter Röhrig
Music: Franz Doelle
Song lyrics: Bruno Balz and C. Amberg
Editing: Arnfried Heyne
Production: UFA
Length: 82 minutes
Country of origin: Germany, 1934
Censor's approval: November 5, 1934
Premiere: November 30, 1934

CAST

Käthe von Nagy (Princess Turandot), Willy Schaeffers (her father, the Emperor of China), Leopoldine Konstantin (the Empress), Willy Fritsch (Calaf), Paul Kemp (Willibald), Inge List (Mian Li), Aribert Wäscher (the judge), Paul Heidemann (the Prince of Samarkand), Gerhard Dammann (the executioner), Ernst Behmer, Angelo Ferrari.

SYNOPSIS

Princess Turandot asks her court dignitaries three riddles, and those who do not answer correctly lose their heads. When young Calaf sees the Prince of Samarkand ride by on the cart of those condemned to death, he decides to put an end to the whims of Turandot, who is the despair of her father, the Emperor of China. Turandot, however, has Calaf brought before the judges, who explain to him that the "executions" are merely a joke invented by the capricious princess to enliven the dreary life at court. Calaf falls in love with Turandot, and in order to see her he devises a plan with the help of a servant and the young Mian Li. At night, Turandot and Calaf meet in the imperial gardens. China rejoices, and only the Lord High Judge of the Society of the Headless is unhappy because there will be no more riddles and beheadings.

With Pierre Blanchar in the French version of "Prinzessin Turandot."

A great new comic film. The set designs are the most elaborate yet to come from Babelsberg. An hour of healthful amusement.

Lokal-Anzeiger,
Berlin, December 1, 1934

Thea von Harbou plays the Chinese flute and weaves an oriental fable. A whim of Fräulein Turandot. . . .The task of Germany's high priestess of the screenplay was to take certain ancient oriental themes and adapt them for today's audience. However, there is no conflict in her fable, whereas there is in the original fable of Turandot. Von Harbou, whose heart obviously beats more for Calaf than for the naughty princess, has even rewritten the brain-twisting riddles. Unfortunately, this film will not hold your attention until the end, primarily because the allegro molto *and* dolcissimo *delights found in Puccini's opera are missing here. [But although]. . .the basic theme has its limitations, this time at least they've given us a lovely bitter almond for dessert—at the end everything resolves itself into a joyous musical pantomime, with a dazzling Willy Fritsch, who has left his tails at home for once. Käthe von Nagy is extremely charming with her silk kimono and impertinent expression. She never stops gesticulating, but is so likable that we would pardon her anything.

C. BRANDT, *Film-Kurier,*
Berlin, December 1, 1934

Käthe von Nagy is certainly the loveliest Princess Turandot that we have ever seen. In this part she is able to display her skill, her imagination and her charm to the maximum. Her smile is like no one else's. . .and Willy Fritsch, enslaved by her beauty, offers her an adoring heart.

R. KUPFER, *Licht-Bild-Bühne,*
Berlin, December 7, 1934

From the left: Pierre Blanchar, Gina Manès and Paul Azais in the French version of "Liebe, Tod und Teufel," 1934.

Liebe, Tod und Teufel   *(1934)*

(Love, Death and the Devil)

Directors: Heinz Hilpert and Reinhart Steinbicker

A French version of this film was done simultaneously, entitled *Le Diable en bouteille* (The Devil in a Bottle), with the same directors and von Nagy, and the French stars Pierre Blanchar and Gina Manès. It is interesting to note that, despite its exotic exteriors, the film was shot entirely in the UFA studios in Babelsberg.

Story: from Robert Louis Stevenson's short story "The Bottle Imp"
Screenplay: Kurt Heuser, Pelz von Felinau and Liselotte Gravenstein
Photography: Fritz Arno Wagner
Set design: Otto Hunte and Willy Schiller
Costumes: Herbert Ploeberger
Music: Theo Mackeben
Song lyrics: Hans Fritz Beckmann
Editing: Wolfgang Becker
Production: UFA
Length: 105 minutes
Country of origin: Germany, 1934
Censor's approval: December 19, 1934 (banned to minors under 18)
Premiere: December 21, 1934, Berlin
Award: Artistic Value

CAST

Käthe von Nagy (Kokua), Albin Skoda (Kiwe), Brigitte Horney (Ruby), Karl Hellmer (Lopaka), Aribert Wäscher (Mounier), Erich Ponto (the old man), Paul Dahlke (the governor), Rudolf Platte (Spunda), Josef Dahmen (Macco), Hans Kettler (Balmer), Karl Hannemann (Hein), Oskar Sima (Kiano), Albert Florath (the notary).

SYNOPSIS

For three years the *Tropic Bird* has plied the seven seas. One day, the seaman Kiwe goes ashore in the port of Kona, in the South Seas, and in a teeming bazaar buys a strange bottle. It grants all a person's wishes—in exchange for the possessor's soul. The only way to get rid of it is to sell it for less than the price paid. Kiwe gives the bottle away, but soon after comes down with leprosy. He tries to get it back, paying one cent for it. Having regained his health, Kiwe marries Kokua, a beautiful native girl, who decides to sacrifice herself for him by buying the cursed bottle. But the middleman, entrusted with selling it, has no fear of the flames of hell; he buys the bottle. Kokua and Kiwe, free at last, prefer a life of poverty and love to being slaves of the devil.

CRITICS' COMMENTS

A film of the South Seas and a tropical island, where reality becomes fantasy and magic, where wishes come true, where the most extraordinary events are commonplace. . . .We haven't seen Käthe von Nagy so relaxed and unaffected in some time. The happy smile of a native girl born in the Tropics imparts a particular warmth to her eyes. She has found an ideal partner in Albin Skoda. . . .Next to them it is a bit of a surprise to find Brigitte Horney, who has finally been given a part that seems made to order for her. She plays a bar girl, common, even vulgar, who, thanks to the bottle, makes her entry into high society. Her song, sung à la Marlene Dietrich, was received with hearty applause. . . .Yesterday's premiere was a great success. Käthe von Nagy and Brigitte Horney were called back to the stage repeatedly.
S.K., Licht-Bild-Bühne,
Berlin, December 22, 1934

Seas of South-UFA, "made in Neubabelsberg." Cramped, claustrophobic sets, stuffed with "exotic" props, evoke only a world hermetically closed to anything real, a synthetic world of pure, uncontaminated sentiments, of endless happiness and of profound doubts. This exotic idyll, this anti-world, all conceived in the sphere of the unattainable, constitutes the real fantasy object of the film. The magic bottle is merely what the "MacGuffin" is in Hitchcock's films—the gimmick, the object upon which all the action hinges, and in the pursuit of which the spectator will happily let himself be carried off into the most absurd cinematic realms. . . .Albin Skoda, whose burning eyes made him wildly popular, seems to be in a permanent state of ecstasy. . . . Brigitte Horney sings, with a disdainful mien and a suitably husky voice, "So oder ist das Leben" [Life Is by Hook or Crook] at the beginning of the film and again at the end for the latecomers.
KRAFT WETZEL and PETER HAGEMANN, *Liebe, Tod und Technik* (Berlin, 1977)

Brigitte Horney in the German version of the film, with Rudolf Platte (left) and Oskar Sima.

LIDA BAAROVA

LIDA BAAROVA WAS BORN IN PRAGUE ON SEPTEMBER 7, 1914, the daughter of a civil servant, and died on October 28, 2000. She attended secondary school and at the same time the dramatic arts school of the State Conservatory in Prague. After gaining experience at the National Theater in Prague, she entered the world of film, and before coming to Berlin had taken part in numerous Czech motion pictures.

Baarova was signed to a contract by UFA, and with her first German film, *Barcarole* (1935), she was on her way to stardom. She reached it in such films as *Einer zuviel an Bord* (One Too Many on Board, 1935), *Ein Teufelskerl* (A Devilish Fellow, 1935) and *Die Stunde der Versuchung* (The Hour of Temptation, 1936)—in the latter two co-starring with her husband, Gustav Fröhlich. Her final German film was *Der Spieler* (The Gambler, 1937).

Her rather short career in German film has an explanation. Gustav Fröhlich, her husband—a celebrated actor, who had starred in Fritz Lang's *Metropolis* in 1927—had earlier been married to Gitta Alpar, a celebrated Hungarian opera star who was the daughter of a rabbi. Gustav and Gitta were obliged to flee Germany to Austria in 1934; they were divorced in 1935 so that the actor might return to his native country. Soon after, he fell in love with and married Baarova—who by this time

was the object of desire of Nazi Minister of Propaganda Joseph Goebbels. Some stories have it that the hot-headed Fröhlich slapped Goebbels' face; it would appear that Fröhlich was interned temporarily in a concentration camp. Finally, American newspapers reported that, on December 21 or 22, 1938, Goebbels "was beaten almost to death." The *New York Daily News* told that the Minister lay in "a closely guarded Berlin clinic, swathed in bandages, his head cut and bruised, both eyes blackened . . ." The *News* explained that Goebbels "was surprised in the flat of a glamorous film star [Baarova] by a group of her husband's friends," that he was punched and pummeled and had a tooth knocked out.

Frau Magda Goebbels had been hinting at divorce for some time by now—when Hitler himself stepped in, assuring that there would be no domestic scandal within his top echelon of officers. Baarova was sent back to Prague, banished from German filmdom. In Czechoslovakia, she took up her screen career once again.

After 1942 Baarova also made films in Italy, such as Enrico Guazzoni's *La fornarina* (The Baker Maid). Here, too, her stay was brief; after Mussolini's fall from power, she was obliged to return to Prague. In 1945 Baarova was accused of collaboration with the Germans, and was sent to the notorious Pankrac Prison in Prague. Shortly before Christmas 1946, she was released, and

These are the eyes that turned Goebbels' head and threatened the respectability of the Nazi regime.

Much Beaten Goebbels Reported a Prisoner As Result of Hitler's Frown on Love Scandal

Report Goebbels Held in Hospital

The British and American press, including the New York Daily News, did not hesitate to play up Goebbels' alleged indiscretion with Lida Baarova and the ire he encountered from her husband, Gustav Fröhlich.

soon afterward she married Jan Kopecky, a relative of the Communist Minister of the Interior. In 1948 the couple tried to flee the country, but were arrested near the border. They were inexplicably released a few days later and sent out of the country. Baarova followed her husband, a theatrical agent, to Argentina, then to Spain.

In the meantime, the Italian film industry had not entirely forgotten her, and she returned to Cinecittà for several forgettable pictures, including *La bisarca* (The Great-grandmother), *Gli amanti di Ravello* (The Lovers of Ravello), *Casa sul lago* (A House by the Lake), *Carne inquieta* (Restless Flesh) and one memorable one, Federico Fellini's *I vitelloni* (The Young and the Passionate, 1953).

Divorced in 1956, Baarova moved to Salzburg,

where she still lives, having acquired Austrian citizenship. In February 1960, for the first time in twenty-two years, she went on stage, appearing at the Theater an der Berliner Allee in Düsseldorf in the adaptation of a play by French dramatist Claude Magnier, *Ein klarer Fall* (A Clear Case). It was a successful comeback. In 1963 she had a supporting role in Czech dramatist/novelist Karel Čapek's *The Makropoulos Affair* at a chamber theater in Heidelberg, winning favorable reviews. In 1975 she again returned to the German stage in Rainer Werner Fassbinder's *Die bitteren Tränen der Petra von Kant* (The Bitter Tears of Petra von Kant).

A resident of Canada for some time, Baarova published her autobiography, *Escapes,* in Toronto in 1983. In 1991 Lida (Baarova) Lundwall was living in Salzburg, Austria.

Barcarole   *(1935)*

Director: Gerhard Lamprecht

Story and screenplay: Gerhard
   Menzel
Photography: Friedl Behn-Grund
Music: Hans-Otto Borgmann (with
   themes from the opera *The Tales
   of Hoffmann* by Jacques
   Offenbach)
Production: UFA
Length: 87 minutes
Country of origin: Germany, 1935
Censor's approval: date uncertain
   (banned to minors under 18)
Premiere: March 4, 1935

CAST

Lida Baarova (Jacinta Zurbarán), Willy
Birgel (her husband), Gustav Fröhlich
(Count Colloredo), Else Wagner, Will
Dohm, Hubert von Meyerinck, Hilde
Hildebrand, Emilie Unda, Gerhard
Dammann, Angelo Ferrari, Karin
Hardt, Michael von Newlinski, Ernst
Rotmund, Ernst Waldow, Werner
Kepich, Edgar Pauly, Otto Stoeckel,
Ludwig Trautmann.

SYNOPSIS

Venice, 1912, the evening of the Feast of
the Barcarole. In an exclusive club,
Count Colloredo has won at gambling
and at love, but when he meets the
beautiful Jacinta Zurbarán, he feels
that he has to conquer her, as well.
Giacinta's life with her cynical, truc-
ulent husband is an unhappy one. That
evening, she and Colloredo wander
happily through Venice, although both
know that their idyll will end the next
day at noon, when she sails back to
Mexico. She gives Colloredo a talisman
of love, which he hopes will help him
win the duel with her husband that is to
take place at dawn. At the first pistol
shot, however, the Venetian nobleman
falls to the ground, clutching the
talisman of Jacinta.

CRITICS' COMMENT

*The director Lamprecht makes remark-
able use of his Venetian setting. There
are no extras, but a happy, noisy mass
of humanity roaming across the bridges
and through the narrow streets, calling
from the gondolas. . . . He is less successful with his actors. The 1912 costumes somehow have the effect of dis-
tancing the characters from us. The
atmosphere created in* Maskerade *is
absent here. Fröhlich's costumes and
makeup are not flattering to him, nor
are his close-ups. Lida Baarova is a
lovely woman with a warm and appealing voice. Her graceful presence
animates every scene in which she appears. Her debut can be considered a
success, and a measure of the credit
must go to Lamprecht. There was pro-
longed applause when the actors came
out on the stage, in particular for the
beautiful Czech guest and the popular
Gustav Fröhlich.*

G.H., *Film-Kurier,*
Berlin, March 5, 1935

With Gustav Fröhlich, as Count Colloredo.

Einer zuviel an Bord   *(1935)*

(One Too Many on Board)

Director: Gerhard Lamprecht

Story: from the novel of the same name by Fred Andreas
Screenplay: Philipp Lothar Mayring, Kurt Heuser and Fred Andreas
Photography: Robert Baberske
Music: Werner Bochmann
Production: UFA
Length: 85 minutes
Country of origin: Germany, 1935
Censor's approval: October 17, 1935 (banned to minors under 18)
Premiere: October 31, 1935

CAST

Lida Baarova (Gerda Hegert), Albrecht Schoenhals (Captain Moltmann), René Deltgen (First Officer Rohlfs), Willy Birgel (State Attorney), Ernest Karchow (Sparkuhl), Annemarie Steinsieck, Jupp Hussels, Alexander Engel, Grethe Weiser.

SYNOPSIS

The Maritime Court in Hamburg decides that Captain Moltmann of the *Ceder* fell overboard during a storm, and that it was not the fault of the crew. But was the cause perhaps the fight between First Officer Rohlfs and the Captain over Rohlfs' wife, Gerda? And why does Sparkuhl hate his captain? Did Moltmann seduce his niece? Or was the captain of the *Ceder* really the victim of an accident? The inquiry is reopened, and the truth gradually emerges: Gerda had been Moltmann's mistress, but had broken off the relationship long before even becoming Rohlf's fiancée. Sparkuhl commits suicide when he hears the truth about his niece, blaming himself. Then, as if by miracle, Captain Moltmann is found to be alive, and can now begin a new life with Gerda — free from suspicion and on good terms with his crew.

CRITICS' COMMENTS

UFA had obviously intended to produce a quality film, but it must be admitted that the result does not correspond to the expectation. And it cannot, given that the philosophical concepts found in Andreas' novel are totally lacking here. But this is not the place to discuss the book; the film stands as an autonomous work . . . The moment at the end when all the plot tangles are straightened out strains one's credulity, and weakens the film. Lamprecht has a good cast to work with, with the exception of Schoenhals, who doesn't seem unprincipled enough

With Albrecht Schoenhals.

to make him suspect. Lida Baarova isn't quite right, either; she is not yet sufficiently mature as an actress to be totally convincing. In sum, it is obvious that the film was made to please the public, and it has evidently succeeded. At the premiere, Lamprecht and his cast were called back to the stage repeatedly. The film is destined to be no less popular than the novel.

BeWe, *Film-Kurier,*
Berlin, November 1, 1935

Lida Baarova's role is not an easy one; her performance, intense yet never excessive, is highly effective. Albrecht Schoenhals is too much the self-confident "bon vivant" for this role, and his performance here is a superficial one. The background music, thankfully, remains in the background, without trying to call attention to itself. The overall sound is UFA's best — the finest there is. The hearty applause was well deserved. This is a film that supplies 85 minutes of excitement and enjoyment.

A.S., *Licht-Bild-Bühne,*
Berlin, November 1, 1935

From the left: Nicole de Rouves, Thomy Bourdelle and Fred Pasquali in the French version of "Einer zuviel an Bord."

Patrioten   *(1937)*

(Patriots)

Director: Karl Ritter

Following World War II, this film was banned in Germany by order of the Allied Military Government.

Story: Karl Ritter
Screenplay: Philipp Lothar Mayring, Felix Lützkendorf and Karl Ritter
Photography: Günther Anders
Music: Theo Mackeben
Production: UFA
Length: 96 minutes
Country of origin: Germany, 1937
Censor's approval: May 14, 1937
Premiere: August 24, 1937, Berlin
Award: Particular Political and Artistic Value

CAST —————————————

Lida Baarova (Thérèse), Mathias Wieman (Peter Thoman), Otz Tollen (French military judge), Bruno Hübner, Hilde Körber, Paul Dahlke, Nikolai Kolin, Kurt Seifert, Edwin Jürgensen, Willi Rose, Ewald Wenck, Ernest Karchow, André Saint-Germain, Karl Hannemann, Karl Wagner, Paul Schwend, Lutz Götz, Gustav Mahnke, Jim Simmons.

SYNOPSIS —————————————

France, 1918. Peter, a German pilot, sets out with two comrades on a mission over the enemy front. The plane crashes, and the only survivor is Peter, who casts off his uniform and tries to reach his own countrymen, behind the German lines. He happens upon a French theatrical company, whose members mistake him for a Frenchman. The young actress Thérèse falls in love with him, but when she discovers his true identity, she is torn between love and duty. She finally decides to denounce him to the military authorities. A trial ensues, during which Peter is accused of espionage. Thérèse's touching testimony saves him, but nonetheless the war divides the two lovers forever.

CRITICS' COMMENTS ——————

Ritter gives us the songs and revue sketches of 1918 that were enjoyed by soldiers on a few days' leave. He has reproduced the atmosphere perfectly, from the "Gobelin" cartoons on the walls of the theater, to the stuccoed ceiling, the period furniture—even the occasonal "Oh, magnifique!" of the French players. The young actress, devastated by the terrible conflict between love and duty, is played movingly by Lida Baarova.

> *Der Deutsche Film,* Munich, pre-premiere assessment, date uncertain

[Bulletin from Paris] The great event of the Paris World's Fair,* the Week of German Culture, began on Friday with the world premiere of the UFA film Patrioten. *Among those present at the gala performance were Secretary of State Walter Funk, Ambassador Count Welczek, the Commissioner of the Fair Labbé, and the Commissioner of the Reich Ruppel. . . . The film's purpose is to show how men can become divided by certain situations, without hating each other. In the film, the general who presides over the French military tribunal (Otz Tollen) is a warm and likable human being. As are the ordinary French soldiers, who show com-*

With Mathias Wieman.

passion for the German prisoners of war. The performances of the leading players pleased the French audience, particularly that of Lida Baarova. She is memorable in the scene in which she weeps before the military tribunal, even though she knows she has done her duty as a French citizen. The Week [of German Culture] could not have been inaugurated with a better film.

H. KOTT, *Licht-Bild-Bühne*,
Berlin, September 4, 1937

The principal virtue of this film is its adherence to reality, and its endeavor to find the man even within the enemy. An enemy should not be considered only as such; it is war that creates hostility between one man and another. We are shown brief excerpts of the theatrical performances given at the front, which, as handled by the director, do not seem at all incongruous, but rather serve to remind us that even in the midst of the greatest calamities, the little joys and sorrows of everyday life do not lose their importance. The cast, headed by Mathias Wieman and Lida Baarova, is admirable, with Baarova better than we have ever seen her. This is a film in which the individual actors are subordinate to the story itself. It was warmly received by the audience at the Berlin premiere.

P. ICKES, *Die Filmwoche*,
Berlin, October 4, 1937

*Forty-two nations exhibited at the 1937 Paris "Exposition Universelle," held in the Palais de Chaillot and Palais de Tokyo. There were an estimated thirty-one million visitors.

Goebbels would have preferred using this net to keep Baarova's rival admirers at bay. She, in turn, played the game well.

MARIKA RÖKK

THE GERMAN AUDIENCE FOR FILM MUSICALS LOVED one star in particular: Marika Rökk. Born in Cairo on November 3, 1913, of Hungarian parents, she became known to German audiences for a series of films made between 1936 and 1939 with the popular and debonair Dutch actor Johannes Heesters. The Rökk-Heesters partnership lasted for only three films: *Der Bettelstudent* (The Beggar Student, 1936) and *Gasparone* (1937)—both of them reworkings of operettas by nineteenth-century composer Carl Millöcker—and *Hallo, Janine!* (1939); just when it seemed that they would achieve the same popularity as the Harvey-Fritsch duo, Heesters left UFA, because he no longer wanted to "make Marika Rökk films, but Johannes Heesters films."[1]

Rökk was happier on her own, anyway, possessed as she was of an iron determination to get ahead that did not exclude below-the-belt blows when deemed necessary—which soon earned her the nickname *Kollegenfresser,* or "partner-eater." After she had begun to be backed by director Georg Jacoby, who later became her husband, Rökk soon found herself in a position to get exactly what she wanted: enormous salaries—without which she threatened to go back to Hungary—and musical films made to order for her, generally following one set pattern. The "Rökk-Filme" usually told the story of an unknown singer and dancer who inevitably becomes a star—not, however, before having endured hard knocks and disappointments. In *Und Du, mein Schatz, fährst mit* (And You, My Darling, Come Along with Me, 1937), she puts a stop to the amorous advances of an American plutocrat, saying, "Die Tiere sind gut, nur die Menschen sind schlecht" (Animals are good; it's men who are bad).

After having studied dance in Budapest, Rökk at fifteen had become the star acrobat of the Berliner Wintergarten, and often went on tour with the Hoffmann-Ensemble. When it broke up, she went to New York, where she studied dance with Ned Wayburn. Rökk met Florenz Ziegfeld in New York, but he made no move to engage her, and in fact she was obliged to return to Europe to further her career. On her return, she joined the Zirkus Renz. It was here that she was spotted by directors Hugo Correl and Gustav Ucicky during a performance in Vienna in October 1934. Won over by her vitality and equestrian talent, they offered her a contract with UFA, which would be the first of many.

In reality, Rökk did not seem ideally cut out for musicals, even though she could tap dance, ride—with or without a saddle—and perform acrobatics, trying to

approximate as closely as possible her idol, American actress/dancer Eleanor Powell. Despite the words of the critic who wrote: "Why do we need Powell? Now we have La Rökk,"[2] the Hungarian actress, who seemed to mistake musicals for lessons in gymnastics, never possessed the skill and polish of her American colleague. In the first place, nature had not endowed her with a dancer's body; she had short, sturdy legs, a waistline that was scarcely sylphlike, and the figure of a healthy, well-fed farm girl rather than that of a slim, long-limbed Hollywood star. Cameraman Konstantin Irmen-Tschet had her stand at specially marked spots on the floor, and photographed her from carefully worked-out angles, hoping to make her appear taller and slimmer. But in vain. Rökk, after all, came from the world of the circus, where flying from one trapeze to another and balancing on top of a trotting stallion, she had acquired muscles of steel rather than long legs and ballerina-like grace.

Rökk's performance in *Kora Terry* (1940), in which she played the dual role of two sisters whose characters were so totally different that, in order to allow her to get more completely into the proper mood, the scenes with Mara (the good one) were shot during the day, and those with Kora (the bad one) in the afternoon, was the beginning of the legend of the versatility of Rökk. It has endured to this day. As for her talent as an actress, she once defined herself as a "dramatic volcano,"[3] alluding perhaps to her continual winking during love scenes, and raising her penciled eyebrows to portray the throes of passion. Nonetheless, despite this "volcanic" nature, which in many musical sequences would prompt her to dance on her hands and do cartwheels across the entire stage, there was never a hair out of place or makeup that was less than perfect. Only a tight-lipped smile betrayed the difficulty of routines that seemed more gymnastic feats than dance numbers.

One of the best-remembered Hollywood-type musicals directed by Rökk's Pygmalion-like husband, Jacoby, was *Die Frau meiner Träume* (The Woman of My Dreams, 1944), in which Marika plays a star named Julia who, during a vacation, falls in love with an engineer (a painfully inhibited Wolfgang Lukschy). The film contains several musical numbers à la Busby Berkeley, such as the initial one, in which Rökk, in an abbreviated gown of black satin trimmed with red roses, sings: "In der Nacht ist der Mensch nicht gern allein" (At Night It Isn't Right to Be Alone), slowly advancing to the front of the stage. In a tight close-up she flutters her eyelashes in what is meant to be a provocative gesture.

The final scene of the film also shows the influence of American choreography of the period, with an incredibly lavish marriage *mise-en-scène* in which Rökk and her partner, Lukschy, both in white, whirl around in a hall filled with chorus girls and gigantic harps. This might be considered the most typical of the "Rökk-Filme," the elaborate musical numbers of which enabled the star to display her unique musico-athletic talents. Nevertheless, despite her energy and her profession-alism, of which she gives tangible proof when she does headstands in the snow or performs gymnastic stunts on a trapeze (as in *Und Du, mein Schatz, fährst mit*), or when she breaks out in a frenzied czardas immediately followed by a lightning-fast tap dance (as in *Karussell*, 1937), somehow the effort was always apparent. Marika Rökk never displayed the easy grace of the naturally talented artist.

In 1991, Marika Rökk was living in Vienna.

Und Du, mein Schatz, fährst mit (1937)

(And You, My Darling, Come Along with Me)

Director: Georg Jacoby

Much of the success of this film was due to the charming musical score by Franz Doelle, perhaps the most gifted composer of film scores of the period. His music had an instantly recognizable quality, and contributed much to the success of such films as *Viktor und Viktoria* (1933), *Amphitryon* (1935) and *Boccaccio* (1936); for *Amphitryon,* he spent over eight months composing 150 separate themes. *Und Du, mein Schatz* begins with a sequence from the French opera *Fra Diavolo*, goes on to several popular songs that became well known, such as the nautical motif "Ja, der Ozean" (Yes, the Ocean) and a brief duet sung by Rökk with a live bear cub, and ends with American-style dance music.

Story: from a novel by Hans Rudolf
  Berndorff
Screenplay: Bobby E. Lüthge and
  Philipp Lothar Mayring
Photography: Herbert Körner
Set design: Hermann Asmus and
  Franz Koehn
Music: Franz Doelle
Song lyrics: Charlie Amberg
Choreography: Sabine Ress
Editing: Herbert Fredersdorf
Production: Universum-Film AG
Length: 97 minutes
Country of origin: Germany, 1936–37
Censor's approval: November 4, 1936
Premiere: January 15, 1937, Berlin

CAST

Marika Rökk (Maria Seydlitz), Hans Söhnker (Dr. Heinz Fritsch), Alfred Abel (William Liners), Paul Hoffmann (Fred Liners, his nephew), Friedl Haerlin (Gloria Liners, Liners' niece), Leopoldine Konstantin (Donna Juana de Villafranca), Oskar Sima (Bel, the magazine editor), Erich Kestin (his assistant), Genia Nikolajewa (Minnie May, a star of the musical revue), Ernst Waldow (Erwin Rückel), Julius E. Hermann (Bum), Kurt Seifert (the jeweler), Franz Schröder-Schrom (the director), Evi Eva, Elfriede Jera, Valy Arnheim, Oskar Eigner, Eduard Bornträger, Hans Eilers, Fred Goebel.

SYNOPSIS

Maria Seydlitz, a singer from the provinces, quits her part in a production of Daniel François Auber's opera *Fra Diavolo* and tears up her contract, to go to Broadway, where she has been invited by the financial magnate William Liners, who has seen her perform and wants to launch her as a star. On board the *Bremen*, Maria tells the German engineer Heinz Fritzsch the story of her marvelous contract with Liners. Among the passengers on the ship are Liners' niece and nephew, who want to impede Maria's career, fearing that Liners may fall in love with her and leave her his entire patrimony. Fred, the nephew, offers Maria ten thousand dollars to break her contract, while his sister, Gloria, steals Maria's passport. An hour before her debut, Maria is arrested for theft; but a telephone call assures that the performance will take place as scheduled. Broadway has a new star, and in the audience Heinz, too, applauds enthusiastically.

CRITICS' COMMENTS

Let us accept this film for what it is; what it offers to the spectator are lavish settings and the artistic talent of Marika Rökk, who can sing while standing on her head. The Broadway sequences offer Marika an opportunity to dance in top hat and tails, à la Powell, and Hans Söhnker to be a manly pillar of strength. . . . Oskar Sima is convincing as an American businessman (of course he's had practice, having played an identical role in Glückskinder*). Much applause, naturally, which no one came*

From the left: Oskar Sima, Erich Kestin and Genia Nikolajewa.

out to receive at the premiere, the cordiality of the public notwithstanding.

F. Röhl, *Der Film*,
Berlin, January 16, 1937

Do you know that feverish excitement that one feels in the theater just before the curtain goes up on opening night? Well, you will feel that same excitement when you see this new UFA film, in which the curtain goes up on a first night, and a young and lovely performer makes her debut. The charming girl around whom the whole film revolves is Marika Rökk, who reveals new talents in each film!

P. Klitze, *8 Uhr-Abendblatt*,
Berlin, January 17, 1937

The principal virtue of this highly entertaining film directed by Jacoby

with verve and humor is the performance of Marika Rökk, whose talents as a dancer and acrobat are displayed to the maximum. The film is a feast for the eyes and the ears, with a compelling plot, agreeable music and opulently staged production numbers. Rökk has no competition in this genre. In addition an extremely likeable Genia Nikolajewa and Oskar Sima give sparkling performances, aided by genuinely amusing dialogue, and were repeatedly applauded during the film, as was La Rökk. The audience was disappointed that Marika was not there in person to receive their applause; she is in Budapest at the moment.

E. Hamann, *Die Filmwoche*,
January 27, 1937

Hallo, Janine! *(1939)*

Director: Carl Boese

This film was to have been presented at the 1939 Venice Film Festival, but the Italian subtitles could not be added in time. On August 29, 1939—three days before Hitler's troops invaded Poland—the board of directors of UFA received an order from the Ministry of Culture and Propaganda to subtitle it in Polish. As Goebbels had often stated, wars are also fought with entertainment.

Story and screenplay: K. G. Külb
Photography: Konstantin
    Irmen-Tschet
Choreography: Edmund N. Leslie
    (American routines)
Set design: Ernst Helmut Albrecht
    and Herbert Frohberg
Music: Peter Kreuder
Song lyrics: Hans Fritz Beckmann
Editing: Milo Harbich
Production: UFA
Length: 93 minutes
Country of origin: Germany, 1939
Censor's approval: May 27, 1939
    (banned to minors under 18)
Premiere: July 1, 1939, Hamburg

CAST

Marika Rökk (Janine), Johannes Heesters (Count René), Rudi Godden (Pierre Tarin), Mady Rahl (Bibi), Else Elster (Yvette), Erich Ponto (Monsieur Pamion), Kate Kühl (Madame Pamion), Hubert von Meyerinck (Jean), Ernst Dumcke (the director), Edith Meinhard (Charlotte), Marjan Lex (Bouboule), Marlise Ludwig (the hostess), Sascha Oscar Schöning.

SYNOPSIS

Janine is just one of the pretty showgirls at the "Moulin Bleu" in Paris, but she can do everything—sing, dance, tap. She dreams of becoming a famous star, but she has competition in the arrogant Yvette, who is no longer so young and is a constant headache to the theatrical impresario. Two friends exchange identities; the unknown composer Pierre

Tarin pretends to be the Count René, who works for the Pamion publishing house, and tries to promote his new magazine *Moulin Bleu*, while the real Count ambles through Paris, passing himself off as Pierre. Janine, pretending to be the Marquise de Bastille, falls in love with the real René. Everything would be fine, if it weren't for Yvette's meddling. Fifty men wearing size-ten gloves attend Janine's opening night, applauding only for her. A star has been born! The real Count asks Janine to marry him.

CRITICS' COMMENTS

This film should be entitled Marika Rökk. UFA has made a genuine star of her, one who is not only a virtuoso dancer (she shows us so many new aspects of her dancing ability here!), but, even more important, a good actress. It can now be said that she can stand comparison with any of her American colleagues; she has more charm and temperament, and, besides, let's not forget—she has paprika in her veins! The creator of her lovely costumes also deserves a bow. The public at the premiere enjoyed themselves immensely, applauding during the film, and greeting the director and players warmly at the end.
G. SCHWARK, *Film-Kurier,*
Berlin, July 12, 1939

It's been a long while since we've seen a German film so lighthearted and amusing! This picture is a return to the best German tradition of the entertainment film of great class. . . . Among the actors, our compliments must go first of all to Marika Rökk, talented both as an actress and a dancer. In the role of Count René, her partner Johannes Heesters is ingratiating. . . . The audience applauded during the film and cheered at the end.
H.-W. BETZ, *Die Filmwelt,*
Berlin, July 21, 1939

A musical with a light touch and bubbling good humor has arrived. We take off our hats to the versatile Marika Rökk, who in this film has surpassed even herself. Her acting is as sparkling

With Georg Alexander in "Karussell," 1937.

On her toes in "Es war eine rauschende Ballnacht," 1939.

as her dancing. Her partner is Johannes Heesters, who has never been better. . . . Kreuder has contributed first-rate music to the production numbers, which have been beautifully staged . . . Marika is dazzling in the Viennese waltz."
W. LÜTHE, *Die Filmwoche,*
Berlin, July 26, 1939

Kora Terry   *(1940)*

Director: Georg Jacoby

Given Marika Rökk's dual role as the "Terry Sisters," she is seen here in several novel dance routines, including one in which one sister balances on the head of the other, in addition to a typical Bavarian folk dance and a belly dance. The composer Peter Kreuder relates that for some of the scenes with both sisters, a stand-in was used, photographed mostly in profile. The girl had been obtained from a concentration camp. At the end of the filming, however, she was not sent back.[4]

Story: from the novel by H. C. von Zobeltitz
Screenplay: Walter Wassermann and C. H. Diller
Photography: Konstantin Irmen-Tschet
Set design: Erich Kettelhut and Hermann Asmus
Costumes: Herbert Ploeberger
Music: Peter Kreuder and Frank Fux
Song lyrics: Günther Schwenn
Choreography: Sabine Ress
Editing: Erich Kobler
Production: UFA
Length: 109 minutes
Country of origin: Germany, 1940
Censor's approval: November 12, 1940 (banned to minors under 18)
Premiere: November 27, 1940, Karlsruhe

CAST

Marika Rökk (Kora Terry and Mara Terry), Will Quadflieg (Michael Varany), Joseph Sieber (Karel Tobias, nicknamed Tobs), Will Dohm (Police Officer Möller), Hans Leibelt (Bartos, director of the Odeon), Ursula Herking (Fräulein Haase), Franz Schafheitlin (Vopescu), Jockel Stahl (solo dancer), Friedl Haerlin, Maria Koppenhöfer, Lotte Spira.

SYNOPSIS

During a performance at the Odeon music hall, the dancer Mara Terry falls, due to the carelessness of her sister, Kora. While Mara is confined to bed for several weeks, Kora takes advantage of the situation to appropriate for herself the services of Varany, the choreographer of the Odeon and a faithful friend of Mara's. One day Kora leaves for Algeria, where she soon finds herself involved in espionage; a certain Vopescu asks her to procure secret military plans. Kora accepts, in return for a considerable sum of money. Mara tries to impede her sister's plans, and accidentally shoots her, without wounding her seriously. Mara's loyal friend Tobs persuades her to perform under her sister's name, and takes the blame himself for the shooting. After a series of triumphs in America, Mara is blackmailed by Vopescu, who thinks she is Kora, and has her brought into court. Two old X-ray plates prove conclusively that "Kora," in reality, is Mara.

CRITICS' COMMENTS

A lively film, more romantic than adventurous, telling the story of two highly different sisters. Jacoby has turned out a singular mixture of sentiment and music, masterfully photographed and effectively interpreted by Marika Rökk playing a dual role, with some highly amusing effects. This spirited film of Jacoby's could represent a turning point for our national film industry.
H. J. ULBRICH, *Film-Nachrichten,* Berlin, November 31, 1940

Kora Terry does a wild and thrilling dance with a cobra wrapped around her neck; for a few moments the spectators' hearts beat faster. But at the end of the dance she has a luminous smile on her face, and the star of Kora Terry *shines brighter than ever in the firmament of the music hall.*
H.O.F., *Filmwelt,* Berlin, December 6, 1940

Noble sentiments and a little espionage, crimes and adventures in far-off countries . . . all hastily whipped together in a shoddy screenplay. But it does have some good musical numbers, such as Marika Rökk in the midst of sarcophagi doing a belly dance that would not be unworthy of the best American musicals. . . . Nevertheless, it is all a bit heavy-handed, much more Berlin than Hollywood.
F. COURTADE and P. CADARS, *Histoire du cinéma nazi* (Paris, 1973)

As Kora, the lying, thieving, stealing sister.

A SELECTED FILMOGRAPHY

HENNY PORTEN

Those readers interested in Henny Porten's films that precede the close of World War I should consult: Gerhard Lamprecht, *Deutsche Stummfilme,* nine volumes and an index, published by Deutsche Kinemathek Berlin, 1968–70.

1919: *Die beiden Gatten der Frau Ruth* (Mrs. Ruth's Two Husbands), dir. Rudolf Biebrach, with Kurt Götz; *Die Fahrt ins Blaue* (Journey into the Blue), dir. Rudolf Biebrach, with Georg Alexander; *Die lebende Tote* (The Living Dead), dir. Rudolf Biebrach, with Paul Bildt; *Die Schuld* (Guilt), dir. Rudolf Biebrach, with Georg H. Schnell; *Ihr Sport* (Her Sport), dir. Rudolf Biebrach, with Hermann Thimig; *Irrungen* (Wanderings), dir. Rudolf Biebrach, with Harry Liedtke; *Monika Vogelsang,* dir. Rudolf Biebrach, with Paul Hartmann and Ernst Deutsch; *Rose Bernd,* dir. Alfred Halm, with Emil Jannings.

1920: *Kohlhiesels Töchter* (Kohlhiesel's Daughters), dir. Ernst Lubitsch, with Emil Jannings; *Anna Boleyn* (Eng. title, *Deception*), dir. Ernst Lubitsch, with Emil Jannings and Paul Hartmann; *Die goldene Krone* (The Golden Crown), dir. Alfred Halm, with Paul Hartmann.

1921: *Die Geierwally* (Wally of the Vultures), dir. E. A. Dupont, with Wilhelm Dieterle; *Hintertreppe* (Backstairs), dir. Leopold Jessner and Paul Leni, with Fritz Kortner and Wilhelm Dieterle; *Frauenopfer* (Women's Sacrifice), dir. Karl Grune, with Albert Bassermann and Wilhelm Dieterle.

1922: *Sie und die drei* (She and the Three), dir. E. A. Dupont, with Hermann Thimig.

1923: *Das alte Gesetz* (The Ancient law), dir. E. A. Dupont, with Ernst Deutsch; *Das Geheimnis von Brinkenhof* (The Secret of Brinkenhof), dir. Svend Gade, with Paul Henckels; *Inge Larsen,* dir. Hans Steinhoff, with Paul Otto; *I.N.R.I.,* (Eng. title, *Crown of Thorns*), dir. Robert Wiene, with Grigori Chmara and Asta Nielsen; *Der Kaufmann von Venedig* (The Merchant of Venice), dir. Peter Paul Felner, with Werner Krauss; *Die Liebe einer Königin* (The Love of a Queen), dir. Ludwig Wolff, with Harry Liedtke.

1924: *Das goldene Kalb* (The Golden Calf), dir. Peter Paul Felner, with Angelo Ferrari; *Gräfin Donelli* (Countess Donelli), dir. G. W. Pabst, with Friedrich Kayssler and Paul Hansen; *Mutter und Kind* (Mother and Child), dir. Carl Froelich, with Erna Morena; *Prater,* dir. Peter Paul Felner, with Ossip Runitsch.

1925: *Das Abenteur der Sybille Brant* (The Adventure of Sybille Brant), dir. Carl Froelich, with Memo Benassi; *Kammermusik* (Chamber Music), dir. Carl Froelich, with Harry Halm; *Tragödie* (Tragedy), dir. Carl Froelich, with Walter Janssen.

1926: *Die Flammen lügen* (The Flames Tell Lies), dir. Carl Froelich, with Grete Mosheim; *Rosen aus dem Süden* (Roses from the South), dir.

Carl Froelich, with Angelo Ferrari; *Wehe, wenn sie losgelassen* (Woe, If They Get Loose), dir. Carl Froelich, with Angelo Ferrari.

1927: *Die grosse Pause* (The Great Pause), dir. Carl Froelich, with Livio Pavanelli and Walter Slezak; *Violantha,* dir. Carl Froelich, with Wilhelm Dieterle and Blandine Ebinger; *Meine Tante, deine Tante* (My Aunt, Your Aunt), dir. Carl Froelich, with Ralph Arthur Roberts.

1928: *Liebe im Kuhstall* (Love in the Barn), dir. Carl Froelich, with Ivan Koval-Samborski; *Liebe und Diebe* (Love and Thieves), dir. Carl Froelich, with Paul Bildt and Kurt Gerron; *Liebfraumilch* (Rhine Wine), dir. Carl Froelich, with Livio Pavanelli; *Lotte,* dir. Carl Froelich, with Walter Jankuhn and Elsa Wagner; *Zuflucht* (Refuge), dir. Carl Froelich, with Franz Lederer and Carl de Vogt; *Die Frau, die jeder liebt, bist Du!* (The Woman Whom Everybody Loves Is You!), dir. Carl Froelich, with Willi Forst.

1929: *Die Herrin und ihr Knecht* (The Mistress and Her Servant), dir. Richard Oswald, with Igo Sym; *Mutterliebe* (Mother Love), dir. Georg Jacoby, with Gustav Diessl.

1930: *Skandal um Eva* (Scandal About Eva), dir. G. W. Pabst, with Oskar Sima; *Kohlhiesels Töchter* (Kohlhiesel's Daughters; Eng. title, *Gretel and Liesel*), dir. Hans Behrendt, with Fritz Kampers.

1931: *24 Stunden aus dem Leben einer Frau* (24 Hours in the Life of a Woman), dir. Robert Land, with Walter Rilla; *Luise, Königin von Preussen* (Luise, Queen of Prussia), dir. Carl Froelich, with Gustav Gründgens.

1933: *Mutter und Kind* (Mother and Child, remake), dir. Hans Steinhoff, with Peter Voss.

1935: *Krach im Hinterhaus* (Trouble in the Tenement), dir. Veit Harlan, with Else Elster.

1938: *Der Optimist,* dir. E. W. Emo, with Viktor de Kowa and Gusti Huber; *War es der im dritten Stock?* (Was It the Stranger on the Third Floor?), dir. Carl Boese, with Walter Steinbeck and Else Elster.

1941: *Komödianten* (The Players), dir. G. W. Pabst, with Käthe Dorsch and Hilde Krahl.

1942: *Symphonie eines Lebens* (Symphony of a Life), dir. Hans Bertram, with Harry Baur and Gisela Uhlen.

1943: *Wenn der junge Wein blüht* (When the New Wine Is in Season), dir. Fritz Kirchhoff, with Otto Gebühr and René Deltgen.

1944: *Familie Buchholz/Neigungsehe* (The Buchholz Family/Love Match), dir. Carl Froelich, with Paul Westermeier, Grethe Weiser and Käthe Dyckhoff.

OLGA TSCHECHOWA

1921: *Schloss Vogelöd (*Eng. title, *Haunted Castle),* dir. F. W. Murnau, with Paul Hartmann and Arnold Korff.

1923: *Nora,* dir. Berthold Viertel; *Der verlorene Schuh* (The Lost Shoe), dir. Ludwig Berger, with Helga Thomas, Paul Hartmann and Mady Christians.

1925: *Die Stadt vor der Versuchung* (The City Before Temptation), dir. Walter Niebuhr, with Julanne Johnston and Malcolm Tod.

1925/ 26: *Der Meister der Welt* (The Master of the World), dir. Gennaro Righelli, with Fred Solm and Xenia Desni.

1926: *Trude, die Sechzehnjährige* (Sixteen-year-old Trude), dir. Conrad Wiene, with Jack Trevor; *Soll man heiraten* (Should One Marry), dir. Manfred Noa, with Vilma Banky and Max Landa.

1926/ 27: *Sein grosser Fall* (His Great Fall), dir. Fritz Wendhausen, with Rudolf Forster and Christa Tordy.

1927: *Die selige Exzellenz* (His Late Excellency), dir. Wilhelm Thiele, with Willy Fritsch and Max Hansen; *Das Meer* (The Sea), dir. Peter Paul Felner, with Heinrich George; *Un Chapeau de paille d'Italie* (An Italian Straw Hat), dir. René Clair, with Albert Préjean (in France).

1927/ 28: *Liebeshölle* (The Torment of Love), dir. Carmine Gallone and Viktor Bieganski, with Angelo Ferrari and Hans Stüwe.

1928: *Moulin Rouge,* dir. E. A. Dupont, with Eve Gray and Jean Bradin (in England); *After the Verdict,* dir. Henrik Galeen, with Malcolm Tod (in England); *Weib in Flammen* (Woman in Flames) dir. Max Reichmann, with Hans Albers and Ferdinand von Alten; *Im 1812* (In 1812), dir. Erich Waschneck, with H. A. Schlettow and Pierre Blanchar; *Die Horde* (The Horde), dir. Erich Waschneck, with Jenny Hasselquist and H. A. Schlettow; *Menschen im Feuer* (People Under Fire), dir. Erich Waschneck, with Henry Stuart and Rudolf Ritter.

1929: *Der Narr, seiner Liebe* (The Fool and His Love), dir. Olga Tschechowa, with Dolly Davis and Jack Trevor (French-German co-production); *Troika,* dir. Vladimir Shtrijevski, with H. A. Schlettow.

1930: *Der Detektiv des Kaisers* (The Kaiser's Detective), dir. Carl Boese, with Käthe Haack; *Liebe im Ring* (Love in the Ring), dir. Reinhold Schünzel, with Max Schmeling and Renate Müller; *Die grosse Sehnsucht* (The Great Longing), dir. Stefan Szekely, with Camilla Horn and Theodor Loos; *Liebling der Götter* (Darling of the Gods), dir. Hans Schwarz, with Emil Jannings and Renate Müller; *Die drei von der Tankstelle* (The Three from the Filling Station), dir. Wilhelm Thiele, with Lilian Harvey and Willy Fritsch; *Zwei Krawatten* (Two Neckties), dir. Felix Basch and Richard Weichert, with Michael Bohnen; *Ein Mädel von der Reeperbahn* (A Girl from the Reeperbahn), dir. Karl Anton, with Trude Berliner and H. A. Schlettow.

1931: *Liebe auf Befehl* (Love on Command), dir. Ernst L. Franck and Johannes Riemann, with Johannes Riemann and Tala Bircll (German-language version of Mal St. Clair's *The Boudoir Diplomat;* filmed in Hollywood); *Mary,* dir. Alfred Hitchcock, with Alfred Abel (German-language version of *Murder;* filmed in England); *Panik in Chicago,* dir. Robert Wiene, with Hans Rühmann; *Das Konzert* (The Concert), dir. Leo Mittler, with Oskar Karlweis and Ursula Grabley (a German-American co-production made in France); *Die Nacht der Entscheidung* (The Night of the Decision), dir. Dimitri Buchowetzi, with Conrad Veidt and Peter Voss (German-language version of the American *The Virtuous Sin); Nachtkolonne* (Night Squad), dir. James Bauer, with Vladimir Gaidarow and Oskar Homolka.

1932: *Trenck,* dir. Heinz Paul and Ernst Neubach, with Hans Stüwe and Dorothea Wieck; *Spione im Savoy-Hotel* (Spies at the Hotel Savoy), dir. Friedrich Zclnik, with the Fratellinis and Alfred Abel; *Liebelei* (Flirtation), dir. Max Ophüls, with Magda Schneider and Gustav Gründgens.

1933: *Der Choral von Leuthen* (The Hymn of Leuthen), dir. Carl Froelich, Arzen von Cserepy and Walter Supper, with Otto Gebühr

and Elga Brink; *Ein gewisser Herr Gran* (A Certain Herr Gran), dir. Gerhard Lamprecht, with Hans Albers; *Wege zur guten Ehe* (Ways to a Good Marriage), dir. Adolf Trotz, with Alfred Abel; *Heideschulmeister Uwe Karsten* (Schoolmaster Uwe Karsten), dir. Carl Heinz Wolff, with Hans Schlenck and Marianne Hoppe; *Der Polizeibericht meldet* (The Police Report States), dir. Georg Jacoby, with Paul Otto and Johannes Riemann.

1934: *Die Welt ohne Maske* (The World Unmasked), dir. Harry Piel, with Harry Piel and Anni Markart; *Maskerade* (Eng. title, *Masquerade in Vienna),* dir. Willi Forst, with Paula Wessely and Adolf Wohlbrück (in Austria); *Was bin Ich ohne Dich?* (What Am I Without You?), dir. Arthur Maria Rabenalt, with Betty Bird and Wolfgang Liebeneiner; *Zwischen zwei Herzen* (Between Two Hearts), dir. Herbert Selpin, with Luise Ullrich and Harry Liedtke; *Abenteuer eines jungen Herrn in Polen* (A Young Man's Adventures in Poland), dir. Gustav Fröhlich, with Gustav Fröhlich; *Regine,* dir. Erich Waschneck, with Luise Ullrich and Adolf Wohlbrück; *Peer Gynt,* dir. Fritz Wendhausen, with Hans Albers and Lucie Höflich.

1935: *Lockspitzel Asew* (Asew, Agent Provocateur), dir. Phil Jützi, with Fritz Rasp and Wolfgang Liebeneiner (in Austria); *Die ewige Maske* (The Eternal Mask), dir. Werner Hochbaum, with Peter Petersen and Mathias Wieman (an Austro-Swiss film); *Ein Walzer um den Stephansturm* (A Waltz Around St. Stephen's Tower), dir. J. A. Hübler-Kahla, with Gusti Huber and Wolf Albach-Retty (in Austria); *Künstlerliebe* (Artists' Love), dir. Fritz Wendhausen, with Inge Schmidt and Wolfgang Liebeneiner; *Liebesträume* (Dreams of Love), dir. Heinz Hille, with Franz Herterich and Erika Dannhoff (in Austria).

1936: *Der Favorit der Kaiserin* (The Empress's Favorite), dir. Werner Hochbaum, with Anton Pointner; *Marja Walewska,* dir. Josef Rovensky, with Maria Andergast and Peter Petersen (in Austria); *Hannerl und ihre Liebhaber* (Hannerl and Her Lover), dir. Werner Hochbaum, with Olly von Flint and Albrecht Schoenhals (in Austria); *Burgtheater* (Town Theater), dir. Willi Forst, with Werner Krauss and Hortense Raky (in Austria); *Seine Tochter ist der Peter* (His Daughter Is Peter), dir. Heinz Helbig, with Carl Ludwig Diehl (in Austria).

1937: *Liebe geht seltsame Wege* (Love Has Strange Ways), dir. H. H. Zerlett, with Carl Ludwig Diehl and K. Hardt; *Unter Ausschluss der Öffentlichkeit* (Public Excluded), dir. Paul Wegener, with Ivan Petrovich and Sabine Peters; *Die gelbe Flagge* (The Yellow Flag), dir. Gerhard Lamprecht, with Hans Albers and Dorothea Wieck; *Gewitterflug zu Claudia* (Stormy Flight to Claudia), dir. Erich Waschneck, with Willy Fritsch and Jutta Freybe.

1938: *Das Mädchen mit dem guten Ruf* (The Girl with a Good Name), dir. Hans Schweikart, with Attila Hörbiger; *Rote Orchideen* (Red Orchids), dir. Nunzio Malasomma, with Albrecht Schoenhals; *Es leuchten die Sterne* (The Stars Are Shining), dir. H. H. Zerlett, with E. F. Fürbringer, La Jana and Vera Bergmann; *Zwei Frauen* (Two Women), dir. H. H. Zerlett, with Irene von Meyendorff and Paul Klinger; *Verliebtes Abenteuer* (Amorous Adventure), dir. H. H. Zerlett, with Paul Klinger.

1939: *Bel Ami, der Liebling schöner Frauen,* dir. Willi Forst, with Willi Forst and Ilse Werner; *Ich verweigere die Aussage* (I Refuse to Testify), dir. Otto Linnekogel, with Albrecht Schoenhals; *Parkstrasse 13,* dir. Jürgen von Alten, with Ivan Petrovich and Hilde Hildebrand; *Die unheimlichen Wünsche* (Sinister Desires), dir. Heinz Hilpert, with Käthe Gold and Hans Holt; *Befreite Hände* (Unfettered Hands), dir. Hans Schweikart, with Brigitte Horney and Ewald Balser.

1940: *Angelika,* dir. Jürgen von Alten, with Albrecht Schoenhals and Marina von Ditmar; *Der Wolf von Glenarvon* (The Wolf of Glenarvon), dir. Max W. Kimmich, with Carl Ludwig Diehl and Ferdinand Marian; *Leidenschaft* (Passion), dir. Walter Janssen, with Hans Stüwe.

1941: *Menschen im Sturm* (People in the Storm), dir. Fritz Peter Buch, with Siegfried Breuer and Gustav Diessl.

1942: *Andreas Schlüter,* dir. Herbert Maisch, with Heinrich George and Dorothea Wieck; *Mit den Augen einer Frau* (With the Eyes of a Woman), dir. Karl George Külb, with Ada Tschechowa and Karl Martell.

1943: *Der ewige Klang* (The Eternal Sound), dir. Günther Rittau, with Elfriede Datzig and Rudolf Prack; *Reise in die Vergangenheit* (A Trip into the Past), dir. H. H. Zerlett, with Margot Hielscher and Ferdinand Marian; *Gefährlicher Frühling* (Dangerous Spring), dir. Hans Deppe, with Winnie Markus and Siegfried Breuer.

1944: *Melusine* (unreleased), dir. Hans Steinhoff, with Siegfried Breuer and Angelika Hauff.

1945: *Mit meinen Augen* (With My Own Eyes), dir. H. H. Zerlett, with Willy Birgel (released in 1948).

LIL DAGOVER

1919: *Harakiri,* (Eng. title, *Butterfly*), dir. Fritz Lang; *Das Kabinett des Dr. Caligari* (The Cabinet of Dr. Caligari), dir. Robert Wiene, with Conrad Veidt, Werner Krauss and Friedrich Feher.

1920: *Kabale und Liebe* (Intrigue and Love), dir. Carl Froelich, with Werner Krauss.

1921: *Der müde Tod* (Eng. title, *Destiny*), dir. Fritz Lang, with Bernhard Goetzke and Walter Janssen.

1922: *Phantom,* dir. F. W. Murnau, with Alfred Abel and Frieda Richard.

1925: *Chronik von Grieshuus* (Eng. title, *At the Grey House*), dir. Arthur von Gerlach, with Paul Hartmann and Gertrud Welcker; *Tartüff* (Tartuffe), dir. F. W. Murnau, with Emil Jannings, Werner Krauss and Lucie Höflich; *Die Brüder Schallenberg* (Eng. title, *The Two Brothers*), dir. Karl Grüne, with Conrad Veidt and Liane Haid.

1926: *Der geheime Kurier, oder Rouge et Noir* (The Secret Courier), dir. Gennaro Righelli, with Ivan Mosjukin.

1927: *Bara en danserska* (Only a Dancing Girl), dir. Olaf Morel (in Sweden); *Hans engeleska fru* (His English Wife), dir. Gustaf Molander (in Sweden).

1928/ *Monte Cristo,* dir. Henry Fescourt, with Jean Angelo, Gaston
29: Modot, Marie Glory and Bernhard Goetzke (in France); *Le Tourbillon de Paris* (The Whirlwind of Paris), dir. Julien Duvivier, with Jacquet, Léon Bary, Hubert Daix and René Lefèvre (in France); *La Grande Passion,* dir. André Hugon, with Rolla Norman, Patricia Allen and Paul Menant (in France).

1929: *Ungarische Rhapsodie* (Hungarian Rhapsody), dir. Hans Schwarz, with Dita Parlo and Willy Fritsch; *Melodie des Herzens* (The Heart's Melody), dir. Hans Schwarz, with Dita Parlo and Willy Fritsch.

1930: *Der weisse Teufel* (The White Devil), dir. Alexander Wolkoff, with Ivan Mosjukin.

1931: *Der Kongress tanzt* (The Congress Dances), dir. Erik Charell, with Lilian Harvey, Willy Fritsch, Conrad Veidt, Otto Wallburg and Adele Sandrock; *The Woman from Monte Carlo* (in the U.S.), dir. Michael Curtiz, with Walter Huston and Warren William.

1932: *Die Tänzerin von Sanssouci* (The Dancer of Sanssouci), dir. Friedrich Zelnik, with Otto Gebühr; *Die letzte Illusion* (The Last Illusion), dir. Erich Waschneck, with Willy Birgel and Lien Deyers; *Das Abenteuer der Thea Roland* (The Adventure of Thea Roland), dir. Hermann Kosterlitz, with Hans Rehmann.

1934: *Ich heirate meine Frau* (I'm Marrying My Wife), dir. Johannes Riemann, with Paul Hörbiger; *Eine Frau, die weiss was sie will* (A Woman Who Knows What She Wants), dir. Viktor Janson, with Anton Edthofer.

1935: *Lady Windermeres Fächer* (Lady Windermere's Fan), dir. Heinz Hilpert, with Walter Rilla; *Der höhere Befehl* (The Higher Command), dir. Gerhard Lamprecht, with Carl Ludwig Diehl.

1936: *Schlussakkord* (Closing Chord), dir. Detlef Sierck, with Willy Birgel and Maria von Tasnady; *Das Mädchen Irene* (The Maiden Irene), dir. Reinhold Schünzel, with Sabine Peters and Geraldine Katt.

1937: *Die Kreutzersonate* (The Kreutzer Sonata), dir. Veit Harlan, with Peter Petersen and Albrecht Schoenhals; *Streit um den Knaben Jo* (Clash Over the Boy Jo), dir. Erich Waschneck, with Willy Fritsch and Maria von Tasnady.

1938: *Dreiklang* (Triad), dir. Hans Hinrich, with Paul Hartmann and Rolf Moebius.

1940: *Die Räuber* (The Brigands), dir. Herbert Maisch, with Horst Caspar, Heinrich George and Hannelore Schroth; *Bismarck,* dir. Wolfgang Liebeneiner, with Paul Hartmann, Friedrich Kayssler and Maria Koppenhöfer.

1942: *Kleine Residenz* (Little Empire), dir. H. H. Zerlett, with Johannes Riemann; *Wien 1910* (Vienna, 1910), dir. E. W. Emo, with Rudolf Forster and Heinrich George.

1944: *Musik in Salzburg,* dir. Herbert Maisch, with Willy Birgel and Hans Nielsen.

BRIGITTE HORNEY

1930: *Abschied* (Farewell), dir. Robert Siodmak, with Aribert Mog.

1934: *Der ewige Traum* (The Eternal Dream), dir. Arnold Franck, with Sepp Rist; *Ein Mann will nach Deutschland* (A Man Wants to Reach Germany), dir. Paul Wegener, with Carl Ludwig Diehl and Siegfried Schürenberg; *Liebe, Tod und Teufel* (Love, Death and the Devil), dir. Heinz Hilpert and Reinhart Steinbicker, with Käthe von Nagy and Albin Skoda.

1935: *Der grüne Domino* (The Green Domino), dir. Herbert Selpin, with Theodor Loos.

1936: *Savoy-Hotel 217,* dir. Gustav Ucicky, with Hans Albers, Alexander Engel and René Deltgen; *Stadt Anatol* (The City of Anatol), dir. Viktor Touriansky, with Gustav Fröhlich.

1938: *Anna Favetti,* dir. Erich Waschneck, with Mathias Wieman; *Du und Ich* (You and I), dir. Wolfgang Liebeneiner, with Joachim Gottschalk and Paul Bildt; *Verklungene Melodie* (Vanished Melody), dir. Viktor Touriansky, with Willy Birgel and Carl Raddatz; *Revolutions Hochzeit* (Revolutionary Wedding), dir. H. H. Zerlett, with Paul Hartmann.

1939: *Aufruhr in Damaskus* (Riot in Damascus), dir. Gustav Ucicky, with Joachim Gottschalk; *Der Gouverneur* (The Governor), dir. Viktor Touriansky, with Willy Birgel, Hannelore Schroth and Ernst von Klipstein; *Befreite Hände* (Unfettered Hands), dir. Hans Schweikart, with Ewald Balser, Carl Raddatz and Olga Tschechowa; *Eine Frau wie Du* (A Woman Like You), dir. Viktor Touriansky, with Joachim Gottschalk.

1941: *Das Mädchen von Fanö* (The Girl from Fanö), dir. Hans Schweikart, with Joachim Gottschalk; *Feinde* (Enemies), dir. Viktor Touriansky, with Willy Birgel and Ivan Petrovich; *Illusion,* dir. Viktor Touriansky, with Johannes Heesters and Theodor Danegger.

1942: *Geliebte Welt* (Beloved World), dir. Emil Burri, with Willy Fritsch.

1943: *Münchhausen* (The Adventures of Baron Münchhausen), dir. Josef von Baky, with Hans Albers, Ilse Werner, Ferdinand Marian and Käthe Haack.

1944: *Am Ende der Welt* (At the End of the World), dir. Gustav Ucicky, with Attila Hörbiger (banned by the censor).

SYBILLE SCHMITZ

1928: *Überfall* (Attack), dir. Ernö Metzner, with Hans Casparius and Kurt Gerron (a short).

1929: *Das Tagebuch einer Verlorenen* (The Diary of a Lost Girl), dir. G. W. Pabst, with Louise Brooks, Fritz Rasp and Valeska Gert.

1932: *Vampyr: l'étrange aventure de David Gray* (Vampire: The Strange Adventure of . . .), dir. Carl Theodor Dreyer, with Julien West, Henriette Gérard, Réna Mandel, Maurice Schutz, Jan Hieronimiko, N. Barbanini and Jane Mora (in France); *F.P.1 antwortet nicht* (F.P.1 Doesn't Answer), dir. Karl Hartl, with Hans Albers.

1933: *Rivalen der Luft* (Rivals of the Air), dir. Frank Wysbar, with Hilde Gebühr and Wolfgang Liebeneiner.

1934: *Musik im Blut* (Music in the Blood), dir. Erich Waschneck, with Hanna Waag, Wolfgang Liebeneiner and Leo Slezak; *Abschiedswalzer* (Farewell Waltz), dir. Geza von Bolvary, with Wolfgang Liebeneiner, Hanna Waag and Richard Romanowsky; *Der Herr der Welt* (Master of the World), dir. Harry Piel, with Siegfried Schürenberg, Walter Franck and Walter Jansen.

1935: *Oberwachtmeister Schwenke* (Police Sergeant Schwenke), dir. Carl Froelich, with Gustav Fröhlich, Marianne Hoppe and Karl Dannemann; *Wenn die Musik nicht wär* (If There Were No Music), dir. Carmine Gallone, with Paul Hörbiger; *Punks kommt aus Amerika* (Punks Arrives from America), dir. Karl Heinz Martin, with Attila Hörbiger and Lien Deyers; *Stradivarius,* dir. Geza von Bolvary, with Gustav Fröhlich, Albrecht Schoenhals, Harald Paulsen and Hilde Krüger; *Ein idealer Gatte* (An Ideal Husband), dir. Herbert Selpin, with Carl Ludwig Diehl, Brigitte Helm and Georg Alexander; *Ich war Jack Mortimer* (I Was Jack Mortimer), dir. Carl Froelich, with Adolf Wohlbrück, Marieluise Claudius and Eugen Klöpfer.

1936: *Die Leuchter des Kaisers* (The Emperor's Candlesticks), dir. Carl Hartl, with Carl Ludwig Diehl and Fritz Rasp (in Austria); *Die*

Unbekannte (The Unknown Woman), dir. Frank Wysbar, with Jean Galland; *Fährmann Maria* (Ferryboat Pilot Maria), dir. Frank Wysbar, with Aribert Mog.

1937: *Unter Ausschluss der Öffentlichkeit* (Public Excluded), dir. Georg Jacoby, with Lida Baarova, Sabine Peters and Ivan Petrovich; *Signal in der Nacht* (Signal in the Night), dir. Richard Schneider-Edenkoben, with Inge List; *Die Kronzeugin* (The Star Witness), dir. Georg Jacoby, with Ivan Petrovich.

1938: *Tanz auf dem Vulkan* (Dance on the Volcano), dir. Hans Steinhoff, with Gustav Gründgens; *Die Umwege des schönen Karl* (The Follies of Handsome Karl), dir. Carl Froelich, with Heinz Rühmann.

1939: *Hotel Sacher,* dir. Erich Engel, with Willy Birgel, Wolf Albach-Retty and Elfie Mayerhofer; *Die Frau ohne Vergangenheit* (The Woman Without a Past), dir. Nunzio Malasomma, with Albrecht Schoenhals.

1940: *Trenck, der Pandur* (Trenck the Hussar), dir. Herbert Selpin, with Hans Albers, Käthe Dorsch, Hilde Weissner and Elisabeth Flickenschildt.

1941: *Wetterleuchten um Barbara* (Storms Over Barbara), dir. Werner Klinger, with Attila Hörbiger; *Clarissa,* dir. Gerhard Lamprecht, with Gustav Fröhlich.

1942: *Vom Schicksal verweht* (Swept Away by Destiny), dir. Nunzio Malasomma, with Albrecht Schoenhals.

1943: *Titanic,* dir. Herbert Selpin and Werner Klinger, with Monika Burg, Charlotte Thiele and Theodor Loos; *Die Hochstaplerin* (The Confidence Woman), dir. Karl Anton, with Carl Ludwig Diehl.

1944: *Das Leben ruft* (Life Calls), dir. Arthur Maria Rabenalt, with Paul Klinger, Gerhild Weber and Otto Wernicke.

ZARAH LEANDER

1930: *Dantes mysterier* (Mysteries of Dante), dir. Paul Merzbach, with Eric Abrahamson and Elisabeth Frisk (in Sweden).

1931: *Falske miljonären* (False Millionaire), dir. Paul Merzbach, with Sture Lagerwall and Håkan Westergren (in Sweden).

1935: *Aktenskapsleken* (Scandal), dir. Ragnar Hyltén-Cavallius, with Einar Axelsson and Karl Gerhard (in Sweden).

1936: *Premiere,* dir. Geza von Bolvary, with Karl Martell and Attila Hörbiger (in Austria).

1937: *Zu neuen Ufern* (Toward New Shores), dir. Detlef Sierck, with Willy Birgel, Viktor Staal, Hilde von Stolz and Erich Ziegel; *La Habanera,* dir. Detlef Sierck, with Ferdinand Marian.

1938: *Der Blaufuchs* (The Blue Fox), dir. Viktor Touriansky, with Willy Birgel, Paul Hörbiger and Jane Tilden; *Heimat* (Homeland), dir.

Carl Froelich, with Heinrich George, Ruth Hellberg, Lina Carstens, Georg Alexander and Leo Slezak.

1939: *Das Lied der Wüste* (The Song of the Desert), dir. Paul Martin, with Friedrich Domin and Gustav Knuth; *Es war eine rauschende Ballnacht* (It Was a Wild Night at the Ball), dir. Carl Froelich, with Hans Stüwe, Aribert Wäscher, Marika Rökk and Leo Slezak; *Das Herz der Königin* (The Heart of the Queen), dir. Carl Froelich, with Willy Birgel, Friedrich Benter and Lotte Koch.

1941: *Der Weg ins Freie* (The Way to Freedom), dir. Rolf Hansen, with Hans Stüwe and Ilse Werner.

1942: *Die grosse Liebe* (The Great Love), dir. Rolf Hansen, with Viktor Staal and Paul Hörbiger.

1943: *Damals* (At That Time), dir. Rolf Hansen, with Rossano Brazzi and Hans Stüwe.

KRISTINA SÖDERBAUM

1936: *Onkel Bräsig* (Uncle Bräsig), dir. Erich Waschneck, with Otto Wernicke.

1938: *Jugend* (Youth), dir. Veit Harlan, with Eugen Klöpfer and Werner Hinz; *Verwehte Spuren* (Covered Tracks), dir. Veit Harlan, with Fritz van Dongen.

1939: *Das unsterbliche Herz* (The Immortal Heart), dir. Veit Harlan, with Heinrich George, Paul Henckels and Paul Wegener; *Die Reise nach Tilsit* (The Journey to Tilsit), dir. Veit Harlan, with Fritz van Dongen, Anna Dammann and Albert Florath.

1940: *Jud Süss* (Jew Süss), dir. Veit Harlan, with Ferdinand Marian, Heinrich George and Werner Krauss.

1942: *Der grosse König* (The Great King), dir. Veit Harlan, with Otto Gebühr and Gustav Fröhlich; *Die goldene Stadt* (The Golden City), dir. Veit Harlan, with Eugen Klöpfer, Paul Klinger and Kurt Meisel.

1943: *Immensee* (Lake Immen), dir. Veit Harlan, with Carl Raddatz, Paul Klinger and Germana Paolieri; *Opfergang* (Sacrifice), dir. Veit Harlan, with Carl Raddatz and Irene von Meyendorff.

1944: *Kolberg,* dir. Veit Harlan, with Heinrich George and Paul Wegener.

LUISE ULLRICH

1932: *Der Rebell* (The Rebel), dir. Luis Trenker and Kurt Bernhardt, with Luis Trenker and Victor Varconi; *Goethe-Film der UFA* (a film on Goethe made by UFA), dir. Fritz Wendhausen, with Theodor Loos, Willy Domgraf-Fassbaender and Else Fink.

1933: *Glück im Schloss* (Happiness in the Castle), dir. Hasso Preis, with Richard Romanowsky, Eduard Wesener and Gay Christie; *Liebelei* (Flirtation), dir. Max Ophüls, with Magda Schneider, Wolfgang Liebeneiner, Gustav Gründgens, Olga Tschechowa and Paul Hörbiger; *Leise flehen meine Lieder* (Eng. title, *Schubert's Unfinished Symphony),* dir. Willi Forst, with Marthe Eggerth, Hans Jaray and Hans Moser (in Austria); *Heimkehr ins Glück* (Return to Happiness), dir. Carl Boese, with Heinz Rühmann, Paul Hörbiger and Paul Heidemann.

1934: *Der Flüchtling aus Chicago* (The Fugitive from Chicago), dir. Johannes Meyer, with Gustav Fröhlich and Lil Dagover; *Liebe dumme Mama* (Dear Foolish Mama), dir. Carl Boese, with Hermann Thimig and Leopoldine Constantin; *Regine,* dir. Erich Waschneck, with Adolf Wohlbrück and Olga Tschechowa; *Vorstadt-varieté* (Playing the Provinces), dir. Werner Hochbaum, with Mathias Wieman, Olly Gebauer and Oskar Sima (in Austria); *Zwischen zwei Herzen* (Between Two Hearts), dir. Herbert Selpin, with Harry Liedtke and Olga Tschechowa.

1935: *Das Einmaleins der Liebe* (The ABC's of Love), dir. Carl Hoffmann, with Paul Hörbiger, Lee Perry and Theo Lingen; *Viktoria,* dir. Carl Hoffmann, with Mathias Wieman, Alfred Abel and Erna Morena.

1936: *Schatten der Vergangenheit* (Shadows of the Past), dir. Werner Hochbaum, with Gustav Diessl and Andrea Pointner (in Austria).

1937: *Versprich mir nichts!* (Promise Me Nothing!), dir. Wolfgang Liebeneiner, with Heinrich George and Viktor de Kowa.

1938: *Ich liebe Dich* (I Love You), dir. Herbert Selpin, with Viktor de Kowa, Olga Limburg and Joachim Rake; *Der Tag nach der Scheidung* (The Day After the Separation), dir. Paul Verhoeven, with Johannes Riemann and Hans Söhnker.

1940: *Liebesschule* (School of Love), dir. G. K. Kulb, with Viktor Staal and Johannes Heesters.

1941: *Annelie: Die Geschichte eines Lebens* (Annelie: The Story of a Life), dir. Josef von Baky, with Werner Krauss, Carl Ludwig Diehl, Käthe Haack, Axel von Ambesser.

1942: *Der Fall Rainer* (The Rainer Case), dir. Paul Verhoeven, with Paul Hubschmid and Karl Schönböck.

1944: *Nora,* dir. Harald Braun, with Viktor Staal, Carl Kuhlmann and Gustav Diessl.

1945: *Kamerad Hedwig* (Comrade Hedwig), dir. Gerhard Lamprecht, with Otto Wernicke and Wolfgang Lukschy (also subject and screenplay in collaboration with Toni Huppertz and Ulrich Erfurth; unfinished).

HEIDEMARIE HATHEYER

1937: *Der Berg ruft* (The Mountain Calls), dir. Luis Trenker, with Luis Trenker, Herbert Dirmoser and Umberto Sacripante.

1938: *Frau Sixta,* dir. Gustav Ucicky, with Gustav Fröhlich.

1939: *Zwischen Strom und Steppe* (Between the River and the Steppe), dir. Geza von Bolvary, with Attila Hörbiger and Margit Symo; *Ein ganzer Kerl* (Quite a Guy), dir. Fritz Peter Buch, with Albert Matterstock and Paul Henckel.

1940: *Die Geierwally* (Wally of the Vultures), dir. Hans Steinhoff, with Sepp Rist, Eduard Köck, Winnie Markus and Leopold Esterle.

1941: *Ich klage an!* (I Accuse!), dir. Wolfgang Liebeneiner, with Paul Hartmann, Mathias Wieman and Harald Paulsen.

1942: *Die Nacht in Venedig* (The Night in Venice), dir. Paul Verhoeven, with Harald Paulsen and Hans Nielsen; *Der grosse Schatten* (The Big Shadow), dir. Paul Verhoeven, with Heinrich George, Will Quadflieg and Marina von Ditmar.

LILIAN HARVEY

1925: *Der Fluch* (The Curse), dir. Robert Land, with Oscar Beregi and Hans Thimig; *Leidenschaft/Die Liebschaften der Hella von Gilsa* (Passion/The Love Affairs of Hella von Gilsa), dir. Richard Eichberg, with Hermann Picha and Otto Gebühr; *Liebe und Trompetenblasen* (Love and Trumpet Playing), dir. Richard Eichberg, with Harry Liedtke; *Die kleine von Bummel* (Little von Bummel), dir. Richard Eichberg, with Hans Brausewetter.

1926: *Der keusche Susanne* (Chaste Susanne), dir. Richard Eichberg, with Willy Fritsch; *Vater werden ist nicht schwer* (Becoming a Father Isn't Difficult), dir. Erich Schönfelder, with Harry Halm.

1927: *Die tolle Lola* (Fabulous Lola), dir. Richard Eichberg, with Hans Junkermann; *Eheferien* (Vacation from Marriage), dir. Victor Janson, with Harry Halm.

1928: *Eine Nacht in London* (Eng. title, A Knight [sic] in London), dir. Lupu Pick, with Robert Irvine; *Du sollst nicht stehlen* (Thou Shalt Not Steal), dir. Victor Janson, with Werner Fütterer; *Ihr dunkler Punkt* (Her Skeleton in the Closet), dir. Johannes Guter, with Willy Fritsch.

1929: *Adieu, Mascotte* or *Das Modell von Montparnasse,* dir. Wilhelm Thiele, with Harry Halm; *Wenn Du einmal Dein Herz verschenkst* (When You One Day Give Your Heart Away), dir. Johannes Guter, with Harry Halm and Igo Sym.

1930: *Liebeswalzer* (Love Waltz), dir. Wilhelm Thiele, with Willy Fritsch; *The Love Waltz* (English version of the preceding film), dir. Wilhelm Thiele, with John Batten; *Hokuspokus*, dir. Gustav Ucicky, with Willy Fritsch; *The Temporary Widow,* dir. Gustav Ucicky, with Laurence Olivier (English version of the preceding film); *Die drei von der Tankstelle* (The Three from the Filling Station), dir. Wilhelm Thiele, with Willy Fritsch; *Le chemin du paradis* (The Road to Paradise), dir. Wilhelm Thiele and Max de Vaucorbeil (French version of the preceding film); *Einbrecher* (Burglars), dir. Hans Schwarz, with Willy Fritsch.

1931: *Nie wieder Liebe* (Love Nevermore), dir. Anatole Litvak, with Harry Liedtke; *Calais-Douvres,* dir. Anatole Litvak, with André Roanne (French version of the preceding film); *Der Kongress tanzt* (The Congress Dances), dir. Erik Charell, with Willy Fritsch, Lil Dagover and Conrad Veidt; *The Congress Dances,* dir. Erik Charell, with Henri Garat and Conrad Veidt (English version of the preceding film); *Le Congrès s'amuse,* dir. Erik Charell, with Henri Garat and Robert Arnou (French version of the preceding film); *Princesse, à vos ordres* (Princess, at Your Orders), dir. Hans Schwarz, with Henri Garat (the French version of Käthe von Nagy's *Ihre Hoheit befiehlt* of the same year).

1932: *Zwei Herzen und ein Schlag* (Two Hearts and One Beat), dir. Wilhelm Thiele, with Wolf Albach Retty; *La fille et le garçon,* dir. Wilhelm Thiele, with Henri Garat (French version of the preceding film); *Quick,* dir. Robert Siodmak, with Hans Albers (a French version was filmed as well, with Pierre Brasseur); *Ein blonder Traum* (A Blonde Dream), dir. Paul Martin, with Willy Fritsch and Willi Forst; *Happy Ever After,* dir. Paul Martin, with Jack Hulbert (English version of the preceding film); *Un Rêve blond* (A Dream Blond), dir. Paul Martin, with Henri Garat (French version of the preceding film).

1933: *Ich und die Kaiserin* (The Empress and I), dir. Friedrich Holländer, with Conrad Veidt; *The Only Girl,* dir. Friedrich Holländer, with Charles Boyer and Maurice Evans (English version of the preceding film); *Moi et l'impératrice,* dir. Friedrich Holländer, with Charles Boyer (French version of the preceding film); *Heart Song,* dir. John Blystone, with John Boles (American version of the preceding film); *My Weakness,* dir. David Butler, with Lew Ayres (in the U.S.); *My Lips Betray,* dir. John G. Blystone, with John Boles (in the U.S.).

1934: *I Am Suzanne,* dir. Rowland V. Lee, with Gene Raymond (in the U.S.).

1935: *Let's Live Tonight,* dir. Victor Schertzinger, with Tullio Carminati (in the U.S.); *Invitation to the Waltz,* dir. Paul Merzbach, with Carl Esmond and Anton Dolin (in England); *Schwarze Rosen* (Black Roses), dir. Paul Martin, with Willy Fritsch and Willy Birgel; *Roses noires,* dir. Paul Martin, with Jean Galland and Jean Worms (French version of the preceding film); *Did I Betray?,* dir. Paul Martin, with Esmond Knight (English version of the preceding film).

1936: *Glückskinder* (Fortune's Children), dir. Paul Martin, with Willy Fritsch; *Les Gais Lurons,* dir. Paul Martin, with Henri Garat (French version of the preceding film).

1937: *Sieben Ohrfeigen* (Seven Slaps), dir. Paul Martin, with Willy Fritsch and Alfred Abel; *Fanny Elssler,* dir. Paul Martin, with Willy Birgel and Rolf Moebius.

1938: *Capriccio,* dir. Karl Ritter, with Victor Staal and Paul Kemp; *Castelli in aria* (Castles in the Air), dir. Augusto Genina, with Vittorio De Sica (in Italy); *Ins Blaue Leben* (Random Living), dir. Augusto Genina, with Vittorio De Sica (German version of the preceding film).

1939: *Frau am Steuer* (Woman at the Wheel), dir. Paul Martin, with Willy Fritsch.

1940: *Sérénade,* dir. Jean Boyer, with Louis Jouvet and Bernard Lancret (in France); *Miquette,* dir. Jean Boyer, with Lucien Baroux and André Lefaur (in France).

RENATE MÜLLER

1928: *Peter der Matrose* (Peter the Sailor), dir. Reinhold Schünzel, with H. H. Twardowsky.

1929: *Teure Heimat* (Beloved Homeland), dir. Carl Wilhelm, with Hans Brausewetter and Hans Albers.

1930: *Liebe im Ring* (Love in the Ring), dir. Reinhold Schünzel, with Max Schmeling; *Revolte im Erziehungshaus* (Revolt in the Reformatory), dir. George Asagaroff, with Veit Harlan; *Liebling der Götter* (Darling of the Gods), dir. Hans Schwarz, with Emil Jannings; *Liebeslied/Canzone d'amore* (Song of Love), dir. Constantin J. David, with Gustav Fröhlich; *Der Sohn der Weissen Berge* (The Son of Mont-Blanc), dir. Mario Bonnard, with Luis Trenker and Michael von Newlinski; *Das Flötenkonzert von Sansouci* (The Flute Concert of Sansouci), dir. Gustav Ucicky, with Otto Gebühr.

1931: *Der kleine Seitensprung* (The Little Escapade), dir. Reinhold Schünzel, with Hermann Thimig; *Die Privatsekretärin* (The Private Secretary), dir. Wilhelm Thiele, with Hermann Thimig; *Sunshine Susie,* dir. Victor Saville, with Owen Nares and Jack Hulbert (English version of the preceding film, released in the United States as *The Office Girl*).

1932: *Mädchen zum Heiraten* (Girl Ready for Marriage), dir. Wilhelm Thiele, with Hermann Thimig and Wolf Albach-Retty; *Marry Me,* dir. William Thiele, with Ian Hunter and Maurice Evans (English version of the preceding film).

1933: *Viktor und Viktoria,* dir. Reinhold Schünzel, with Hermann Thimig; *Saison in Cairo* (A Season in Cairo), dir. Reinhold Schünzel, with Willy Fritsch; *Walzerkrieg* (War of the Waltzes), dir. Ludwig Berger, with Willy Fritsch and Hanna Waag.

1934: *Die englische Heirat* (The English Marriage), dir. Reinhold Schünzel, with Adolf Wohlbrück.

1935: *Liselotte von der Pfalz* (Liselotte of the Palatinate), dir. Carl Froelich, with Dorothea Wieck.

1936: *Allotria* (name of a mythical country), dir. Willi Forst, with Adolf Wohlbrück, Jenny Jugo and Heinz Rühmann (in Austria); *Eskapade*, dir. Erich Waschneck, with Georg Alexander, Grethe Weiser, and Walter Franck.

1937: *Togger*, dir. Jürgen von Alten, with Paul Hartmann and Mathias Wieman.

GRETHE WEISER

1930: *Kasernenzauber* (Miracle in the Barracks), dir. Carl Boese, with Igo Sym, Fritz Schulz and Lucie Englisch.

1933: *Grethel zieht das grosse Los* (Grethel Wins the Grand Prize), dir. Carl Boese, with Lucie Englisch, Hans Brausewetter and Jacob Tiedtke; *Kind, ich freue mich auf Dein Kommen* (Little One, I'm Glad You've Come), dir. Kurt Gerron, with Magda Schneider, Wolf Albach-Retty and Otto Walburg.

1934: *Schützenkönig wird der Felix* (Felix Will Be the Winner at Targetshooting), dir. Carl Boese, with Rudolf Platte, Ursula Grabley and Paul Heidemann.

1935: *Familie Schimek* (The Schimek Family), dir. E. W. Emo, with Hans Moser, Käthe Haack, Hilde Schneider; *Lady Windermeres Fächer* (Lady Windermere's Fan), dir. Heinz Hilpert, with Lil Dagover, Hanna Waag and Walter Rilla; *Frischer Wind aus Kanada* (Cool Wind from Canada), dir. H. Kenter and H. Holder, with Dorit Kreyssler, Paul Hörbiger and Max Gülstorff; *Einer zuviel an Bord* (One Too Many on Board), dir. Gerhard Lamprecht, with Lida Baarova, Albrecht Schoenhals and René Deltgen; *Der Mann mit der Pranke* (The Man with the Paw), dir. Rudolph van der Noss, with Paul Wegener, Rose Stradner and Johannes Riemann; *Anschlag auf Schweda* (Assault on Schweda), dir. Karl Heinz Martin, with Marianne Hoppe, Peter Voss and Hanna Waag.

1936: *Alles für Veronika* (Everything for Veronica), dir. Veit Harlan, with Thekla Ahrens, Willy Eichberger and Hans Moser; *Der Raub der Sabinerinnen* (The Rape of the Sabines), dir. R. A. Stemmle, with Bernhard Wildenhain, Max Gülstorff and Maria Koppenhöfer; *Männer vor der Ehe* (Men Before Marriage), dir. Carl Boese, with Carola Höhn, Paul Klinger and Rolf Weih; *Der verkannte Lebemann* (The Unknown Playboy), dir. Carl Boese, with Ralph Arthur Roberts, Trude Marlen and Theo Lingen; *Martha,* dir. Karl Anton, with Carla Spletter, Helge Roswaenge and Fritz Kampers; *Hilde und die vier PS* (Hilde and the Four Horsepower Automobile), dir. Heinz Paul, with Ludwig Manfred Lommel, Hilde Schneider and Franz Zimmermann; *Engel mit kleinen Fehlern* (Angels with Little Imperfections), dir. Carl Boese, with Rudolf van der Noss, Arthur Roberts, Charlotte Daudert and Jack Trevor; *Geheimnis eines alten Hauses* (The Secret of an Old House), dir. Rudolph van der Noss, with Magda Schneider, Wolf Albach-Retty and Kurt Vespermann; *Eskapade,* dir. Erich Waschneck, with Renate Müller, Georg Alexander and Walter Franck.

1937: *Mädchen für alles* (Maid of All Work), dir. Carl Boese, with Ralph Arthur Roberts, Ellen Frank Irmgard Nowak; *Gabriele: eins, zwei, drei* (Gabriele: One, Two, Three), dir. Rolf Hansen, with Marianne Hoppe, Gustav Fröhlich and Will Dohm; *Meine Freundin Barbara* (My Girlfriend Barbara), dir. F. Kirchhoff, with Paul Hoffmann, Franz Zimmermann and Elisabeth Ried; *Menschen ohne Vaterland* (People Without a Country), dir. Herbert Maisch, with Willy Fritsch, Maria von Tasnady and Willy Birgel; *Die göttliche Jette* (The Divine Jette), dir. Erich Waschneck, with Viktor de Kowa, Marina von Ditmar and Kurt Meisel.

1938: *Frauen für Golden Hill* (Women for Golden Hill), dir. Erich Waschneck, with Viktor Staal, Kirsten Heiberg and Karl Martell; *Unsere kleine Frau* (Our Little Woman), dir. Paul Verhoeven, with Käthe von Nagy, Albert Matterstock and Jola Jobst.

1939: *Verdacht auf Ursula* (Suspicion About Ursula), dir. Karl Heinz Martin, with Luli Hohenberg, Anneliese Uhlig and Viktor Staal; *Frau am Steuer* (Woman at the Wheel), dir. Paul Martin, with Lilian Harvey, Willy Fritsch and Leo Slezak; *Hochzeitsreise zu Dritt* (Honeymoon for Three), dir. Ernst Marischka, with Maria Andergast, Johannes Riemann and Paul Hörbiger; *Marguerite: 3* (Marguerite Times Three), dir. Theo Lingen, with Gusti Huber, Hans Holt and Franz Schafheitlin; *Liebe streng verboten* (Love Strictly Forbidden), dir. H. Helbig, with Hans Moser, Carola Höhn and Wolf Albach-Retty; *Irrtum des Herzens* (Error of the Heart), dir. B. Hofmann, with Paul Hartmann, Käthe Dorsch and Leny Marenbach; *Die Geliebte* (The Beloved), dir. Gerhard Lamprecht, with Viktoria von Ballasko, Willy Fritsch and Karl Martell; *Ehe in Dosen* (Marriage in Small Doses), dir. Johannes Meyer, with Leny Marenbach, Johannes Riemann and Ralph Arthur Roberts; *Das Glück wohnt nebenan* (Happiness Lives Next Door), dir. Ernst Marischka, with Maria Andergast, Olly Holzmann and Wolf Albach-Retty.

1940: *Links der Isar—rechts der Spree* (To the Left of the Isar, to the Right of the Spree), dir. P. Ostermayr, with Charlotte Schellhorn, Fritz Genschow and Fritz Kampers; *Mein Mann darf es nicht wissen* (My Husband Should Not Know), dir. P. Heidemann, with Mady Rahl, Hans Nielsen and Günther Lüders; *Zwischen Hamburg und Haiti* (Between Hamburg and Haiti), dir. Erich Waschneck, with Gisela Uhlen, Gustav Knuth and Walter Franck; *Wie konntest Du, Veronika?* (How Could You, Veronica?), dir. M. Harbich, with Gusti Huber, Wolf Albach-Retty and Ralph Arthur Roberts; *Alles Schwindel* (It's All a Swindle), dir. B. Hofmann, with Gustav Fröhlich, Ruth Hellberg and Hans Brausewetter; *Der rettende Engel* (The Redeeming Angel), dir. F. Dörfler, with Carla Rust, Sepp Rist and Gustav Waldau; *Polterabend* (Eve of the Wedding Day), dir. Carl Boese, with Camilla Horn, Rudi Godden and Ralph Arthur Roberts.

1941: *Sonntagskinder* (Sunday's Children), dir. Jürgen von Alten, with Johannes Riemann, Carola Höhn and Rudolf Platte; *Oh, diese Männer!* (Oh, These Men!), dir. Ernst Marischka, with Johannes Riemann, Paul Hörbiger and Jane Tilden; *Krach im Vorderhaus* (Trouble in the Front Block), dir. P. Heidemann, with Mady Rahl, Rotraut Richter and Carl-Heinz Schroth.

1942: *Die grosse Liebe* (The Great Love), dir. Rolf Hansen, with Zarah Leander, Viktor Staal and Paul Hörbiger; *Wir machen Musik* (We Make Music), dir. Helmut Käutner, with Ilse Werner, Viktor de Kowa and Edith Oss.

1943: *Ein Walzer mit Dir* (A Waltz with You), dir. Ernst Marischka, with Lizzi Waldmüller, Albert Matterstock and Rudolf Platte; *Drei tolle Mädels* (Three Terrific Girls), dir. Ernst Marischka, with Carola Höhn, Else von Möllendorff and Lucie Englisch; *Alles aus Liebe* (All Because of Love), dir. Ernst Marischka, with Heli Finkenzeller, Wolf Albach-Retty and Rudolf Carl.

1944: *Familie Buchholz/Neigungsehe* (The Buchholz Family/Love Match), dir. Carl Froelich, with Henny Porten, Paul Westermeier and Käthe Dyckhoff; *Der Meisterdetektiv* (The Master Detective), dir. Ernst Marischka, with Rudolf Platte, Erich Ponto and Georg Alexander; *Die Frau meiner Träume* (The Woman of My Dreams), dir. Georg Jacoby, with Marika Rökk, Wolfgang Lukschy and Walter Müller; *Hundstage* (Dog Days), dir. G. von Cziffra, with Maria Holst, Olly Holzmann and Wolf Albach-Retty.

1945: *Ich glaube an Dich* (I Believe in You), dir. Rolf Hansen, with Heidemarie Hatheyer, Viktor Staal and Paul Klinger; *Das alte Lied* (The Old Song), dir. Fritz Peter Buch, with Winnie Markus, Ernst von Klipstein and Hannes Keppler; *Shiva und die Galgenblume* (Shiva and the Gallows Flowers), dir. Hans Steinhoff, with Hans Albers, Aribert Wäscher and Elisabeth Flickenschildt; *Verlobte Leute* (Engaged People), dir. Karl Anton, with Alex von Ambesser, Günther Lüders and Gretl Schörg.

MARIANNE HOPPE

1933   *Judas von Tirol* (The Tyrol Judas), dir. Franz Z. Osten, with Fritz Rasp and Camilla Spira; *Heideschulmeister Uwe Karsten* (Schoolmaster Uwe Karsten), dir. Carl Heinz Wolff, with Hans Schlenck, Brigitte Horney and Olga Tschechowa.

1934:   *Der Schimmelreiter* (The Rider of the White Steed), dir. Curt Oertel and Hans Deppe, with Hans Deppe and Mathias Wieman; *Krach um Jolanthe* (Trouble About Iolanthe), dir. Carl Froelich, with Marieluise Claudius; *Schwarzer Jäger Johanna* (Black Hunter Johanna), dir. Johannes Meyer, with Gustav Gründgens.

1935:   *Oberwachtmeister Schwenke* (Police Sergeant Schwenke), dir. Carl Froelich, with Gustav Fröhlich and Harald Paulsen; *Alles hört auf mein Kommando* (Everyone Obeys My Command), dir. Georg Zoch, with Adele Sandrock and Wolfgang Liebeneiner.

1936:   *Eine Frau ohne Bedeutung* (A Woman of No Importance), dir. Hans Steinhoff, with Gustav Gründgens.

1937:   *Der Herrscher* (The Ruler), dir. Veit Harlan, with Emil Jannings, Paul Wagner, Maria Koppenhöfer, Hilde Körber and Käthe Haack.

1938:   *Capriolen* (Caprices), dir. Gustav Gründgens, with Gustav Gründgens and Fita Benkhoff.

1939:   *Der Schritt vom Wege* (The False Step), dir. Gustav Gründgens, with Carl Ludwig Diehl; *Kongo-Express,* dir. Eduard von Borsody, with René Deltgen.

1941:   *Auf Wiedersehen, Franziska!* (Till We Meet Again, Franziska!), dir. Helmut Käutner, with Hans Söhnker, Rudolf Fernau and Aribert Wäscher.

1942:   *Stimme des Herzens* (Voice of the Heart), dir. Johannes Meyer, with Ernst von Klipstein and Eugen Klöpfer.

1943:   *Romanze in Moll* (Romance in a Minor Key), dir. Helmut Käutner, with Ferdinand Marian, Paul Dahlke and Siegfried Breuer.

1944:   *Ich brauche Dich* (I Need You), dir. Hans Schweikart, with Willy Birgel and Paul Dahlke.

ILSE WERNER

1938:   *Frau Sixta,* dir. Gustav Ucicky, with Franziska Kinz and Gustav Fröhlich; *Das Leben kann so schön sein* (Life Can Be So Beautiful), dir. Rolf Hansen, with Rudi Godden, Hedwig Bleibtreu and Gustav Waldau; *Die unruhigen Mädchen,* (The Restless Girls), dir. Geza von Bolvary, with Käthe von Nagy, Elfriede Datzig and Lucie Englisch.

1939:   *Fräulein,* dir. Erich Waschneck, with Erik Frey, Mady Rahl and Roma Bahn; *Drei Väter um Anna* (Three Fathers for Anna), dir. Carl Boese, with Hans Stüwe, Theodor Danegger and Beppo Brem; *Ihr erstes Erblenis* (Her First Experience), dir. Josef von Baky, with Johannes Riemann, Wolker von Collande and Charlotte Daudert.

1940:   *Bal paré* (Fancy-dress Ball), dir. Karl Ritter, with Paul Hartmann, Hannes Stelzer and Käthe Haack; *Wunschkonzert* (Request Concert), dir. Eduard von Borsody, with Carl Raddatz, Joachim Brennecke and Ida Wüst.

1941:   *U-Boote westwärts* (U-Boats Westward), dir. G. Rittau, with Herbert Wilk, Heinz Engelmann and Joachim Brennecke; *Die schwedische Nachitgall* (The Swedish Nightingale), dir. Peter Paul Brauer, with Carl Ludwig Diehl, Joachim Gottschalk and Aribert Wäscher.

1942:   *Wir machen Musik* (We Make Music), dir. Helmut Käutner, with Viktor de Kowa, Georg Thomalla and Grethe Weiser; *Hochzeit auf Bärenhof* (Wedding at Bärenhof), dir. Carl Froelich, with Heinrich George, Paul Wegener and Ernst von Klipstein.

1943:   *Münchhausen* (The Adventures of Baron Münchhausen), dir. Josef von Baky, with Hans Albers, Brigitte Horney, Ferdinand Marian and Käthe Haack.

1944:   *Grosse Freiheit Nr. 7* (Great Freedom No. 7), dir. Helmut Käutner, with Hans Albers, Hans Söhnker and Gustav Knuth.

1945:   *Ein toller Tag* (A Crazy Day), dir. O. F. Schuh, with Paul Hartmann, Lola Müthel and Kurt Meisel; *Das seltsame Fräulein Sylvia* (The Strange Fräulein Sylvia), dir. Paul Martin, with Paul Hubschmid, Gerti Soltau and Willi Rose (unfinished).

PAULA WESSELY

1934:   *Maskerade* (Eng. title, *Masquerade in Vienna*), dir. Willi Forst, with Willy Fritsch, Adolf Wohlbrück, Olga Tschechowa, Peter Petersen, Hilde von Stolz, Paul Hörbiger and Walter Janssen (in Austria); *So endete eine Liebe* (Thus Ended a Love), dir. Karl Hartl, with Willi Forst, Rose Stradner and Gustav Gründgens.

1935:   *Episode,* dir. Walter Reisch, with Carl Ludwig Diehl, Friedl Czepa, Erika von Wagner and Georg Tressler (in Austria).

1936:   *Die Julika,* dir. Geza von Bolvary, with Attila Hörbiger and Gina Falckenberg (in Austria).

1937:   *Die ganz grossen Torheiten* (The Very Greatest Follies), dir. Carl Froelich, with Rudolf Forster and Kurt Meisel.

1938:   *Spiegel des Lebens* (Mirror of Life), dir. Geza von Bolvary, with Attila Hörbiger and Peter Petersen (in Austria).

1939:   *Maria Illona,* dir. Geza von Bolvary, with Willy Birgel and Paul Christian Hubschmid.

1940:   *Ein Leben lang* (For a Lifetime), dir. Gustav Ucicky, with Joachim Gottschalk, Annie Rosar and Lina Woiwode.

1941:   *Heimkehr* (Homecoming), dir. Gustav Ucicky, with Peter Petersen, Attila Hörbiger, Ruth Hellberg, Carl Raddatz, Hermann Thimig and Hans Holt.

1943:   *Späte Liebe* (Late Love), dir. Gustav Ucicky, with Attila Hörbiger; *Die kluge Marianne* (Clever Marianne), dir. Hans Thimig, with Attila Hörbiger and Hermann Thimig.

1944:   *Das Herz muss schweigen* (The Heart Must Be Silent), dir. Gustav Ucicky, with Mathias Wieman and Werner Hinz.

KÄTHE VON NAGY

1927: *Männer vor der Ehe* (Men Before Marriage), dir. Constantin J. David, with Nina Vanna and Hanni Weisse; *Wien, du Stadt meiner Träume* (Vienna, City of My Dreams), dir. Viktor Janson, with Liane Haid and Luigi Serventi; *Die Sandgräfin* (The Countess of Sand), dir. Hans Steinhoff, with Christa Tordy and Jack Trevor.

1928: *Gustav Mond, Du gehst so stille* (. . . You Walk So Softly), dir. Reinhold Schünzel, with Jacob Tiedtke and Yvette Darnys; *Republik der Backfische* (Teenagers' Republic), dir. Constantin J. David, with Ilse Stobrawa and Ernst Stahl-Nachbaur; *Le Bateau de verre* (The Glass Boat), dir. Constantin J. David and Jacqueline Millet, with André Nox, Eric Barclay and Françoise Rosay (French-German co-production); *Die Durchgängerin* (The Runaway Girl), dir. Hans Schwarz, with Hans Brausewetter.

1929: *Der Weg durch die Nacht* (The Way Through the Night), dir. Robert Dinesen, with René Navarre; *Maskottchen* (Mascots), dir. Felix Basch, with Paul Morgan and Jeanne Hellbling; *Rotaie* (Rails), dir. Mario Camerini, with Maurizio D'Ancora (in Italy).

1930: *Les Saltimbanques* (The Mountebanks), dir. Robert Land and Jacquelux, with Nicolas Koline and Georges Melchior; *Der Andere* (The Other One), dir. Robert Wiene, with Fritz Kortner and Heinrich George.

1931: *Ihre Majestät die Liebe* (Her Majesty Love), dir. Joe May, with Franz Lederer (German-language remake of U.S. film *Her Majesty Love*, 1930, with Marilyn Miller and W. C. Fields); *Ihre Hoheit befiehlt* (Her Highness Commands), dir. Hans Schwarz, with Willy Fritsch; *Meine Frau, die Hochstaplerin* (My Wife, the Promoter), dir. Kurt Gerron, with Heinz Rühmann; *Ronny*, dir. Reinhold Schünzel, with Willy Fritsch and Otto Wallburg; *Ronny*, dir. Roger Le Bon, with Marc Dantzer and Lucien Baroux (French version of the preceding film); *Le Capitaine Craddock*, dir. Hans Schwarz and Max de Vaucorbeil, with Jean Murat (French version of *Bomben auf Monte Carlo,* with Anna Sten and Hans Albers, a 1931 German film).

1932: *Der Sieger* (The Victor), dir. Hans Hinrich and Paul Martin, with Hans Albers; *Le Vainqueur,* with Jean Murat (French version of the preceding film); *Ich bei Tag, Du bei Nacht* (I by Day, You by Night), dir. Ludwig Berger, with Willy Fritsch; *A moi le jour, à toi la nuit,* dir. Ludwig Berger and Claude Heymann, with Fernand Gravey (French version of the preceding film).

1933: *La Belle Aventure* (The Wonderful Adventure), dir. Reinhold Schünzel, with Lucien Baroux and Jean Périer (in France); *Flüchtlinge* (Refugees), dir. Gustav Ucicky, with Hans Albers; *Au bout du monde* (To the End of the World), dir. Gustav Ucicky and Henri Chomette, with Pierre Blanchar (French version of the preceding film).

1934: *Die Töchter ihrer Exzellenz* (Her Excellency's Daughters), dir. Reinhold Schünzel, with Dagny Servaes and Willy Fritsch; *La Jeune Fille d'une nuit* (A Girl for One Night), dir. Reinhold Schünzel and Roger Le Bon, with Lucien Baroux (French version of the preceding film); *Einmal eine grosse Dame sein* (To Be a Great Lady Just Once), dir. Gerhard Lamprecht, with Wolf Albach-Retty; *Un jour viendra* (A Day Will Come), dir. Gerhard Lamprecht and Serge Veber, with Jean-Pierre Aumont and Charbonnier (French version of the preceding film); *Der junge Baron Neuhaus* (The Young Baron Neuhaus), dir. Gustav Ucicky, with Viktor de Kowa; *Nuit de mai,* dir. Gustav Ucicky and Henri Chomette, with Fernand Gravey (French version of the preceding film); *Die Freundin eines grossen Mannes* (The Girlfriend of a Great Man), dir. Paul Wegener, with Carl Ludwig Diehl; *Prinzessin Turandot,* dir. Gerhard Lamprecht, with Willy Fritsch; *Turandot, princesse de Chine,* dir. Gerhard Lamprecht and Serge Veber, with Pierre Blanchar (French version of the preceding film); *Liebe, Tod und Teufel* (Love, Death and the Devil), dir. Heinz Hilpert and Reinhardt Steinbicker, with Brigitte Horney and Albin Skoda; *Le Diable en bouteille* (The Devil in the Bottle), dir. Heinz Hilpert and Reinhardt Steinbicker, with Gina Manès and Pierre Blanchar (French version of the preceding film).

1935: *La Route impériale* (The Imperial Road), dir. Marcel L'Herbier, with Pierre Richard-Willm (in France); *Die Pompadour* (Madame Pompadour), dir. Willy Schmidt-Gentner, Heinz Helbig and Veit Harlan, with Willy Eichberger (in Austria).

1936: *Ave Maria,* dir. Johannes Riemann, with Beniamino Gigli.

1937: *Cargaison blanche* or *Le Chemin de Rio* (Eng. title, *Traffic in Souls*), dir. Robert Siodmak, with Jules Berry, Jean-Pierre Aumont and Suzy Prim (in France); *La Bataille silencieuse* (The Silent Battle), dir. Pierre Bilon, with Pierre Fresnay and Michel Simon (in France).

1938: *Nuit de princes* (Night of Princes), dir. Vladimir Striyevsky, with Jean Murat (in France); *Unsere kleine Frau* (Our Little Wife), dir. Paul Verhoeven, with Albert Matterstock (in Italy); *Am seidenen Faden* (By a Silken Thread), dir. Robert A. Stemmle, with Willy Fritsch; *Die unruhigen Mädchen* (The Restless Girls), dir. Geza von Bolvary, with Ilse Werner, Lucie Englisch and Hans Holt (in Austria).

1939: *Accord final* (Final Agreement), dir. J. R. Bay, with Georges Rigaud (a French-Swiss film); *Renate im Quartett* (Renata in the Quartet), dir. Paul Verhoeven, with Gustav Fröhlich.

1943: *Mahlia la métisse* (Mahlia the Mestiza), dir. Walter Kapps, with Jean Servais (in France).

LIDA BAAROVA

1931: *Kariéra Pavla Camrdy* (The Career of Pavla Camrdy), dir. J. M. Krnansky, with Antonie Nedosinka (in Czechoslovakia).

1932: *Madla z sihelny* (Madla of the Brickyard), dir. Vladimir Slavinsky, with Hugo Haas (in Czechoslovakia).

1933: *Okénko* (Scatterbrain), dir. Vladimir Slavinsky and Hugo Haas, with Hugo Haas; *Jeji lekai* (Her Doctor), dir. Vladimir Slavinsky, with Jaroslav Proucha (both in Czechoslovakia).

1935: *Barcarole,* dir. Gerhard Lamprecht, with Gustav Fröhlich, Elsa Wagner and Rudolf Klein-Rogge; *Ein Teufelskerl* (A Devilish Fellow), dir. Georg Jacoby, with Gustav Fröhlich, Georg Alexander and Adele Sandrock; *Einer zuviel an Bord* (One Too Many on Board), dir. Gerhard Lamprecht, with Albrecht Schoenhals, Willy Birgel and René Deltgen.

1936: *Die Stunde der Versuchung* (The Hour of Temptation), dir. Paul Wegener, with Gustav Fröhlich, Harald Paulsen and Theodor

Loos; *Verräter* (Traitor), dir. Karl Ritter, with Willy Birgel, Irene von Meyendorff and Theodor Loos.

1937: *Unter Ausschluss der Öffentlichkeit* (Public Excluded), dir. Georg Jacoby, with Sabine Peters, Ivan Petrovich and Sybille Schmitz; *Patrioten* (Patriots), dir. Karl Ritter, with Paul Dahlke, Edwin Jürgensen and Bruno Hübner; *Panenstvi* (Virginity), dir. Otokar Vàvra, with Jaroslav Proucha and Ladislav Bohàc (in Czechoslovakia); *Der Spieler* (The Gambler), dir. Gerhard Lamprecht, with Albrecht Schoenhals and Hilde Körber.

1939: *Ohnivé léto* (Exciting Summer), dir. František Cap, with Zorca Janu, V. Sova and Svatopluck Beneš; *Divka v modrem* (The Girl in Blue), dir. O. Vavra, with Oldrich Novy; *Maskovana milenka* (The Masked Mistress), dir. O. Vavra, with G. Nezval and Ewald Balser; *Turbina* (Power Machine), dir. O. Vavra, with Oldrich Novy (all in Czechoslovakia).

1942: *La fornarina* (The Baker Maid), dir. Enrico Guazzoni, with Loredana and Massimo Serato; *Il cappello del prete* (The Priest's Hat), dir. Ferdinando Poggioli, with Rolando Lupi, Loris Gizzi and Carlo Lombardi; *Ti conosco, mascherina!* (You Can't Fool Me!), dir. Eduardo De Filippo, with Eduardo and Peppino De Filippo (all in Italy).

1943: *L'ippocampo* (Hippocampus), dir. Gian Paolo Rosmino, with Vittorio De Sica and Maria Mercader (in Italy).

MARIKA RÖKK

1932: *Csokoli meg édes* (Kiss Me, Dear), dir. Béla Gáal, with Erzsi Somogyi and Kálman Rozsahegyi (in Hungary).

1933: *Kisértetek vonata* (Phantom Train), dir. Lajos Lazar, with Jenö Törzs, Ella Gombaszögi and Oskar Beregi (in Hungary).

1935: *Leichte Kavallerie* (Light Cavalry), dir. Werner Hochbaum, with Heinz von Cleve and Fritz Kampers.

1936: *Der Bettelstudent* (The Beggar Student), dir. Georg Jacoby, with Johannes Heesters, Carola Höhn and Fritz Kampers; *Heisses Blut* (Hot Blood), dir. Georg Jacoby, with Hans Stüwe and Paul Kemp.

1937: *Und Du, mein Schatz, fährst mit* (And You, My Dear, Come Along with Me), dir. Georg Jacoby, with Hans Söhnker and Alfred Abel; *Gasparone,* dir. Georg Jacoby, with Johannes Heesters, Heinz Schorlemmer and Edith Schollwer; *Karussell* (Carousel), dir. Alwin Elling, with Georg Alexander and Paul Henckels.

1938: *Eine Nacht im Mai* (A Night in May), dir. Georg Jacoby, with Karl Schönböck and Oskar Sima.

1939: *Hallo, Janine!,* dir. Carl Boese, with Johannes Heesters and Rudi Godden; *Es war eine rauschende Ballnacht* (It Was a Wild Night at the Ball), dir. Carl Froelich, with Hans Stüwe, Zarah Leander and Leo Slezak.

1940: *Kora Terry,* dir. Georg Jacoby, with Will Quadflieg and Will Dohm; *Wunschkonzert* (Request Concert), dir. Eduard von Borsody, with Ilse Werner, Carl Raddatz and Joachim Brennecke.

1941: *Frauen sind doch bessere Diplomaten* (Women Are the Best Diplomats), dir. Georg Jacoby, with Willy Fritsch, Aribert Wäscher and Hans Leibelt (first German color film); *Tanz mit dem Kaiser* (Dance with the Emperor), dir. Georg Jacoby, with Wolf Albach-Retty, Axel von Ambesser and Maria Eis.

1942: *Hab' mich lieb* (Take My Love), dir. Harald Braun, with Viktor Staal, Hans Brausewetter and Mady Rahl.

1944: *Die Frau meiner Träume* (The Woman of My Dreams), dir. Georg Jacoby, with Wolfgang Lukschy, Walter Müller and Georg Alexander.

NOTES

Introduction

1. Cited in C. Belling, *Der Film in Staat und Partei* (Berlin, 1939).
2. *Der Kinematograph,* March 30, 1933.
3. *NS-Monatshefte,* December 1931.
4. *Filmwoche,* February 10, 1933.
5. *Berlin-Glieniker Brücke* (Berlin, 1978).
6. Bundesarchiv (Koblenz), R 109 I/1033, 76.
7. *German Resistance to National Socialism* (Press and Information Office of the Federal Government, Bonn, n.d.).
8. *Protokoll des Reichsfilmarchivs,* June 2, 1933.
9. Cited in C. Belling, *Der Film in Staat und Partei.*
10. Cited in W. Becker, *Film und Herrschaft* (Berlin, 1973).
11. First published, edited by L. Lochner, in Zurich in 1948 as *Goebbels Tagebücher,* and translated the same year into English as *The Goebbels Diaries* (Garden City, NY: Doubleday).
12. V. Harlan, *Im Schatten meiner Filme* (Gütersloh, 1966).
13. Ibid.
14. A. M. Rabenalt, *Film in Zwielicht: über den unpolitischen Film und die Begrenzung des totalitären Anspruchs* (Munich, 1958).
15. Cited in O. Kalbus, *Vom Werden deutscher Filmkunst* (Hamburg, 1935, Vol. II).
16. D. S. Hull, *Film in the Third Reich: A Study of the German Cinema 1933–1945* (Berkeley and Los Angeles: University of California Press, 1969).
17. G. L. Mosse, *La nazionalizzazione delle masse* (Bologna, 1975).
18. H. P. Bleuel, *Strength Through Joy* (London, 1973).
19. A. M. Rabenalt, *Tanz und Film* (Berlin, 1960).
20. The author was unable to locate the title, publisher, and date of this work.
21. *Filmwelt,* February 2, 1940.
22. C. Rosten, *Das Abc des Nationalsozialismus* (Berlin, 1933).
23. Ibid.
24. J. Rosenberg, *Der Mythos des 20. Jahrhunderts* (n.p., 1930).
25. W. Reich, *Psicologia di massa del fascismo* (Mailand, 1971).
26. Cited in R. Grunberger, *A Social History of the Third Reich* (Harmondsworth, 1974).
27. V. Harlan, *Im Schatten meiner Film.*
28. F. Hippler, *Betrachtungen zum Filmschaffen* (Berlin, 1942).
29. G. Puccini, *Galleria: Lil Dagover,* in *Cinema,* April 10, 1939.
30. F. Savio, *Visione privata* (Rome, 1972).
31. C. Riess, *Das gab's nur einmal* (Vienna/Munich, 1977).
32. Cited in S. Sontag, "Fascinating Fascism," in B. Nichols (ed.), *Movies and Methods* (University of California, 1975).

Olga Tschechowa

1. G. P. Straschek, *Handbuch wider das Kino* (Frankfurt, 1975).

Kristina Söderbaum

1. V. Harlan, *Im Schatten meiner Filme* (Gütersloh, 1966).
2. J. Wulf, *Theater und Film im Dritten Reich* (Gütersloh, 1964).

Zarah Leander

1. Z. Leander, *Es war so wunderbar* (Hamburg, 1973).
2. Ibid.
3. *Der Angriff,* Berlin, September 15, 1937.

Luise Ullrich

1. D. S. Hull, *Film in the Third Reich: A Study of the German Cinema 1933–1945* (Berkeley and Los Angeles: University of California Press, 1969).

Heidemarie Hatheyer

1. C. Reiss, *Das gab's nur einmal* (Vienna and Munich: Molden-Taschenbuch-Verlag, 1977).

Grethe Weiser

1. H. Borgelt, *Grethe Weiser* (Berlin, 1971).

Marianne Hoppe

1. G. Sadoul, *Histoire générale du cinéma* (Paris, 1946–47).

Lida Baarova

1. E.g., West Germany's *Bunte Illustrierte,* January 1960.

Marika Rökk

1. M. Rökk, *Herz mit Paprika* (Berlin, 1974).
2. Ibid.
3. Ibid.
4. P. Kreuder, *Nur Puppen haben keine Tränen: Ein Lebensbericht* (Bergisch-Gladbach, 1973).

Opposite: Sybille Schmitz in "Fährmann Maria" (Ferryboat Pilot Maria), 1936.

BIBLIOGRAPHY

Bächlin, Peter. *Der Film als Ware*. Basel, 1945.

Bauer, Alfred. *Deutscher Spielfilm-Almanach 1929–1950*. Berlin, 1950.

Belling, Curt. *Der Film in Staat und Partei*. Berlin, 1936.

Boelcke, Willi A. *Kriegspropaganda 1939–1941: Geheime Ministerkonferenzen im Reichspropagandaministerium*. Stuttgart, 1966.

Bramstedt, Ernest. *Goebbels and National Socialist Propaganda*. Lansing, MI, 1965.

Brenner, Hildegard. *La politica culturale del nazismo*. Bari, 1965.

Courtade, Francis, and Pierre Cadars. *Histoire du cinéma nazi*. Paris, 1973.

Fest, Joachim C. *Das Gesicht des Dritten Reiches: Profile einer totalitären Herrschaft*. Munich, 1963.

Fraenkel, Heinrich, and Roger Manvell, *Vita e morte del dottor Goebbels*. Milan, 1961.

Goebbels, Joseph. *Vom Kaiserhof zur Reichskanzlei: Eine historische Darstellung in Tagebuchblättern* (January 1, 1932–May 1, 1933). Munich, 1934.

Goebbels, Joseph. *Das eherne Herz: Reden und Aufsätze aus den Jahren 1942–43*. Munich, 1943.

Gregor, Ulrich, and Enno Patalas. *Geschichte des Films*. Gütersloh, 1962.

Harlan, Veit. *Im Schatten meiner Filme*. Gütersloh, 1966.

Heiber, Helmut. *Joseph Goebbels*. Berlin, 1962.

Hinkel, Hans. *Handbuch der Reichskulturkammer*. Berlin, 1937.

Hippler, Fritz. *Betrachtungen zum Filmschaffen*. Berlin, 1942 and 1943, edition VI.

Hitler, Adolf. *Mein Kampf*. Munich, 1941.

Hofer, Walther. *Der Nationalsozialismus: Dokumente 1933–1945*. Frankfurt, 1957.

Hull, David Stewart. *Film in the Third Reich: A Study of the German Cinema 1933–1945*. Berkeley and Los Angeles: University of California Press, 1969. Translated into Italian, Rome, 1972.

Kochenrath, P. *Der Film im Dritten Reich*. Cologne, 1963.

Kracauer, Siegfried. *Cinema tedesco: Dal "Gabinetto dei dottor Caligari" a Hitler*. Milan, 1954.

Krauss, Werner. *Das Schauspiel meines Lebens: Einem Freund erzählt*. Stuttgart, 1958.

Kreuder, Peter. *Nur Puppen haben keine Tränen: Ein Lebensbericht*. Bergisch-Gladbach, 1973.

Kriegk, Otto. *Der deutsche Film im Spiegel der Ufa: 25 Jahre Kampf und Vollendung*. Berlin, 1943.

Lehnich, Oswald. *Jahrbuch der Reichsfilmkammer*. Berlin, 1937, 1938, 1939.

Leiser, Erwin. *Nazi Cinema*. London, 1974.

Mayer, J. P. *Sociology of Film: Studies and Documents*. London, 1946.

Oertel, Rudolf. *Filmspiegel: Ein Brevier aus der Welt des Films*. Vienna, 1941.

Petzet, Wolfgang. *Verbotene Filme*. Frankfurt, 1971.

Rabenalt, Arthur Maria. *Film im Zwielicht: Über den unpolitischen Film und die Begrenzung des totalitären Anspruchs*. Munich, 1958.

Sontag, Susan. "Fascinating Fascism," *Movies and Methods*. Berkeley and Los Angeles: University of California Press, 1975.

Stephenson, Jill. *Women in Nazi Society*. London, 1975.

Wetzel, Kraft, and Peter Hagemann. *Liebe, Tod und Technik*. Berlin, 1977.

———. *Zensur: Verboten deutsche Filme*. Berlin, 1978.

Witte, Karsten. "Die Filmkomödie im Dritten Reich," *Die deutsche Literatur im Dritten Reich*. Stuttgart, 1976.

Wolf, Kurt. "Entwicklung und Neugestaltung der deutschen Filmwirtschaft seit 1933." Dissertation, Heidelberg University, 1938.

Wulf, Joseph. *Theater und Film im Dritten Reich: Eine Dokumentation*. Gütersloh, 1974.

Zglinicki, Friedrich von. *Der Weg des Films*. Berlin, 1956.